Sustainable Consumption

CW00541316

Sustainable Consumption: Key Issues provides a concise introduction to the field of sustainable consumption, outlining the contribution of the key disciplines in this multi-disciplinary area, and detailing the way in which both the problem and the potential for solutions are understood.

Divided into three parts, the book begins by introducing the concept of sustainable consumption, outlining the environmental impacts of current consumption trends, and placing these impacts in social context. The central section looks at six contrasting explanations of sustainable consumption in the public domain, detailing the stories that are told about why people act in the way they do. This section also explores the theory and evidence around each of these stories, linking them to a range of disciplines and approaches in the social sciences. The final section takes a broader look at the solutions proposed by sustainable consumption scholars and practitioners, outlining the visions of the future that are put forward to counteract damage to the environment and society. Each chapter highlights key authors and real-world examples to encourage students to broaden their understanding of the topic and to think critically about how their daily lives intersect with environmental and ethical issues.

Exploring the ways in which critical thinking and an understanding of sustainable consumption can be used in daily life as well as in professional practice, this book is essential reading for students, academics, professionals and policy-makers with an interest in this growing field.

Lucie Middlemiss is Associate Professor in Sustainability, and Co-director of the Sustainability Research Institute, in the School of Earth and Environment at the University of Leeds, UK.

Key Issues in Environment and Sustainability

This series provides comprehensive, original and accessible texts on the core topics in environment and sustainability. The texts take an interdisciplinary and international approach to the key issues in this field.

Low Carbon Development: Key Issues
Edited by Frauke Urban and Johan Nordensvärd

Sustainable Business: Key Issues
Helen Kopnina and John Blewitt

Sustainability: Key Issues
Helen Kopnina and Eleanor Shoreman-Ouimet

Ecomedia: Key Issues
Edited by Stephen Rust, Salma Monani and Sean Cubitt

Ecosystem Services: Key Issues
Mark Everard

Sustainability Science: Key Issues
Edited by Ariane König and Jerome Ravetz

Sustainable Business: Key Issues (2nd Ed.)
Helen Kopnina and John Blewitt

Sustainable Consumption: Key Issues
Lucie Middlemiss

'Sustainable consumption is a grand challenge of our time, and this long-awaited textbook positively fizzes with clarity and curiosity, guaranteed to spark engagement and inspiration. Middlemiss expertly relates major real-world problems and solutions to our everyday lives, grounding complex debates in an accessible, no-nonsense style. She helps us think critically about the stories we tell ourselves, about how we will live in the future, and the political action we need to take us there. Unashamedly infused with a passion for social justice, this is essential reading for students and scholars of sustainable consumption.'
– *Gill Seyfang, Reader in Sustainable Consumption, University of East Anglia, UK*

'This innovative textbook in the growing field of sustainable consumption studies tackles questions of power, social equity and environmental limits, whilst it also considers different representations of consumption in relation to everyday life. Middlemiss grapples with big questions in a highly accessible and inviting manner. I look forward to putting the book to immediate use in my classroom.' – *Marlyne Sahakian, founding member of the Sustainable Consumption Research and Action Initiative (SCORAI) Europe, and Assistant Professor of Sociology, University of Geneva, Switzerland*

'This book marks a milestone in the evolution of research and policy practice on the unsustainability of contemporary consumption in many parts of the world. Students and others will benefit enormously from Middlemiss's careful work to digest and make meaningful a Himalayan-sized expanse of material on an extremely significant, but thus far largely underappreciated, topic. The volume embodies impressive ambition and will propel to new heights readers who take its insights to heart.' – *Maurie J. Cohen, Professor of Sustainability Studies, New Jersey Institute of Technology, and co-founder of the Sustainable Consumption Research and Action Initiative (SCORAI), USA*

'Middlemiss brings together the perspectives of a wide range of disciplines to frame an accessible picture of the academic landscape surrounding sustainable consumption – an evolving field. An excellent resource for anyone wishing to understand the role of consumption in the social, economic and environmental challenges of the modern world.' – *Garrette E. Clark, Sustainable Lifestyles Programme Officer, UN Environment, France*

'This book provides a timely and highly needed textbook for classes on sustainable consumption across disciplines. Middlemiss does a wonderful job of highlighting the relevance of the topic, the enormous challenges involved, and, most importantly, the need to adopt systemic approaches if one seriously aims to solve the problems arising from our high-consumption lifestyles.' – *Doris Fuchs, Professor of International Relations and Sustainable Development, University of Münster, Germany*

'Middlemiss has given instructors and students an invaluable resource! Instructors will appreciate the use of concrete examples to make clear the complexity of sustainable consumption. Students will be grateful for the real-life illustrations that connect their own lives to large-scale sociological and cultural drivers of unsustainable resource use patterns.' – *Emily Huddart Kennedy, Assistant Professor of Sociology, Washington State University, USA*

Sustainable Consumption

Key Issues

Lucie Middlemiss

LONDON AND NEW YORK

First published 2018
by Routledge
2 Park Square, Milton Park, Abingdon, Oxon OX14 4RN

and by Routledge
711 Third Avenue, New York, NY 10017

Routledge is an imprint of the Taylor & Francis Group, an informa business.

British Library Cataloguing-in-Publication Data
A catalogue record for this book is available from the British Library

Library of Congress Cataloging-in-Publication Data
Names: Middlemiss, Lucie, author.
Title: Sustainable consumption : key issues / Lucie Middlemiss.
Description: Abingdon, Oxon ; New York, NY : Routledge, 2018.
    Series: Key issues in environment and sustainability | Includes
    bibliographical references and index.
Identifiers: LCCN 2018004832 | ISBN 9781138645639 (hbk :
    alk. paper) | ISBN 9781138645660 (pbk : alk. paper) | ISBN
    9781315628035 (ebk : alk. paper)
Subjects: LCSH: Consumption (Economics)—Environmental aspects.
Classification: LCC HB820 .M53 2018 | DDC 339.4/7—dc23
LC record available at https://lccn.loc.gov/2018004832

ISBN: 978-1-138-64563-9 (hbk)
ISBN: 978-1-138-64566-0 (pbk)
ISBN: 978-1-315-62803-5 (ebk)

Typeset in Goudy
by Swales & Willis Ltd, Exeter, Devon, UK

Contents

Figures

Tables

Boxes

Foreword

Garrette Clark and Alexia Legrand from
UN Environment

Individuals make dozens if not hundreds of decisions every day. For the lucky amongst us, we decide what to wear, what to eat, how to get to school or work, what to do when we go home, and where to go on vacation. Add together these individual decisions and we have a mass consumer base whose preferences, attitudes and behaviours shape citizens' decisions, and ultimately help drive global patterns of production and consumption.

Research shows that global resource consumption is increasingly occurring in urban contexts, where most of the world's population lives.[1] By 2050, some two-thirds of the global population, or 6.3 billion people – and most of them young – will be living in cities. If we are serious about meeting Sustainable Development Goals, we need to take a closer look at how people make decisions and how they can be encouraged to make more sustainable choices, at scale. In particular, influencing the consumption patterns of the younger generation will be crucial in paving the path towards achieving Sustainable Development Goals. But these decisions are often shaped by the choice architecture and availability as well as supply of goods, products and services.[2]

How do people consume and make decisions about their daily behaviour? People do not wake up in the morning with the intention to harm the planet. Nor do they necessarily wake up motivated to conserve energy or water, or to find the least polluting way to get to work. People wake up, eat, prepare for the day, get to work, school or chores, in accordance with habits and make decisions based on their needs and aspirations for family, friends and those around them. Sustainability, as such, is not *the* main lifestyle motivating factor. Rather, individual choices depend on variables such as time, costs, routine, information, culture, social belonging, convenience, etc. Furthermore, we know that human decisions are not always rational. Therefore, to make everyday choices more sustainable, available options must be easy, simple, comfortable, affordable and accessible. Yet this is not the situation today, due to lack of infrastructure, limited viable options and mass consumption messaging.

What can be done to avail and encourage more sustainable choices? The private sector has many lessons to teach; the success of a business has always been dependent on its ability to create, anticipate and respond to consumer demand. Businesses regularly develop strategies from market research and insights on actual consumer behaviour. Some companies already integrate sustainability criteria into their business models, recognising that resource scarcity, energy costs and environmental impacts affect bottom lines. Others acknowledge that customers are increasingly picky about responsible resourcing and simply find it 'good business' to adopt sustainable corporate practices.

Where do policy-makers stand? Policy-makers are faced with the challenge to advance sustainability agendas while simultaneously encouraging economic growth. They must encourage sustainable production and consumers from businesses as well as customers – which includes the public and private sectors as well as citizens. The government, too, can play a role in influencing individual and organisational decision-making for better sustainability by taking attitudes and behaviour into account when designing and implementing policies. Better data (hotspots where action should be taken), more innovative policy-making, and better communication of the benefits of sustainable choices can contribute to the common goal.

Sustainable lifestyles are on the international agenda, as policy-makers and other stakeholders have recognised that there are opportunities to increase quality of life for all and are beginning to develop indicators beyond Gross Domestic Product growth. The 2030 Agenda for Sustainable Development includes 17 Sustainable Development Goals (SDGs) that promote implicitly and explicitly the adoption of more sustainable consumption and production to address global societal and environmental issues. The COP21 Paris Agreement and intergovernmental processes like the 10-Year Framework of Programmes on Sustainable Consumption and Production also highlight the importance of sustainable patterns of consumption and production to address climate change, reduce poverty and protect the environment.

Hearteningly, change is under way. Around the globe, individuals, businesses and policy-makers are beginning to understand the consequences of our current consumption path and increasingly weave sustainability into their daily decisions. Simple initiatives such as urban gardening, waste-reduction campaigns, or vehicle-sharing are increasingly adopted. Not only do they make an impact, but they may actually also enhance livelihoods.

While these trends are promising, building a more sustainable and inclusive society needs to focus on education. Educators need to develop a holistic, compelling and pragmatic understanding of what drives, defines and results from sustainable consumption. The youth of today are driving consumption trends and will be tomorrow's decision-makers. As 2–3 billion new consumers are anticipated to come in the next decades, education about sustainable consumption is essential to enable the transition to a more low-carbon, resource-efficient and socially inclusive economy. We need to empower youth with the understanding and tools to make informed lifestyle choices. Together we can build a world where sustainable lifestyles are desirable, accessible and encouraged by all sectors of society.

Notes

1 Cities are associated with 60–80 per cent of GHG emissions, consume 75 per cent of natural resources and account for 50 per cent of waste (UNEP, 2012).
2 This is complemented by the increasing numbers of people who are unable to meet even their basic needs. And the aspirations and systems in place that are feeding the decision making, are setting and fixing the production and consumption patterns that will determine our future.

Acknowledgements

The inspiration for writing this book was my third-year undergraduate module on Sustainable Consumption (SOEE 3202) which I have taught at the University of Leeds since 2009. There is so much intellectual stimulation to be had in talking to a group of engaged and critical students about these topics. For me, teaching this topic is about bringing together theory and daily life, and I have many treasured memories of the 'learning moments' my students have experienced along the way. The module, and indeed this book, is designed to draw out the intellectual lessons from this highly practical topic, and I hope to encourage a more critical approach to understanding daily life in the process. Teaching the module has been essential in shaping both my own views on the topic, and my research interests as it forces me to read and think more widely than I otherwise would.

As such I owe a 'thank you' to the students I have worked with over the years. More specifically, I also want to thank the following students who kindly read a chapter of the book to check that it was pitched appropriately: Lliam Bennett, Becky Ewen, Anna Lawson, George Middlemiss, Lewis Mitchell, Eleanor Scull and Rosie Watson.

Setting out to write the whole of this book was an exciting prospect, and I have very much enjoyed the process. Having said that, it has also involved a mammoth reading exercise on my part: summarising a huge body of literature from a wide range of social science disciplines was a challenge. For my own reassurance, and indeed for quality control, I engaged disciplinary experts who kindly read a chapter each of the book in exchange for an e-book copy. Any remaining errors are no doubt my own. Thank you to Manisha Anantharaman, Lina Brand Correa, Milena Buchs, Tim Foxon, Tom Hargreaves, Cindy Isenhour, Marlyne Sahakian, Kate Scott, Gill Seyfang, Anne Tallontire, Andrea Taylor, Gerald Taylor-Aiken and Dan Welch.

Chapter 12 was greatly inspired by a separate piece of work, which was funded thanks to the goodwill of my colleague Anna Wesselink, who also had some input into the development of these ideas.

I started writing this book on a sabbatical granted by my research institute, the Sustainability Research Institute at the University of Leeds. I am indebted to my parents-in-law, Liz and Jim Revill who hosted me in their attic where I hid in order to make space and time to write. Jim, a retired physics book publisher, also kindly helped me gain the permission to reproduce the images here.

Finally, most of my own consumption happens in collaboration with my husband Derek, and my two sons George and Ralph. Derek's support of my work, in particular in holding the fort when I am at sustainable consumption conferences, and in co-parenting the rest of the time is both essential and deeply appreciated. George and Ralph give me a sense of perspective: after all, it is their future being planned for, not my own.

Part 1

Introducing sustainable consumption

1 Introduction

Every January I have the privilege to stand in front of a new cohort of sustainable consumption students at the University of Leeds in the United Kingdom. This is always an exciting moment for me. Most of my students are third years, about to finish their undergraduate degrees, but they are a diverse bunch. Many come from other university departments than my own: earth and environment. Over the years, I have encountered business students, engineers, physicists, human geographers, environmental social scientists, biologists and more. My students have come from five continents of the world, some on exchange programmes from their home university. I have taught students who are environment or human rights activists, and others who are aiming for graduate programmes in big corporations. Each of my students comes with their own perspective on the world, and that perspective is often the starting point for their studies.

Indeed, the beauty of studying sustainable consumption is that it is about bringing academic understanding together with everyday life. Everyone has experience of everyday life, so this is an easy starting point. The connection with everyday life makes the academic work that we do on sustainable consumption the theory – more approachable. If we take an example from our own life and think it through using theory, we not only understand how that theory works, but also start to get a sense of its shortcomings, to think about what it does and does not explain. When we talk about the theories of everyday life, we also begin to reveal the assumptions that are made in the world about what makes people act in particular ways.

Another great thing about studying sustainable consumption is that it brings together a wide range of social science disciplines to look at possible solutions to environmental and social problems. From the beginning, these disciplines disagree. An economist does not understand the problem of unsustainable consumption in the same way that a psychologist, sociologist, or anthropologist does. Very often the disagreements between disciplines amount to a disagreement in politics: a difference of opinion on what the problem is and what should be done about it. As a result we encounter questions such as 'what is most important – individual freedom or the well-being of society?', or 'how should access to environmental resources be distributed?', or 'who bears responsibility here?' By the end of this book, you will have a flavour of how each of these disciplines works, and a sense of which (if any) chimes most closely with your own way of thinking.

The best way to approach this topic is to start with an open mind, and be prepared to challenge your own assumptions and beliefs. This is likely to involve thinking about what kind of a background you have, your gender, age and ethnic heritage, and attempting to understand how this makes you think in particular ways. It also might mean that you need to be honest about the basic beliefs that you have about why people do what they do, and be prepared to revise these. When teaching this topic, the best moments for me are when people have to confront the fact that they hold inconsistent views, and decide what they will do about this. I hope that, after reading this book, you will have understood the wide variety of approaches to sustainable consumption, and worked out where you stand on this topic. In the Conclusion, I will also offer you some advice on how you might want to approach the world given your standpoint.

What is sustainable consumption?

Consumption, in its simplest sense, means using up resources in order to live our daily lives. We all need to consume in order to survive, there are still many people on the planet that consume too little. Researchers, policy-makers and practitioners who work on sustainable consumption, would agree that high-consumption lifestyles have negative impacts on the environment and on other people (UNEP, 2001; Cohen and Murphy, 2001b; Jackson, 2006; Seyfang, 2009; Lorek and Vergragt, 2015; Urban Sustainability Director's Network, 2016).

Box 1.1 Summary: what is sustainable consumption?

For the purposes of this book the study and practice of sustainable consumption concerns:

- Understanding the impact of high-consumption lifestyles on the environment and on other people, through the intersection of people's daily lives with environmental problems.
- Exploring the opportunities for consuming less (for e.g. less resource intensity, longer product life, energy efficiency and sufficiency) and consuming differently (for e.g. sharing not owning, replacing one practice with another) with regards to the purchase, use and disposal of stuff.
- Understanding the way in which high-consumption lifestyles are embedded in the material, social, cultural and political world.

(See also Jackson, 2006; Lorek and Vergragt, 2015.)

By 'high consumption', I mean lifestyles which use a lot of resources and create a lot of waste, the kinds of lifestyles that many people in the global North, and more affluent people in the global South tend to live (see Chapter 2). The impacts of high-consumption lifestyles are often indirect: we consume goods and services, and as a result, either the environment, other people, or both, are adversely affected (at some point in the chain of production, purchase, use and disposal). In its simplest sense, the term 'sustainable consumption' refers to efforts to understand how these impacts on environment or on other people might be avoided.

In other words, the key question here is: how might our current consumption patterns be made more environmentally and socially sustainable? To be more specific, people working in the field of sustainable consumption are aiming to answer some important questions about the world, including:

- What impacts do our high-consumption lifestyles have on the environment and on other people?
- Why do people consume in the way they do?
- What can we do to reduce negative environmental and social impacts of high-consumption lifestyles?
- What are the opportunities for transformation towards a more just, environmentally benign world?

These questions also suggest that sustainable consumption research, policy and practice sits somewhere between the environmental, social and economic worlds. In general, work on sustainable consumption does not question whether environmental problems exist; instead we focus on how consumption impacts on these problems, and what can be done to reduce these impacts.

Sustainable consumption is a topic which we can access through thinking about daily life. Very often, we are talking about the mundane realities of people's everyday lives, such as how they choose to live, or how they are constrained by their circumstances, what values they hold and how these play out in their decisions, and the influence that personal identity has on a person's practices. When I say 'mundane', I do not mean that this is dull – quite the opposite! For me, thinking about sustainable consumption is exciting because it makes us connect the details of people's daily lives to bigger ideas about society, and theories of how the world works. In my experience, this topic makes theory very accessible to students like yourself, as many of the examples we draw on to explain theory come from people's daily lives, and these are instinctively understood.

The precise term 'sustainable consumption' is most at home among policymakers, particularly at an international and national level, where changes in consumption patterns are talked about in more abstract terms, with the objective of reducing impacts. Some academics also use the term 'sustainable consumption' to talk about these issues, and the international Sustainable Consumption Research and Action Initiative, with its associated conferences, events and networks is a good example of this (SCORAI, 2017). This is a multi-disciplinary field, however, and academics from different disciplines use a very wide range of concepts and associated theories in thinking about this topic, including pro-environmental behaviour (psychology), practice (sociology), ethical consumption (business studies and cultural studies), and environmental citizenship (political science). Practitioners engage an even wider range of concepts to talk about their activities in this area, concepts specific to their particular field of interest. A transport planner might talk about 'travel mode change' for instance, or an energy efficiency advisor about 'alleviating fuel poverty'.

In this book, I take a very broad view of 'what counts' as sustainable consumption, including all of the concepts listed above and more in my understanding of the term. I do this for several reasons. First, because pragmatically there is value in engaging with all these different disciplinary, policy and practitioner perspectives, in order to gain both a deeper understanding of these problems, and the possible solutions to them. If I just looked at thinking, policy and practice that called itself 'sustainable consumption' I would miss out a lot of interesting and useful work. Second, because in writing this book I am encouraging you to develop a critical perspective on this field. By helping you to understand what sustainable consumption means from a variety of perspectives, I hope this will also help you understand the merits and shortfalls of each of these perspectives. Indeed all of the chapters will include a critical commentary on the assumptions that each perspective takes, and the limitations that these assumptions place on us understanding and addressing the problem. Note that taking such a broad definition is rather risky: plenty of authors would argue that even ethical consumption is too broad to be definable (Lewis and Potter, 2011; Littler, 2011). It also situates this book, and indeed the topic of sustainable consumption as a multi-disciplinary endeavour, which starts with a real-world problem (the unsustainable use and distribution of resources) and attempts to understand it using all the academic tools at our disposal.

By taking both a multi-disciplinary starting point, and by looking at this work rather critically, I also expose the fact that this is a topic of contention: that there is no 'right answer' to the many questions that this topic raises. In this book, you will see that different people have very different perspectives on what the 'real problem' is, what causes that problem, and how it might be resolved. For instance, the problem of unsustainable consumption is explained variously as a problem of individuals not meeting their responsibilities, a problem of structural, social forces preventing people from acting how they would like to, or a problem of people not understanding the need for change. For me, this reveals sustainable consumption to be a highly political topic: how you see the problem, its causes and its solutions will depend very much on what you think is important (your politics). I hope you can use this book to develop your own opinions, and indeed your own politics on this topic.

Box 1.2 Why 'sustainable consumption'?

To start as we mean to go on, it is worth thinking critically about why this book is called 'sustainable consumption' at all. As an academic working in this area, I feel quite ambivalent about the term: on the one hand, it does not really do justice to the range of work done in this area; on the other hand, it connects me to a community of scholars and practitioners who have common interests. I list some of the advantages and disadvantages of the term here:

Advantages:

- The term 'sustainable consumption' is multi-disciplinary. As such, it does not 'take sides' in the way that other terms would (e.g. if the book was called 'pro-environmental behaviour', you would expect to read only psychological insights).
- The term 'sustainable consumption' is where international and national policy-makers often start to engage with this topic. This means work conducted under this label attracts their attention.
- Consumption is a social science category, not a natural science category like energy, food or water. The term therefore tends to bring together social scientists to talk about sustainability issues, and to help us see how consumption of energy and water (for instance) might have things in common.

Disadvantages:

- The word 'consumption' tends to make people think of shopping, rather than the vast range of interactions people have with the environment and with other people. I include political activism, boycotts, voluntary simplicity and all of resource-consuming daily life in the category of sustainable consumption, but many would restrict their definition to 'shopping'.
- The word 'consumption' tends to be interpreted as 'using up resources'. This can become a very technocratic framing of the problem: which focuses on which resources are used, losing sight of the people using the resources, and the power structures that impact on the distribution of resources.
- The word 'consumption' may also imply that we are only interested in individuals and how they choose to live according to their values. As you will see, this is not at all the case! Many scholars of sustainable consumption make it their business to focus on how social structures result in people consuming in specific ways.

Key ideas in sustainable consumption

Rather than give a straightforward history of sustainable consumption here, I want to outline some of the key ideas that have influenced thinking in this field since its inception. Academic work in this field is relatively new. As a research field, the term 'sustainable consumption' began to take off in the early 2000s, with the first book using the term in its title published in 2001 (Cohen and Murphy, 2001b). In this section, I will take you through mainstream (from population control to ecological modernisation), radical (degrowth and new economics) and embedded (practice approaches, ethical consumption) ideas of sustainable consumption. These to some extent map onto the categories of reformist, revolutionary and reconfiguration identified by Geels and colleagues (Geels et al., 2015). Note that histories of sustainable consumption, tracking the development of the idea in policy and practice are available elsewhere (Cohen, 2001; Fuchs and Lorek, 2005; Rumpala, 2011; Chappells and Trentmann, 2015).

In the policy world, these concepts have been commonplace for somewhat longer. 'Sustainable consumption and production' have been referred to in many of the international agreements on environmental issues since the 1992 Rio Earth Summit, including most recently the Paris agreement. This recognises that 'sustainable lifestyles and sustainable patterns of consumption and production, with developed country parties taking the lead, play an important role in addressing climate change' (UNFCCC, 2015, 2). The Sustainable Development goals also include '12. Responsible consumption and production' (UNDESA, 2016). Some national governments have included sustainable consumption and production in their environmental policies, including Finland, Sweden and the UK (Berg, 2011). In some pioneering initiatives, local governments are also engaging with these issues, including for instance the work of urban sustainability directors in the US (Urban Sustainability Director's Network, 2016). To some extent, the corporate world is also engaging with these issues, through initiatives on product design and durability (see Chapter 10). Finally, the third sector, or non-profit world is also engaged in action on sustainable consumption (see Chapter 11).

Mainstream views of sustainable consumption

As a concept, sustainable consumption exists very much in the shadows of sustainable development, or indeed the environmental agenda. As a result, the way it is understood (or its 'framing') is strongly linked to broader environmental and sustainability framings. For a long time, the central framing of environmental issues was as a problem of *over-population*: too many people consuming too much stuff, creates environmental damage, exacerbated by population growth. Politically this is highly contentious. As Cohen puts it: 'By defining global environmental problems in terms of population growth, wealthy nations managed for several decades to successfully sidestep their own complicity' (Cohen, 2001, 21). In other words, defining sustainable consumption as a population problem implies that the developing world should be held responsible for environmental damage (since developing countries tend to have higher population growth), despite the highly evident disparity in environmental impact caused by citizens of the developed world (see Chapter 2). More recently, this problem definition has changed, as it became more and more difficult to ignore the impact of affluence on consumption effects.

The mainstream framing of the problem of sustainable consumption is now more likely to refer to market and technology failure, and the resulting need for economic and technical solutions (Cohen and Murphy, 2001a; Geels et al., 2015). In this perspective, commonly known as *ecological modernisation*, there is optimism about the possibility to make a growing economy work for environmental protection, through technological innovation. In such a 'weak sustainability' approach, the appropriate response to unsustainable consumption is to correct market failure; as Jackson puts it: 'to ensure that the market allows people to make efficient choices about their own actions' (Jackson, 2005b, 3). Most global North governments which act on sustainable consumption take an ecological modernisation, or at least a weak sustainability approach, emphasising efficiency (consuming better) above sufficiency (consuming less) (Berg, 2011; Cohen, 2001; Hobson, 2004). This involves decoupling economic growth from environmental damage, and governments have had some success with this (O'Rourke and Lollo, 2015).

The shift to an ecological modernisation framing produced further changes in the way that sustainable consumption is talked about, particularly with regards to the onus of responsibility. In 2001, Maurie Cohen and Joe Murphy argued that until then, the approach to solving environmental problems had been producer-oriented, with responsibility for change being attributed to the producer: 'For the past two centuries, and particularly during the last thirty years, solving environmental problems has been construed as a producer responsibility and consumers have been placed at a distance from the assignment of culpability' (Cohen and Murphy, 2001a, 4).

Tackling consumer behaviour is more challenging for a number of reasons: because it involves the state getting involved in people's everyday lives, and because producers are less numerous than consumers, and as such easier to target (ibid.). There are further barriers to talking about consumption in public life, however. As Princen and colleagues put it, writing around the same time: 'No one in public life dares – or needs – to ask why people consume, let alone to question whether people or societies are better off with their accustomed consumption patterns' (Princen et al., 2002, 5).

In some contexts, this fear of talking about (and particularly making moral judgements about) consumption persists. On the other hand, if we are to see market failure as a one of the central causes of environmental problems, and to link this market failure to the actions of individuals, it is an easy step to transfer responsibility to the consumer, for failing to correctly respond to market signals (Seyfang, 2009). Such individualisation of responsibility for environmental problems is widespread, and subject to extensive criticism (Maniates, 2001; Hobson, 2004; Berg, 2011; Middlemiss, 2014). The individualisation of responsibility is also an example of neo-liberal rollback: of consumers 'inheriting the regulatory responsibilities that the state has cast off' (Cohen, 2001, 34).

More radical concerns

Alongside these mainstream ideas about sustainable consumption, there is a history of more radical concern with environment, and with sustainable consumption issues, sometimes called 'strong sustainable consumption' (Lorek and Fuchs, 2013). Radical concerns stem from the broader environmental movement, which tends to widen the critique of environmental problems by identifying causal structures in society (particularly the growth imperative, and neo-liberal economics) and calling for their transformation. As Geels and colleagues put it, in 'revolutionary' perspectives: 'many proponents share the diagnosis that contemporary environmental problems are symptoms of deeper (socio-cultural and politico-economic) problems in modern capitalist societies' (Geels et al., 2015, 4).

Revolutionary or radical perspectives also propose different social goals, and mechanisms by which these goals can be achieved. In the context of sustainable development research, much radical attention is paid to degrowth research, which contests the idea that economic growth is of value to humanity (ibid. and see Chapter 13) and proposes that nations should focus on more positive social goals. Means to achieve degrowth, or at least to achieve a 'new economics of sustainable consumption' (which prioritises people and planet above profits) might include: localisation, reducing ecological footprints, community building, collective action and building new infrastructures of provision (Seyfang, 2009).

As we begin to see in Seyfang's vision of a 'new economics' above, these radical perspectives position both human well-being, and local or community action more centrally in crafting solutions. This includes a commitment to incorporating issues of national and global equity into sustainable consumption. For instance, in Dobson's idea of ecological citizenship, the ecological footprint (see Chapter 7) is interpreted as an entitlement to a certain amount of ecological space: people have a responsibility not to use too many resources, but also a right to a decent life (Dobson, 2003). Maurie Cohen says that to overcome the potential negative effects of reducing consumption, there is a need to cultivate income equality within nations (thus developing a culture that does not look to consumption for status), as well as solidarity with developing countries (which could lose out from reduced consumption) (Cohen, 2004). A further body of work argues that more sustainable lifestyles actually increase people's well-being (Jackson, 2005a). Tim Jackson's idea of the 'double dividend' (see Chapter 12) is that consuming less might have benefits both for the environment and for people's well-being.

Radical perspectives challenge many of the 'truths' implied in the mainstream approach: that economic growth is essential (see Chapter 13), that consumption makes you happy, that existing distributions of wealth are appropriate. This is useful because it helps us to be more critical of the assumptions we make (that some of these things are part of the 'natural order'). On the other hand, these perspectives have also tended to start with a rather naïve and moralistic vision of the future, and the means by which we might reach it (Geels et al., 2015). Further, the specific vision of a future in which local communities hold more power, and in which we aim to be happy rather than rich, is not to everyone's taste. Indeed, such a vision is most appropriate for a rather wealthy, educated and middle-class demographic, in which adopting voluntary simplicity or 'downshifting' is a viable option. Both mainstream and radical perspectives on sustainable consumption need to take into account social difference (see Chapter 3) in their thinking. This brings us to our final key idea.

Consumption is embedded

More recent advances in thinking on sustainable consumption, partly in reaction to the individualisation apparent in mainstream policy, and the corresponding focus on radical possibilities for action, have emphasised the social, historical, political, cultural, material and systemic embeddedness of any act of consumption (see Chapters 8, 9 and 13). By embeddedness, I mean that each act of consumption, or indeed each individual, cannot be understood independently from its world. This shift in thinking marks the engagement of the social sciences with this topic, with contributions from sociology (Shove, 2003), anthropology (Wilk, 2002), science and technology studies (Geels et al., 2015) and others. There is a

> need to see consumption not just as an individual's choice among goods but as a stream of choices and decisions winding its way through the various stages of extraction, manufacture, and final use, embedded at every step in social relations of power and authority.
>
> (Princen et al., 2002, 12)

Note also that this tendency towards understanding actions in context is a reaction to the disciplines of psychology and economics, which typically aim to build theory that can be applied more universally to a number of behaviours (e.g. people react to monetary incentives; or people's values affect their behaviours). The social sciences tend instead to take an interest in context: starting with an assumption that people act differently because of their circumstances, rather than an assumption that everyone acts the same, and attempting to understand how those differences play out.

In the context of sustainable consumption, these ideas are somewhat younger than the mainstream or radical approaches, and as such they are only beginning to think about how change happens (see, for instance, Spurling et al., 2013). They are not strongly represented in political thinking, partly because their message is somewhere between the revolution and business as usual. Geels and colleagues characterise these ideas as 'reconfiguration', and argue that changes in this context 'entail co-evolutionary changes in technologies, markets, institutional frameworks, cultural meanings and everyday life practices, but do not necessitate the overthrowing of some hypostasized totality (such as capitalism, consumerism or materialism)' (Geels et al., 2015, 2).

Most fundamental to this set of ideas is that change will only happen systemically, and if we understand, and account for the contexts in which people live (O'Rourke and Lollo, 2015). Changing prices (economics) or the way people think and feel about things (psychology) is not enough. These are difficult messages for government, as they imply substantial investment in both research and implementation, and this may account for the persistence of less holistic ideas in policy and practice.

A multi-disciplinary or interdisciplinary field?

One of the key characteristics of sustainable consumption research is that it is not owned by one discipline. Indeed, as I pointed out in the Introduction, the term is most often used by people working on environmental policy at a national or international level, and some academics. Different academic disciplines use different terminology, and practitioners working on specific aspects of sustainable consumption will also draw on different languages. In a sense then, sustainable consumption is the object that we study, and we study it from many different perspectives.

I would argue that sustainable consumption is a mostly a multi-disciplinary field, in that a number of different disciplines have engaged with the topic, applying their discipline-specific theories and methods to answer questions about sustainable consumption, and to some extent they have engaged in conversation across disciplines. There have also been a number of attempts to look at sustainable consumption from an interdisciplinary perspective: disciplines working together to create new forms of knowledge about sustainable consumption. All the disciplines that engage with this topic sit principally in the social sciences, although the natural sciences are instrumental in helping to characterise the problem (see Chapter 2).

Economics, psychology, politics, sociology and cultural studies all make contributions here, with an interdisciplinary body of work also existing. As discussed, each of these disciplines uses different terminology to talk about sustainable consumption. The main concepts are shown across the top of Figure 1.1, each of these will be explained in more detail in later chapters. I have also characterised the disciplines in relation to their substantive focus in the field in this figure: some are more preoccupied with questions of policy and sustainable consumption, others with questions about how people practice (un)sustainable consumption in daily life.

The challenges that stem from working in a multi-disciplinary field are multiple. The key one for me is the use of different languages by different disciplines to explain the world. In a simple sense, this becomes a problem of understanding and translation: when people from one discipline understand the world through one set of terminology, they can find it hard to communicate with people from another discipline with different words. I would argue that the power of language

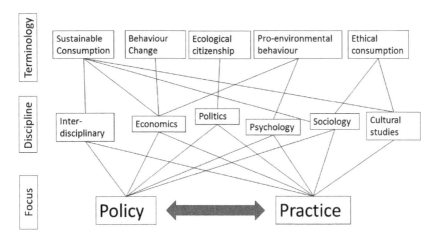

Figure 1.1 A map of the terminology, disciplines and focus engaged in the field of
   sustainable consumption

goes further than this, however. In a seminal study of 'defense intellectuals' (people who manage nuclear weapons in the US) and the language they use, Carol
Cohn found that their language structured the kinds of questions they are able to
ask, and the kinds of values that they can incorporate in decision-making (Cohn,
1987). It is difficult, for instance, for people who think and speak from the point
of view of the weapon to incorporate more human considerations into their decisions. A parallel with this in our field, might be that if you use the language of
neo-classical economics, there is limited or even no place for discussing society
or collective action.

   Some important consequences stem from the multi-disciplinary nature of the
field. First, the relationships between the different disciplines are important to
understand. There is sometimes antagonism between the disciplines, witness the
'ABC' debate begun by Elisabeth Shove (sociology) and continued by psychologists and beyond, which you can read more about in Chapter 8 (Shove, 2010;
Whitmarsh et al., 2011; Wilson and Chatterton, 2011). Some of this antagonism
no doubt stems from perceptions of the power held by the ideas and theories promoted by each discipline. Certainly in the UK (where this debate took place),
there is a common understanding that power in the two relevant government
departments, the Department of Energy and Climate Change (DECC) and the
Department of Environment, Food and Rural Affairs (DEFRA), is held by psychologists and economists, and there is some frustration among other disciplines
about their ideas not being used in policy-making. In other cases, work within
each individual discipline completely ignores work on the others. The sociologists and cultural studies scholars are unlikely to engage with psychology and

economics (and vice versa) because each of these disciplines speaks such a different language, and has such a different world-view.

In response to this world in which groups of scholars defend and promote their own ideas in opposition to others, we often see calls for interdisciplinarity (meaning the disciplines working together to create new forms of knowledge). Richard Wilk, for instance, argues that academics should try to avoid methodological purism, and to understand that a combination of approaches will be essential to address the problem of unsustainable consumption (Wilk, 2002). Others have produced interdisciplinary frameworks in order to attempt to break down these kinds of barriers (Kollmuss and Agyeman, 2002; Barr and Gilg, 2006; Young and Middlemiss, 2012). Multi-disciplinarity can be confusing for students in this field. My advice: be prepared to listen to a range of explanations of how things happen, be open minded, and do not expect a simple answer!

A critical approach

We now have some understanding of the concept of sustainable consumption, some key ideas in this field and its multi-disciplinary nature. Before we jump in to the details of this research, policy and practice area in more detail, I want to say some words about my approach to this topic, and its impact on the way this book is written. In this book, I take a critical approach to understanding sustainable consumption. This does not mean that I spend the next fourteen chapters telling you what a waste of time and energy this agenda is! Far from it – I work in this area because I care about environmental issues, about inequality and human suffering, and about the intersection between these two. However, as an academic I also care about uncovering the political motivations, justifications and implications of knowledge. Further, I care that knowledge is used appropriately and with a good understanding of its politics. This is particularly important in a multi-disciplinary topic area such as sustainable consumption.

My fellow environmental social scientists, as in many disciplines, have varying degrees of, often public, commitment to a number of political causes. My colleagues include deep green environmentalists, advocates for corporate sustainability, and enthusiastic proponents of a well-being objective for society. The effect of these political positions on our research is often left unstated, or merely assumed to be negligible. In my experience, while we are rather good at recognising mainstream politics, and its limitations, we are less good at recognising our own politics, and the limits that this places on our research. One of the tasks for me as the writer, and you as the reader of this book, is to uncover these politics and to think about how they affect the world.

Academic disciplines are also a form of politics. For instance, in the study of environmental issues, the first discipline to address the environment was economics, a 'science' which has a huge amount of leverage in contemporary society. The fact that economics was first to the party, and that it is the language of an accepted and powerful discourse in society, allows it to have an impact which other interesting and valuable knowledge forms (such as cultural studies, for instance) do not. Further, the type of knowledge that (especially mainstream) economics promotes (quantitative, financial) means that answers to questions such as 'what matters?', 'what should we do?', 'who should do it' are rather predetermined.

Box 1.3 Some critical questions about sustainable consumption

How is the problem being defined?

Being critical involves stepping outside of the world which the proponents of a particular perspective inhabit, and unpicking how they think. It is useful to start by asking how they are defining the problem (in this case, how they are defining sustainable consumption). In asking this question, we should also look for what is not included in their problem definition.

Who is the subject?

Sustainable consumption deals with everyday life, and as such is often concerned with discussing why and how people do things. To think about this critically it helps to ask 'who is the subject' of a particular perspective, in other words 'what does this perspective think people are like?' So, for instance, neo-classical economics thinks that people are rational and that they act in their own interests. When we know how the subject is understood, we can also see what kinds of solution are (and are not) possible from that perspective.

How is the solution understood?

The way in which the problem is defined, and the subject understood will have a big impact on how a perspective sees the solutions. To some extent, this question is asking 'what are the possibilities for action of a given starting point?' We can also dig deeper into a given solution to ask 'what is this solution being used to do?' (probably to solve a sustainable consumption problem, but it may also be reinforcing other agendas).

Note that a 'perspective' could be that of a discipline, an organisation, or an individual. You probably have your own assumptions about the problem, subject and solution. It is my job in this book to help you think more deeply about your own perspective, to challenge it, and hopefully to change it a bit in the process!

So what does being 'critical' mean? Some of the hallmarks of a critical approach include: understanding that 'facts' are affected by the people who define them, understanding that facts and politics are intertwined, and as a result refusing to accept facts and politics at face value (Horkheimer, 1972). Critical scholars and thinkers often want to know how a problem is being understood (or 'problematised') as this can have a huge impact on what possible solutions can be put forward to solve that problem (Rose, 1999; Bacchi, 2015). You will see in this book that different disciplines understand the problems of sustainable consumption differently, and this also has an impact on what kinds of policy recommendations they are able to make. Being critical also suggests being careful not to accept at face value attempts to 'improve the way things are done' (Horkheimer, 1972). This is particularly important in sustainability studies, as while writers often have good intentions (trying to solve environmental and social problems) they cannot always see how their own prejudices are affecting their recommendations. In the social sciences, being critical also means engaging with social theory to help explain a social phenomenon such as sustainable consumption. This often helps us see things about that social phenomenon that we would otherwise have missed.

Some useful critical questions are included in Box 1.3. These are questions that I will be addressing throughout the book in the various chapters on disciplinary perspectives or research areas. They also might be useful for you in thinking about this topic and further afield.

About this book

The book is organised into three parts, titled: 'Introducing sustainable consumption', 'Explaining sustainable consumption', and 'Visions of the future in sustainable consumption'.

The first part outlines my understanding of the problem of sustainable consumption: its environmental (Chapter 2) and social (Chapter 3) characteristics. Clearly we have to understand the scope of the environmental and social problem before we start to think about how it can be solved. In Chapter 2, I also talk about means of measuring unsustainable consumption, and developments in the scholarship of measurement. The social context to sustainable consumption is also important to understand, and in my view rather neglected. In Chapter 3, I explore how social difference categories (such as class, gender, ethnic origin, disability, or wealth) impact on people's inclusion in the environmental agenda and their ability to take action.

In the middle part of the book (Chapters 4–9), I critically assess a series of received opinions on the root cause of sustainable consumption: 'People don't understand'; 'People are selfish'; 'It's all about values'; 'The personal is political'; 'We don't have a choice'; 'Consumption is meaningful!'. Each of these 'received opinions' or 'stories' represents a disciplinary perspective on the problem of sustainable consumption, although admittedly the debates are rather oversimplified by these titles! You also might recognise your own assumptions in one of these titles. I use these six chapters to outline a series of theoretical perspectives, and to critically explore what such assumptions mean about the problem definition and the possible solutions stemming from each discipline.

In the third part of the book, I look at the various solutions that have been brought forward by academics, policy-makers and/or practitioners in this space, to address problems of sustainable consumption. These solutions are not bounded by discipline, indeed each chapter shows how a group of political ideas and disciplinary perspectives have been brought together to offer some form of resolution. This section includes Chapter 10, which covers the claims for looking at sustainable consumption in the context of production, rather than understanding it as a separate entity. Chapter 11 looks at how ideas of the 'collective' have been mobilised in this field. In Chapter 12, we look at the arguments around well-being and happiness mobilised in favour of promoting sustainable consumption. Finally, Chapter 13 explores systemic explanations of change, grounded in the transitions literature and degrowth movements.

In the concluding chapter (14), I offer some guidance on how to make sense of this large body of work. It can at times be overwhelming to be studying such a disparate field, with a wide variety of strong theoretical starting points from the different disciplines, and no clear 'right' or 'wrong' answers, despite the very clear environmental problem I outline in Chapter 2. Here I suggest some strategies for managing this uncertainty in your future engagement with this topic, with the hope of leaving you confident to take this agenda forward in your own world.

Further resources

Sustainable Consumption Research and Action Initiative (SCORAI) website, mailing list and discussion group – http://scorai.org/.

References

BACCHI, C. 2015. The turn to problematization: Political implications of contrasting interpretive and poststructural adaptations. *Open Journal of Political Science*, 5, 1–12.

BARR, S. & GILG, A. 2006. Sustainable lifestyles: Framing environmental action in and around the home. *Geoforum*, 37, 906–920.

BERG, A. 2011. Not roadmaps but toolboxes: Analysing pioneering national programmes for sustainable consumption and production. *Journal of Consumer Policy*, 34, 9–23.

CHAPPELLS, H. & TRENTMANN, F. 2015. Sustainable consumption in history: Ideas, resources and practices. In: REISCH, L. & THØGERSEN, J. (eds) *Handbook of Research on Sustainable Consumption*. Cheltenham, UK: Edward Elgar.

COHEN, M. 2001. The emergent environmental policy discourse on sustainable consumption. In: COHEN, M. & MURPHY, J. (eds) *Exploring Sustainable Consumption: Environmental Policy and the Social Sciences*. Oxford, UK: Pergamon.

COHEN, M. 2004. *Sustainable consumption and global citizenship: An empirical analysis. In:* BOSTROM, M., FOLLESDAL, A., KLINTMAN, M., MICHELETTI, M. & SOERENSEN, M. P. (eds) *Political Consumerism: Its motivations, power and conditions in the Nordic Countries and elsewhere, 2004 Oslo.* Proceedings from the 2nd International Seminar on Political Consumerism.

COHEN, M. & MURPHY, J. 2001a. Consumption, environment and public policy. *In:* COHEN, M. & MURPHY, J. (eds) *Exploring Sustainable Consumption: Environmental Policy and the Social Sciences.* Oxford, UK: Pergamon.

COHEN, M. & MURPHY, J. 2001b. *Exploring Sustainable Consumption: Environmental Policy and the Social Sciences.* Oxford, UK: Pergamon.

COHN, C. 1987. Sex and death in the rational world of defense intellectuals. *Signs*, 12, 687–718.

DOBSON, A. 2003. *Citizenship and the Environment.* Oxford, UK: Oxford University Press.

FUCHS, D. A. & LOREK, S. 2005. Sustainable consumption governance: A history of promises and failures. *Journal of Consumer Policy*, 28, 261–288.

GEELS, F. W., MCMEEKIN, A., MYLAN, J. & SOUTHERTON, D. 2015. A critical appraisal of Sustainable Consumption and Production research: The reformist, revolutionary and reconfiguration positions. *Global Environmental Change*, 34, 1–12.

HOBSON, K. 2004. Sustainable consumption in the United Kingdom: The 'responsible' consumer and government at 'arm's length'. *Journal of Environment and Development*, 13, 121–139.

HORKHEIMER, M. 1972. Traditional and critical theory. *In:* IDEM. *Critical Theory: Selected Essays.* New York: The Continuum Publishing Company.

JACKSON, T. 2005a. Live better by consuming less? Is there a 'double dividend' in sustainable consumption? *Journal of Industrial Ecology*, 9, 19–36.

JACKSON, T. 2005b. *Motivating Sustainable Consumption: A review of evidence on consumer behaviour and behavioural change* [Online]. Sustainable Development Research Network. Available: www.sustainablelifestyles.ac.uk/sites/default/files/motivating_sc_final.pdf.

JACKSON, T. 2006. Readings in sustainable consumption. *In:* JACKSON, T. (ed.) *The Earthscan Reader in Sustainable Consumption.* London: Earthscan.

KOLLMUSS, A. & AGYEMAN, J. 2002. Mind the gap: Why do people act environmentally and what are the barriers to pro-environmental behaviour? *Environmental Education Research*, 8, 239–260.

LEWIS, T. & POTTER, E. 2011. Introducing ethical consumption. *In:* LEWIS, T. & POTTER, E. (eds) *Ethical Consumption: A Critical Introduction.* Abingdon, UK: Routledge.

LITTLER, J. 2011. What's wrong with ethical consumption? *In:* LEWIS, T. & POTTER, E. (eds) *Ethical Consumption: A Critical Introduction.* Abingdon, UK: Routledge.

LOREK, S. & FUCHS, D. 2013. Strong sustainable consumption governance–precondition for a degrowth path? *Journal of Cleaner Production*, 38, 36–43.

LOREK, S. & VERGRAGT, P. J. 2015. Sustainable consumption as a systemic challenge: Inter-and transdisciplinary research and research questions. *In:* REISCH, L. & THØGERSEN, J. (eds) *Handbook of Research on Sustainable Consumption.* Cheltenham, UK: Edward Elgar.

MANIATES, M. F. 2001. Individualization: Plant a tree, buy a bike, save the world? *Global Environmental Politics*, 1, 31–52.

MIDDLEMISS, L. 2014. Individualised or participatory? Exploring late-modern identity and sustainable development. *Environmental Politics*, 23, 929–946.

O'ROURKE, D. & LOLLO, N. 2015. Transforming consumption: From decoupling, to behavior change, to system changes for sustainable consumption. *Annual Review of Environment and Resources*, 40, 233–259.

PRINCEN, T., MANIATES, M. & CONCA, K. 2002. Confronting consumption. *In:* PRINCEN, T., MANIATES, M. & CONCA, K. (eds) *Confronting Consumption.* London: MIT Press.

ROSE, N. 1999. *Governing the Soul: The Shaping of the Private Self.* London: Free Association Books.

RUMPALA, Y. 2011. 'Sustainable consumption' as a new phase in a governmentalization of consumption. *Theory and Society*, 40, 669–699.

SCORAI. 2017. *Sustainable Consumption Research and Action Initiative Website* [Online]. Available: http://scorai.org/.

SEYFANG, G. 2009. *The New Economics of Sustainable Consumption: Seeds of Change.* Basingstoke, UK: Palgrave Macmillan.

SHOVE, E. 2003. *Comfort, Cleanliness and Convenience: The Social Organization of Normality.* Oxford, UK: Berg Publishers.

SHOVE, E. 2010. Beyond the ABC: Climate change policy and theories of social change. *Environment and Planning A*, 42, 1273–1285.

SPURLING, N., MCMEEKIN, A., SHOVE, E., SOUTHERTON, D. & WELCH, D. 2013. *Interventions in Practice: Re-framing Policy Approaches to Consumer Behaviour* [Online]. Sustainable Practices Research Group. Available: www.sprg.ac.uk/projects-fellowships/theoretical-development-and-integration/interventions-in-practice---sprg-report [Accessed 18 December 2017].

UNITED NATIONS DEPARTMENT OF ECONOMIC AND SOCIAL AFFAIRS (UNDESA). 2016. *Sustainable Development Goals* [Online]. Available: https://sustainabledevelopment.un.org/sdgs [Accessed 18 December 2017].

UNITED NATIONS ENVIRONMENT PROGRAMME (UNEP). 2001. *Consumption Opportunities: Strategies for Change.* United Nations Environment Programme.

UNITED NATIONS FRAMEWORK CONVENTION ON CLIMATE CHANGE (UNFCCC). 2015. *Paris Agreement* [Online]. Available: http://unfccc.int/files/essential_background/convention/application/pdf/english_paris_agreement.pdf [Accessed 18 December 2017].

URBAN SUSTAINABILITY DIRECTOR'S NETWORK. 2016. *Sustainable Consumption Toolkit* [Online]. Available: http://sustainableconsumption.usdn.org/ [Accessed 18 December 2017].

WHITMARSH, L., O'NEILL, S. & LORENZONI, I. 2011. Climate change or social change? Debate within, amongst, and beyond disciplines. *Environment and Planning A*, 43, 258–261.

WILK, R. 2002. Consumption, human needs, and global environmental change. *Global Environmental Change*, 12, 5–13.

WILSON, C. & CHATTERTON, T. 2011. Multiple models to inform climate change policy: A pragmatic response to the 'beyond the ABC' debate. *Environment and Planning A*, 43, 2781–2787.

YOUNG, W. & MIDDLEMISS, L. 2012. A rethink of how policy and social science approach changing individuals' actions on greenhouse gas emissions. *Energy Policy*, 41, 742–747.

2 Measuring sustainable consumption

In this chapter, I will outline the problem of sustainable consumption from an environmental perspective. The focus is on the environment here, because of the environmental focus of the field as a whole: particularly for those writers using the term 'sustainable' rather than 'ethical' consumption. It is also important to establish the scope of the environmental problem, in order to understand what the efforts that are profiled in the rest of the book are aiming to change. In basic terms, richer people live lifestyles that have a substantially detrimental effect on the environment. By the end of this chapter, you will have a sense of both what these detrimental effects are, and how they can be measured.

On the whole, I leave a discussion of social difference and sustainable consumption, which includes comment on the social effects of unsustainable consumption, to the next chapter. However, as soon as we talk about measuring sustainable consumption, we quickly see that there are wealth and spatial effects of unsustainable consumption. These have enormous social implications. The very fact that wealthier people consume more and have a bigger detrimental impact on the environment is highly political, and has become a central focus of international negotiations on environmental issues (e.g. climate change). Indeed, the idea of 'consumption-based accounting' profiled below, is an attempt to attribute the impacts of consumption to the consumer rather than to the producer (who might see less of the benefits of their product). The consumption histories of the richer nations have resulted in a legacy of environmental damage, as well as a sense of entitlement to consume to the unsustainable levels we currently do.

This leads to the spatial dimension of unsustainable consumption. Environmental damage does not respect national borders. This is particularly the case with climate change, for instance, where emissions from the US or Canada can have impacts on the other side of the world, in the low-lying islands of Vanuatu. We have also seen richer nations exporting their polluting industries to poorer nations as they develop knowledge or service economies, yet continuing to benefit from the manufactured imports that have a detrimental effect on the health and environment of their source nations. Both wealth and spatial effects will therefore come up throughout this chapter.

In writing this chapter, I found myself very frequently referring to human impacts on the environment in the form of carbon emissions, as opposed to the many other impacts on the environment that humans have. This is likely because of a substantial increase in political interest in the topic of climate change, and the impact of consumption on the climate. When politicians become interested in topics, they also fund research on them! In profiling climate change-related research here, my intention is to show you the state of research in the field, rather than to make a political point about the importance of this topic relative to other forms of environmental degradation. There are plenty of studies around about other forms of environmental degradation including water scarcity (Lenzen et al., 2013), biodiversity (Lenzen et al., 2012; Wilting et al., 2017), and land use (Weinzettel et al., 2013) among others.

I start here by briefly profiling the state of the environment, explaining who impacts on the environment and by how much (at a nation state level), and outlining the main ways in which environmental impacts have been measured. I then discuss how the various measurement tools allow us to make comparisons within nations. Finally, I point to the risks inherent in defining and measuring this problem, offering a critical take on a variety of approaches.

The state of the environment

To get an impression of the state of the environment we are looking to assess the condition of resources that we might want and need to consume, and the potential for waste 'sinks' to store any by-products of our consumption. Herman Daly (1990), ecological economist and one of the early writers in this field, defines the 'conditions for the sustainable use of natural resources' according to three principles:

1   We should use renewable resources at a rate which allows them to regenerate.
2   We should develop renewable replacements for non-renewable resources before they run out.
3   Waste should be generated at a rate, or to a concentration, that the natural environment can absorb and withstand.

In these principles, Daly outlines the limits of the world's resources and the rules we should have for consuming them and disposing of them in order to ensure that they are available to us in perpetuity. One of the concepts used in environmental studies to reflect these limits to human activities is the 'carrying capacity': the maximum level of resource use and waste disposal that can take place without earth systems being compromised.

There is a substantial body of evidence on the state of the world's resources and waste sinks, and the impact of consumption patterns on these. One of the helpful ways of summarising these impacts that has emerged in recent years is the concept of planetary boundaries: the limits that define a 'safe operating space' for humanity (Rockström et al., 2009; Steffen et al., 2015). Here, natural scientists look to characterise the state of a number of natural stocks (such as fresh water or biodiversity) and man-made impacts (ozone depletion, biochemical flows, climate change), in order to provide an analysis of the fragility of our existence on the planet, and an indication of where the dangerous impacts are being/likely to be felt. One of the objectives of this kind of work is for it to be useful to non-specialists, and a summary diagram to that effect is available in Figure 2.1.

Figure 2.1 is shaded to show where we are operating safely (light grey zone: here freshwater use or stratospheric ozone depletion), where there is increasing uncertainty (mid grey zone: here climate change and land system change), and where we are substantially overshooting in our impact on natural resources (dark grey zone: here biochemical flows, genetic diversity). In some cases, it is not yet possible to define the planetary boundary (question marks '?': here atmospheric aerosol loading). The safe zone for all of these planetary boundaries is the border between light and mid grey, and as we can see, four of these boundaries have already been transgressed. Further, these scientists assert that climate change and biosphere integrity are 'core boundaries', which, when transgressed, will fundamentally alter the state of the earth. In other words, as human inhabitants of the earth, we are not sticking to Daly's conditions above, and as such we are not using

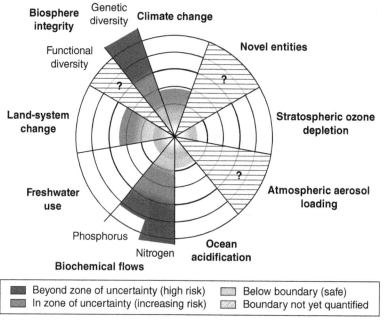

Figure 2.1 Current state of the control variables for seven of the planetary boundaries (from Steffen et al., 2015; reprinted with permission from AAAS)

the earth's resources in a sustainable way. This means that our human population faces shortages of key non-renewable resources, the risks associated with poor storage of waste, and transformations to the environment itself, through processes such as climate change.

Who impacts and by how much?

So this brief foray into the state of the environment gives us a fairly bleak analysis as to some of the challenges that we face as a result of the impacts of our social world on the earth system. It also provides a detailed picture as to the level and nature of the impact of our actions on natural stocks and waste sinks. This is not the end of the story however. Given that we are interested in consumption, we also need to understand who consumes, in order to get to grips with the level and nature of the contribution of people from different social units to this problem. In the first instance, this is something we need to understand on a global scale, given the global nature of many environmental problems, and the fact that pollution does not respect national borders. Further, the differing contribution of rich and poor nations, as a result of their differentiated consumption profiles, is critical. This is also a phenomenon that has to be understood over time: emissions change over time as nations develop.

Bill Rees characterises the world as divided into rich and poor, with the consumption of the rich having detrimental environmental impacts on the lives of the poor.

> The rich live in the world's most ecologically healthy habitats, whereas the poor (particularly racial minorities) are increasingly confined to urban slums and degraded landscapes characterised by toxic waste, polluted air and water, and contaminated food . . . the world is witnessing the emergence of a new form of 'eco-apartheid' characterised by the income-related segregation of people along environmental gradients.
>
> (Rees, 2008, 696)

This argument is confirmed in the context of climate change by Oxfam's analysis that the poorest 50 per cent of the population of the world are responsible for only 10 per cent of carbon emissions, while being most exposed to the effects of climate change (Oxfam, 2015). On the other hand, the richest 10 per cent of the global population are responsible for 50 per cent of global carbon emissions (ibid.).

The true picture is rather more complex than this, however, as nations have a range of different consumption profiles and development trajectories (Steinberger et al., 2013), and within nations there is also diversity (see Chapter 3). Both rich and poor can also be exposed to environmental 'ills'. Some countries in the global South have very low consumption impacts, with low levels of pollution from industry, and subsistence or near subsistence lifestyles. The block of nations known as BRICS (Brazil, Russia, India, China, and South Africa) are substantially industrialised, producing many goods for export, and having major environmental impacts as a result. Typically, these nations had relatively limited impacts in the past, before they began to grow economically. They also have an emerging middle class whose consumption impacts are similar to their counterparts in the global North (see for instance Parikh et al., 2009). Countries in the global North tend to have peaked in terms of their domestic impact on the environment, with many of the industries that create environmental damage replaced with service or knowledge economies, and a greater value placed on the quality of the domestic environment. This does not mean that richer countries have less impact internationally: countries achieve lower impacts by importing goods from abroad (Spangenberg, 2001), and in any case maintain higher impacts overall.

A recent comparison of per capita income with per capita carbon emissions, for instance, is shown in Figure 2.2 (Hubacek et al., 2017b). Here there is a clear relationship between these two variables, albeit with differing variations from the regression line, and with some outliers. Figure 2.2 shows that residents of richer countries on average consume more than those of poorer countries, and as a result have higher impacts on the environment. Hubacek and colleagues also argue that the inequality in distribution of carbon emissions, which is clearly linked to the inequality in distribution of income (as a proxy for consumption), means that if the incomes of the very poor increase, the incomes of the rich will also have to decrease in order to meet carbon targets (Hubacek et al., 2017a). This relationship between wealth and distribution of resources is not a simple one: there are varying degrees of inequality. In a detailed global scale analysis, Steinberger and colleagues find that different resources have different distributions. While control of material use is less unequal than that of energy, land ownership and income (GDP), the wealthiest 10 per cent globally still consume 27 per cent of materials (Steinberger et al., 2010).

As well as highlighting the distribution of environmental harm across nations and its relationship to wealth, a considerable amount of work has been done to understand the relationships between nations, in terms of their environmental impact. Figure 2.3 shows a useful pictorial representation of the flows of trade around the globe, in particular revealing the flow of carbon emissions from one country to another through trade (measured in megatonnes of carbon) (Peters et al., 2012). While Figure 2.3 only shows the twelve largest flows of carbon, it is clear that the largest arrows lead from China (and Russia), to Europe and the US, with smaller flows of trade going back and forth between Europe and the US. None of the twelve largest flows leads to China: in other words, because China is a net exporter, many of the emissions it produces are to service other economies around the world (Weber et al., 2008).

Figure 2.3 ultimately reveals how globalisation, de-industrialisation in the global North, and the manufacturing (and economic) boom in China have resulted in a global pattern of emissions which does not really work when understood as a function of nation states. Indeed, taking account for the trading relationship between states is essential to understand which has the biggest impacts on environmental problems; otherwise we may be misled into thinking

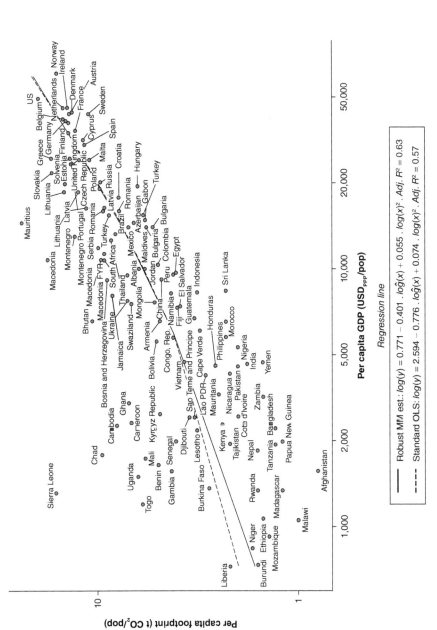

Figure 2.2 Per capita carbon footprints versus per capita GDP by nation state (from Hubacek et al., 2017b, reprinted by permission from Springer)

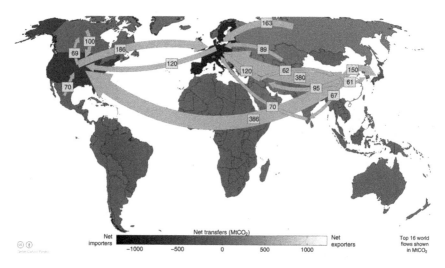

Figure 2.3 This diagram shows the largest flows of carbon between regions, when we count the carbon that is 'embodied' in trade; in other words, the carbon emissions that were released in making and distributing stuff from one part of the world to another. The largest flow here is from China to USA (98 MtC) (reproduced with permission from the author, Peters et al., 2012, and under the terms of the CC BY 3.0 License)

that high-emitting nations such as China are a bigger cause of the problem than the nations that consume the products produced there.

I have discussed the distribution of consumption between nations at some length, but the differences within nations are also extremely important. A more detailed discussion of social differences and their impact on people's ability to engage with a sustainable consumption agenda can be found in Chapter 3. There are some interesting quantitative findings in the body of work on measuring sustainable consumption that merit further coverage here, however. The relationship between wealth and detrimental environmental impacts, tends to hold true on a national level. Fundamentally, the more materials people buy, use and dispose of, the more environmental impact they are likely to have.

When we disaggregate data to look at subnational differences, we notice a range of drivers, however. Minx and colleagues, for instance find a strong relationship between income and carbon footprint in the UK (higher-income households have higher per capita carbon footprints) as well as a similar relationship with education (higher-educated households have higher per capita carbon footprints) (Minx et al., 2013). Density of settlement and number of people in the household, on the other hand, tend to have a positive impact on carbon emissions, with higher-density settlements or large households both resulting in lower emissions per capita (ibid.). A more nuanced discussion of the impact of household size can be found in Chapter 11 (see the section 'Household dynamics'). Druckman and

Jackson (2009) compare household carbon footprints from a range of different neighbourhood types (see Figure 2.4). Here we can see (again) that the more prosperous communities ('prospering suburbs') are emitting more than those that are 'constrained by circumstances' (less economically wealthy). It is also interesting that 'multicultural' and 'city living' have rather low emissions.

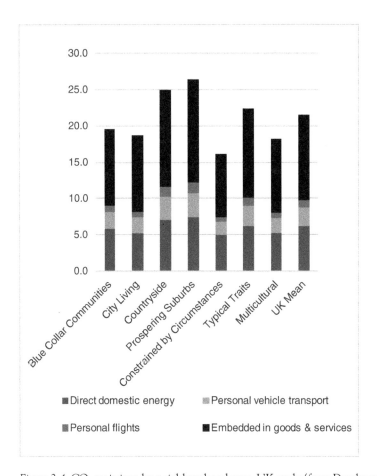

Figure 2.4 CO$_2$ emissions by neighbourhood type, UK study (from Druckman and Jackson, 2009; reprinted with permission from Elsevier)

Consumption-based accounting

Consumption-based accounting has emerged as a way of attributing responsibility for emissions in the light of the wealth inequality and spatial issues outlined above. The formal measurements of greenhouse gas emissions which are used during climate change negotiations are currently based on production-based accounting: the number of emissions which occurred in the country where goods were produced.

As you can imagine, this rather prejudices against those nations that consume relatively little per capita, but produce and export a lot of goods. Consumption-based accounting offers an alternative way of attributing both emissions and responsibility: by counting the number of emissions linked to consumption, and by attributing distribution and production emissions to the consumer (see Afionis et al., 2017 for a summary of the research in this field).

This way of counting emissions makes a substantial difference to the overall emissions of a nation. For instance, if we look at UK emissions from a production perspective, they reduced more than 10 per cent between 1992 and 2004, while if we measure these from a consumption perspective, they increased by more than 8 per cent in these years (Minx et al., 2009). Note that since the global recession in 2008, emissions measured on a consumption basis in the UK have been declining (DEFRA, n.d.). Academics are engaging with government using these insights: my colleague John Barrett and his associates produced a report for the UK government, pointing out that 55 per cent of household emissions are produced outside of the UK (associated with imported goods and services) (Barrett et al., 2011). In Figure 2.5, we can see that for some products and services most emissions occur overseas (e.g. electronic equipment), and even products we

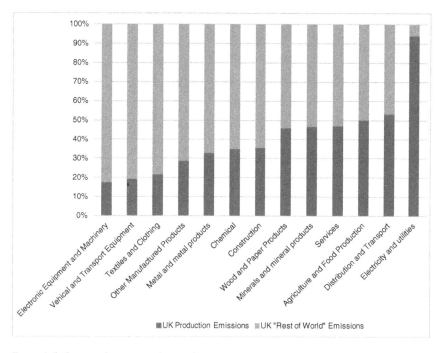

Figure 2.5 Origin of emissions for goods consumed in the UK, showing a large proportion of emissions occurring outside of national borders (from Barrett et al., 2011; contains public sector information licensed under the Open Government Licence v3.0)

might assume would be more domestically provided (e.g. agriculture and food production) have substantial emissions associated with imports.

Consumption-based accounting is not yet taken into account in global governance, but there have been attempts to get national governments to take heed in the UK (Barrett et al., 2013) and Sweden (Isenhour and Feng, 2016). Managing consumption-based accounting is difficult because of the political limits of nation states. For instance, the electricity sector in China emits more than 30 Mt CO_2 equivalent to provide the UK with goods and services (Barrett et al., 2011). Chinese power stations are on average substantially less efficient than UK plants, and as such, Chinese electricity is more carbon intensive: that is, more emissions are released to produce each unit of electricity (ibid.). Clearly the UK government has limited control over electricity production in China, so when it thinks about governing carbon emissions, it is more likely to be drawn to addressing this problem as a domestic (production) issue. In the Swedish context, where the government is directly attempting to address consumption-based emissions, Isenhour and Feng (2016) find that it has been rather tame in its efforts. There is a tension between carbon reduction ambitions on the one hand, and wanting to avoid to be seen as interfering in household management on the other.

Measuring sustainable consumption

There are number of ways of measuring consumption, and the resulting impacts of that consumption. Here I profile a few of these. Note that these include both measurement of specific forms of consumption that we know is environmentally detrimental (or indeed beneficial), measurement of overall impact (e.g. ecological and carbon footprinting), and measurement of the overall resources used at a given unit of analysis (e.g. input-output analysis). It is possible to measure the impacts of a specific behaviour, a product or service, an individual or household, a city or nation state, or at a global scale. As we will see, measurements at each of these scales can, and will be used for political ends.

Note also that this section is not a comprehensive summary of all the forms of measurement that exist; instead, I have picked some of the key measurement types to give you a taste of the possibilities in this field.

Measurement of specific forms of consumption

There are endless possibilities for measuring specific forms of consumption, and many data sources are available publicly to help us do so. For instance, in many nations, governments conduct surveys about people's daily lives; sometimes these are also complemented by international data sets (e.g. through the European Union, or globally). Governments frequently collect data on choice of transport mode, use of water or energy within the home, people's gardening practices, or how people make shopping decisions. Further, corporations also gather information about markets which have relevance to our work. The advantage of government data is that it is often possible to look at a number of variables (people's demographic or spatial characteristics) and to see if these have an impact on the specific variable we want to understand (the specific form of unsustainable consumption).

To give one short example which illustrates this point: there is a lot of attention paid to the environmental impacts of aviation, and how detrimental aviation is to climate change (for details of impacts, see Penner, 1999). Part of the reason this is talked about so often is that flying is perceived (and indeed experienced) as a real benefit to people, and the implication of the damage that it causes is that we probably should not be doing it so often! Inevitably, this leads to much soul searching, something that I see frequently among colleagues and students who study sustainability. Figure 2.6 complicates that discussion somewhat. The data here is from a public survey run by the UK government (DEFRA, 2009), and it shows us which UK residents actually flew for leisure purposes in the last twelve months, and how frequently they flew. I think this is particularly enlightening because, if we were to tap into the public debate on this issue we might imagine that 'giving up flying' would be a sacrifice for everyone. In fact, most of the population took no flights at all for leisure in this period (59 per cent said no to this question, just 41 per cent said yes). Further, the data shows that it is the upper-middle class and middle class (AB refer to these social categories) that fly most, with the amount of flights gradually diminishing through the social categories (lower-middle class (C1), skilled working class (C2), working class (D), subsistence (E)). Knowing how this data breaks down into social categories gives us a more meaningful insight into both how this resource (access to flights) is distributed and what impacts any restriction to flying might have.

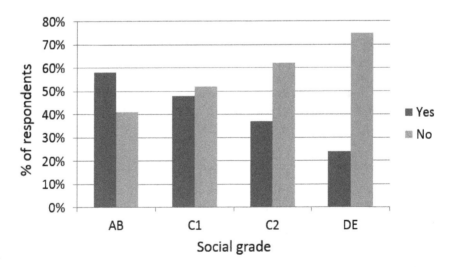

Figure 2.6 Data from DEFRA Survey of Public Attitudes and Behaviours toward the Environment (2009), responses to the question: 'Have you taken any flights in the last 12 months for leisure, holidays or visiting friends or family?'

Ecological/carbon footprinting

Ecological or carbon footprinting is used to give an impression of the overall impact of human activities on the earth. The footprint is used as a metaphor for human impact: we can characterise each person's impact (and sometimes that of other units of analysis) by translating the effects he or she has into a single (more approachable) measure. Ecological footprints, conceived of by Wackernagel and Rees (1996), take a wide variety of impacts (e.g. use of polluting chemicals, destruction of biodiversity, carbon emissions, etc.) and translate them into hectares of productive land space (Sutcliffe et al., 2008). Ecological footprints are measured by assimilating data on food and other consumption, transport choices, energy use, waste production and housing type, often from an individual. You can calculate your own ecological footprint at www.footprintcalculator.org/, where you will be required to answer indicative questions about your lifestyle, which the calculator then models into an overall impact on the earth (presented in hectares).

One of the values of the ecological footprint is that it allows us to say that in the global North, people have ecological footprints that surpass the carrying capacity of the earth, as they use more productive land space than is available on average (based on a division of total productive land space by the population of the earth) (Wackernagel and Rees, 1996). It also allows for easy comparisons between nations, individuals, or other units of analysis. On the Global Footprint Network website you can play around with the data that exists on different nations' ecological footprints, and find out, for instance, that while the carrying capacity of the earth allows for 1.7 global hectares of land per person, in 2013 the average ecological footprint per person in a selection of countries (including lowest and highest) was as shown in Table 2.1.

At a national scale, the ecological footprint calculator exposes the fact that the average Luxemburgish citizen has a huge amount more impact than the average Eritrean. Broadly speaking, there is a connection between lifestyles, wealth and ecological footprint, although this is not a simple relationship. The contrast between neighbours Luxembourg and Germany will give some indication of this.

Table 2.1 Data from Global Footprint Network (2017)

Nation	Ecological footprint (in global hectares of land)	Ranking
Luxembourg	13.1	1
Trinidad and Tobago	8.8	4
Kazakhstan	6.5	15
Germany	5.5	31
Suriname	4.0	59
Costa Rica	2.5	102
Syria	1.4	143
India	1.1	169
Eritrea	0.5	192

Further, within nations there will also be considerable disparities, so for instance, some people in India are likely to have a similar impact to those in the global North, despite the low average here, because they lead similar lifestyles, while others consume considerably less.

Note that the term 'carbon footprint' means the carbon emissions associated with a particular unit of analysis (person, product, country, etc.), as, for instance, in Figure 2.2. This is a much simpler measure in some ways, because it only takes into account the carbon emissions impacts (in tonnes of CO_2), rather than the broader environmental impacts (biodiversity loss, fresh water availability, etc.) measured by the ecological footprint. It still requires a comprehensive understanding of how carbon is emitted throughout the life cycle of products, from cradle to grave, however.

The ecological or carbon footprints are useful not only for the kinds of country comparisons I have made here, but also for comparing products or even individuals. Not everyone is convinced by their value, however. The spatial effects of people's impacts are rather hidden in an ecological or carbon footprint: for instance, my impacts as a UK consumer might be felt all over the world, but this is not apparent in a 'global hectares' measurement. The tendency to conceptualise the ecological footprint as the property of an individual, leads to individualised policy recommendations: such as how 'you' can reduce your footprint, rather than how you can be enabled to do so by a more environmentally conscious culture and infrastructure (Middlemiss, 2010). Van den Bergh and Grazi (2014) think that the ecological footprint is only useful in so far as it reveals the difference between the carrying capacity and our current rate of consumption, and a number of authors point out methodological flaws in the way that the footprint is calculated (Wiedmann and Barrett, 2010; Blomqvist et al., 2013; van den Bergh and Grazi, 2014). Perhaps this is inevitable given the fact that the ecological footprint is attempting to simplify a highly complex set of impacts. Wiedmann and Barrett (2010) also argue that while it is useful as a communications tool, it can only be useful for policy as part of a basket of indicators.

Input-output analysis

Input-output analysis is a method whereby the inputs (resources in) and outputs (waste out) of a given entity are measured. Input-output analysis will typically start with data about which resources a sector of the economy uses (e.g. the value of steel, fabric, energy and electronics bought by the car manufacturing industry) and use this to create a picture of the sector's overall impacts (e.g. carbon emissions, waste water, other pollutants). This can be done for a range of units, including household, business (either private or public sector), city, region, or nation state. Much of the work in this area tends to focus at the state level, however, in 'Multi Region Input Output Analysis' or MRIOA. There are some studies undertaken with smaller units of analysis (see Van der Wal and Noorman, 1998, on household metabolism). This is also the method behind consumption-based accounting as profiled above.

Given the potential complexity of this method, studies often focus on specific themes, and lots of work using this method in recent years has focused on carbon emissions. This work allows authors to illustrate how nations are developing, and the key challenges for these nations in curbing their carbon emissions. Peters and colleagues' study of carbon emissions in China, for instance, shows a substantial growth of CO_2 emissions in recent years, driven principally by the construction of new infrastructure and increases in household consumption (Peters et al., 2007). Efficiency improvements in China have been outpaced by these drivers of growth (ibid.). This kind of study also allows us to see how much of a contribution is made to Chinese CO_2 emissions by its booming export markets (Weber et al., 2008). China is the largest emitter of CO_2 in the world. Figure 2.7, drawn from a later study, gives us a sense of the spatial effect of western consumption, given the substantial chunk of emissions that are caused by exports (between 20 and 30 per cent since 1997) (Pan et al., 2017).

In an Indian study, input-output analysis was used to profile the nation's key inputs to carbon emissions, and compare the impact of different sectors and parts of the population (Parikh et al., 2009). Here we see that the electricity sector, manufacturing, steel production and road transportation are the key high emission industries (ibid.), all driven by the demands for products associated with construction and manufacturing. This is as would be expected, given the

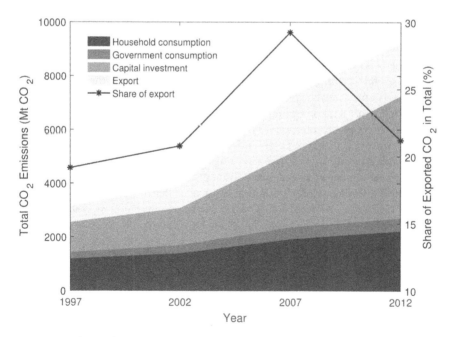

Figure 2.7 China's domestic CO_2 emissions, showing the proportion of emissions that are driven by exports, government consumption, household consumption and capital investment since 1997 (from Pan et al., 2017; American Geophysical Union, licensed under CC BY 2.0)

development trajectory of the nation. The contrast between emissions associated with the urban rich and the rural poor in India are also revealed here, and show striking disparities in impact (and consumption): the former emits 3,416 kg of CO_2 per year, the latter just 141kg of CO_2 per year (ibid.).

Clearly this method is very useful for bringing out spatial effects (whether within nation or between nations) of consumption, and for mapping the resources used and disposed of. While it is most frequently used to aggregate national consumption, showing how consumption at a national level uses and disposes of resources, it can also be used to show how specific resources flow through the system. This means that as a concept it is less tangible than the ecological or carbon footprint, but more transparent – as it is possible to see the inputs and outputs more clearly.

Definition as measurement (and measurement as definition)

How we define the problem of sustainable consumption is important, because it shapes how we measure it, and in turn, this influences how we further define the problem (Rose, 1999). The choices we make about definition and measurement have a big impact on what can be said about the problem, and in some cases what can be done about it. If we measure the problem as a characteristic of the individual, for instance, the solutions that are thrown up tend to be individualising (Maniates, 2001; Shove, 2010; Middlemiss, 2014). The problem of sustainable consumption could actually be understood as a problem of the individual, household, community, product, or nation state, or even as a global problem. We could also seek to solve this problem at any of these scales.

It is useful at this point to think in more detail about how the problem definition can impact on measurement. For instance, Tim Jackson (2006) makes a distinction between consuming less and consuming differently, with the former being a deeper green interpretation of sustainable consumption than the latter. This is mirrored in Sylvia Lorek and Doris Fuchs's ideas of 'weak' and 'strong' sustainable consumption (2013). How might these different perspectives play out in the measurement of sustainable consumption as a problem? We can imagine that our achievement of 'consuming less' would depend on a measurement of overall consumption decreasing, and this might be something we could measure at different scales (globally, at nation scale, for a community, or individual). We could measure this as a decrease in money spent on consuming products and services, or, as a decrease in material throughput itself. The input-output analysis approach outlined above is a method that has been developed to do the latter.

On the other hand, if we wanted to achieve 'consuming differently' we might want to measure specific markets that exist for alternative forms of consumption. The amount of spending in a number of 'ethical' markets in the UK (including food and drink, travel, home, money and boycotts among others) has increased substantially (*Ethical Consumer*, 2017). Note that this shows an encouraging and increasing interest in ethical issues among consumers, and the ability of producers to respond to this by offering ethical products and services. However, despite this increase in the value of 'ethical' markets, we saw in 'the state of the environment' above that these are clearly not solving the problem. The UK is not a nation that consumes sustainably, despite evidence of us 'consuming differently'.

Another very common way of defining the problem of sustainable development, which touches on consumption is the so-called IPAT formula: Impact= Population x Affluence x Technology ($I = P * A * T$). This was developed in the early 1970s, through a debate around which element had the most influence on environmental degradation (Chertow, 2000). Increasing population was thought by many at the time to make the most substantial contribution to environmental harm, and this in a sense is why the debate came about, as people saw the flaws in this argument (more people from Eritrea have a lot less impact than more people from Luxembourg, for instance). We can imagine how this might be used to measure sustainable consumption: you could count the number of people in a nation (with an eye on birth rates), multiply that by the average level of affluence (richer people can consume more) and then again by a proxy for their access to technology (assuming that technology causes harm).

IPAT is based on problematic assumptions, however (Hartmann, 1995). For instance, seeing increasing population as having a negative impact is rather too simplistic: humans can both take from and give to environment (ibid.). Further, people give and take in different ways: gender, ethnicity and class play a role as we will see in Chapter 3 (ibid.). The way people are distributed in space makes a big difference to their consumption patterns (suburban versus high density), as does the distribution of affluence within society (inequality levels). With regards to technology, highly political choices are made that structure people's access to appropriate technology. For instance, the investment in private over public transport infrastructures in many parts of the world has a negative environmental effect, which is not merely a function of the technology itself, but of the choice to invest in a particular way (ibid.). Indeed, technology can play a positive role in compensating for increased affluence and population (Chertow, 2000), when, for instance, energy efficiency reduces the impact of appliances. As Betsy Hartmann puts it: 'The main problem with the equation, however, is what it leaves out, namely the question of social, economic, and political power, and the systems by which current power relations are enforced' (Hartmann, 1995, 23–24). If we adopt IPAT as a means of measuring sustainable consumption, we also risk forgetting about these important drivers of the problem.

From this discussion, we can see that each framing of the problem of sustainable consumption has a substantial impact on the way in which it is measured, and the kinds of data needed to allow an entity (government, city, household) to aim towards it. Once the problem begins to be measured in a particular way, we tend to define it more narrowly, according to the data we have gathered. This is a theme that will reoccur throughout this book, as I outline how the various disciplines engaged in this topic understand the problem of and solutions to sustainable consumption. In the meantime I would encourage you to use the questions in Chapter 1: 'how is the problem being defined?' and 'how is the solution understood?', to ensure a critical appreciation of any reading matter on this topic.

Conclusions

One of the key challenges in measuring sustainable consumption is working out where the boundaries of measurement should be. This is a really complex problem, and accounting for each act of consumption can result in an intricate web of cause and effect which reaches into many aspects of human and ecological life, some of which are difficult to quantify. Both defining the boundaries of the problem and choosing the unit of analysis is challenging, and political. As we have seen, measuring the impacts of the individual, or measuring production-based emissions suggests that responsibility lies with the individual consumer or the producer respectively. Consumption-based accounting represents an attempt to attribute responsibility to those nation states who have built their wealth through consumerism over time. Academics have also attempted to incorporate both producer and consumer responsibility when measuring the problem (Lenzen et al., 2007).

As a result of the complexity of the problem of sustainable consumption, the various forms of measurement profiled here are works in progress. You will find that if you try to work out your own carbon or ecological footprint using different online tools, for instance, you will get different results, depending on the model that makes the calculation. This causes problems when talking to people about their impact: if there are different results, which should they believe? There is also confusion about the optimal solutions to environmental problems. As Gjerris and colleagues (2016) point out, this is not through people's lack of understanding, but rather because it is sometimes genuinely unclear as to what the best option is, and of course because what is 'best' is always political. Further, if people only have the choice between a number of unsatisfactory options (from an environmental or personal point of view), it is very challenging for them to do the 'right thing'.

Fundamentally, however, what we have learned in this chapter is that we are already overshooting the earth's carrying capacity in our use of resources and our production of waste. You should also now understand that people's impact on the environment is not uniform, and that some people and nations have a bigger impact than others. This comes across clearly in the various measurements that exist to understand the extent of unsustainable consumption. In the rest of the book, I will be evaluating to what extent a consumption-driven understanding of this problem can produce convincing solutions.

Resources

Gapminder: www.gapminder.org/tools allows you to explore data on carbon footprints and other environmental, economic and social indicators.
Global Carbon Atlas: www.globalcarbonatlas.org/
Global Footprint Network: http://data.footprintnetwork.org allows you to explore ecological footprint data from around the world.

References

AFIONIS, S., SAKAI, M., SCOTT, K., BARRETT, J. & GOULDSON, A. 2017. Consumption-based carbon accounting: Does it have a future? *Wiley Interdisciplinary Reviews: Climate Change*, 8.

BARRETT, J., OWEN, A. & SAKAI, M. 2011. *UK Consumption Emissions by Sector and Origin* [Online]. Report to the UK Department for Environment, Food and Rural Affairs by University of Leeds. Available: http://randd.defra.gov.uk/Document.aspx?Document=FINALEV0466report(2).pdf [Accessed 18 December 2017].

BARRETT, J., PETERS, G., WIEDMANN, T., SCOTT, K., LENZEN, M., ROELICH, K. & LE QUÉRÉ, C. 2013. Consumption-based GHG emission accounting: A UK case study. *Climate Policy*, 13, 451–470.

BLOMQVIST, L., BROOK, B. W., ELLIS, E. C., KAREIVA, P. M., NORDHAUS, T. & SHELLENBERGER, M. 2013. Does the shoe fit? Real versus imagined ecological footprints. *PLoS Biol*, 11, 1–6.

CHERTOW, M. R. 2000. The IPAT equation and its variants. *Journal of Industrial Ecology*, 4, 13–29.

DALY, H. E. 1990. Toward some operational principles of sustainable development. *Ecological Economics*, 2, 1–6.

DEFRA. 2009. *2009 Survey of Public Attitudes and Behaviours towards the Environment* [Online]. UK Department for Environment, Food and Rural Affairs. Available: http://webarchive.nationalarchives.gov.uk/20110704135447/http://archive.defra.gov.uk/evidence/statistics/environment/pubatt/index.htm [Accessed 18 December 2017].

DEFRA. n.d. *UK's Carbon Footprint 1997–2014* [Online]. Department for Environment, Food and Rural Affairs. Available: www.gov.uk/government/uploads/system/uploads/attachment_data/file/629880/Consumption_emissions_July17_Final.pdf [Accessed 1 January 2018].

DRUCKMAN, A. & JACKSON, T. 2009. The carbon footprint of UK households 1990–2004: A socio-economically disaggregated, quasi-multi-regional input-output model. *Ecological Economics*, 68, 2066–2077.

ETHICAL CONSUMER. 2017. *Markets Report 2017* [Online]. Available: www.ethicalconsumer.org/researchhub/ukethicalmarket.aspx [Accessed 31 January 2018].

GJERRIS, M., GAMBORG, C. & SAXE, H. 2016. What to buy? On the complexity of being a critical consumer. *Journal of Agricultural and Environmental Ethics*, 29, 89–110.

GLOBAL FOOTPRINT NETWORK. 2017. *Ecological Footprint per Capita* [Online]. Available: www.footprintnetwork.org/content/documents/ecological_footprint_nations/ecological_per_capita.html.

HARTMANN, B. 1995. *Reproductive Rights and Wrongs: The Global Politics of Population Control*. Boston, MA: South End Press.

HUBACEK, K., BAIOCCHI, G., FENG, K. & PATWARDHAN, A. 2017a. Poverty eradication in a carbon constrained world. *Nature Communications*, 8, 1–9.

HUBACEK, K., BAIOCCHI, G., FENG, K., CASTILLO, R. M., SUN, L. & XUE, J. 2017b. Global carbon inequality. *Energy, Ecology and Environment*, 2, 361–369.

ISENHOUR, C. & FENG, K. 2016. Decoupling and displaced emissions: On Swedish consumers, Chinese producers and policy to address the climate impact of consumption. *Journal of Cleaner Production*, 134, 320–329.

JACKSON, T. 2006. Readings in sustainable consumption. *In:* JACKSON, T. (ed.) *The Earthscan Reader in Sustainable Consumption*. London: Earthscan.

LENZEN, M., MURRAY, J., SACK, F. & WIEDMANN, T. 2007. Shared producer and consumer responsibility – Theory and practice. *Ecological Economics*, 61, 27–42.

LENZEN, M., MORAN, D., KANEMOTO, K., FORAN, B., LOBEFARO, L. & GESCHKE, A. 2012. International trade drives biodiversity threats in developing nations. *Nature*, 486, 109–112.

LENZEN, M., MORAN, D., BHADURI, A., KANEMOTO, K., BEKCHANOV, M., GESCHKE, A. & FORAN, B. 2013. International trade of scarce water. *Ecological Economics*, 94, 78–85.

LOREK, S. & FUCHS, D. 2013. Strong sustainable consumption governance – Precondition for a degrowth path? *Journal of Cleaner Production*, 38, 36–43.

MANIATES, M. F. 2001. Individualization: Plant a tree, buy a bike, save the world? *Global Environmental Politics*, 1, 31–52.

MIDDLEMISS, L. 2010. Reframing individual responsibility for sustainable consumption: Lessons from environmental justice and ecological citizenship. *Environmental Values*, 19, 147–167.

MIDDLEMISS, L. 2014. Individualised or participatory? Exploring late-modern identity and sustainable development. *Environmental Politics*, 23, 929–946.

MINX, J., BAIOCCHI, G., WIEDMANN, T., BARRETT, J., CREUTZIG, F., FENG, K., FÖRSTER, M., PICHLER, P.-P., WEISZ, H. & HUBACEK, K. 2013. Carbon footprints of cities and other human settlements in the UK. *Environmental Research Letters*, 8, 1–10.

MINX, J. C., WIEDMANN, T., WOOD, R., PETERS, G. P., LENZEN, M., OWEN, A., SCOTT, K., BARRETT, J., HUBACEK, K. & BAIOCCHI, G. 2009. Input-output analysis and carbon footprinting: An overview of applications. *Economic Systems Research*, 21, 187–216.

OXFAM. 2015. *Extreme Carbon Inequality* [Online]. Oxfam Media Briefing. Available: www.oxfam.org/sites/www.oxfam.org/files/file_attachments/mb-extreme-carbon-inequality-021215-en.pdf [Accessed 1 January 2018].

PAN, C., PETERS, G. P., ANDREW, R. M., KORSBAKKEN, J. I., LI, S., ZHOU, D. & ZHOU, P. 2017. Emissions embodied in global trade have plateaued due to structural changes in China. *Earth's Future*, 5, 934–946.

PARIKH, J., PANDA, M., GANESH-KUMAR, A. & SINGH, V. 2009. CO2 emissions structure of Indian economy. *Energy*, 34, 1024–1031.

PENNER, J. E. 1999. *Aviation and the Global Atmosphere: A Special Report of the Intergovernmental Panel on Climate Change*. Cambridge, UK: Cambridge University Press.

PETERS, G. P., DAVIS, S. J. & ANDREW, R. 2012. A synthesis of carbon in international trade. *Biogeosciences*, 9, 3247–3276.

PETERS, G. P., WEBER, C. L., GUAN, D. & HUBACEK, K. 2007. China's growing CO2 emissions: A race between increasing consumption and efficiency gains. *Environmental Science and Technology*, 41, 5939–5944.

REES, W. E. 2008. Human nature, eco-footprints and environmental injustice. *Local Environment*, 13, 685–701.

ROCKSTRÖM, J., STEFFEN, W., NOONE, K., PERSSON, Å., CHAPIN, F. S., LAMBIN, E. F., LENTON, T. M., SCHEFFER, M., FOLKE, C. & SCHELLNHUBER, H. J. 2009. A safe operating space for humanity. *Nature*, 461, 472–475.

ROSE, N. 1999. *Governing the Soul: The Shaping of the Private Self*. London: Free Association Books.

SHOVE, E. 2010. Beyond the ABC: Climate change policy and theories of social change. *Environment and Planning A*, 42, 1273–1285.

SPANGENBERG, J. H. 2001. The environmental Kuznets curve: A methodological artefact? *Population and Environment*, 23, 175–191.

STEFFEN, W., RICHARDSON, K., ROCKSTRÖM, J., CORNELL, S. E., FETZER, I., BENNETT, E. M., BIGGS, R., CARPENTER, S. R., DE VRIES, W. & DE WIT, C. A. 2015. Planetary boundaries: Guiding human development on a changing planet. *Science*, 347, 1259855.

STEINBERGER, J. K., KRAUSMANN, F. & EISENMENGER, N. 2010. Global patterns of materials use: A socioeconomic and geophysical analysis. *Ecological Economics*, 69, 1148–1158.

STEINBERGER, J. K., KRAUSMANN, F., GETZNER, M., SCHANDL, H. & WEST, J. 2013. Development and dematerialization: An international study. *PloS one*, 8, e70385.

SUTCLIFFE, M., HOOPER, P. & HOWELL, R. 2008. Can eco-footprinting analysis be used successfully to encourage more sustainable behaviour at the household level? *Sustainable Development*, 16, 1–16.

VAN DEN BERGH, J. C. J. M. & GRAZI, F. 2014. Ecological footprint policy? Land use as an environmental indicator. *Journal of Industrial Ecology*, 18, 10–19.

VAN DER WAL, J. & NOORMAN, K. 1998. Analysis of household metabolic flows. *In*: NOORMAN, K. J. & UITERKAMP, T. S. (eds) *Green Households? Domestic Consumers, Environment, and Sustainability*. London: Earthscan.

WACKERNAGEL, M. & REES, W. E. 1996. *Our Ecological Footprint: Reducing Human Impact on the Earth*. Gabriola Island, B.C.: New Society Publishers.

WEBER, C. L., PETERS, G. P., GUAN, D. & HUBACEK, K. 2008. The contribution of Chinese exports to climate change. *Energy Policy*, 36, 3572–3577.

WEINZETTEL, J., HERTWICH, E. G., PETERS, G. P., STEEN-OLSEN, K. & GALLI, A. 2013. Affluence drives the global displacement of land use. *Global Environmental Change*, 23, 433–438.

WIEDMANN, T. & BARRETT, J. 2010. A review of the ecological footprint indicator – Perceptions and methods. *Sustainability*, 2, 1645–1693.

WILTING, H. C., SCHIPPER, A. M., BAKKENES, M., MEIJER, J. R. & HUIJBREGTS, M. A. 2017. Quantifying biodiversity losses due to human consumption: A global-scale footprint analysis. *Environmental Science & Technology*, 51, 3298–3306.

3 Sustainable consumption in social context

In Chapter 2, we concentrated on understanding how consumption impacts on the environment, and the resulting imperative to consume within environmental limits. As I wrote in the Introduction, the topic of sustainable consumption sits on the intersection between the physical, economic and social worlds. If we are to think about how to change our consumption, in order to solve these physical world problems, we must also understand the social context in which consumption occurs. By the end of this chapter, you will understand how different types of people consume, as well as how different types of people might be affected by attempts to change consumption.

My focus here is on social difference (gender, class, age, ethnic origin, disability status, geographical location, etc.), and how belonging to specific social categories relates to how people consume. I will look at different concepts that are useful for theorising about social difference and sustainable consumption, including justice, responsibility, identity, distinction and stigma. I will also think about how social difference affects the potential to introduce sustainable consumption measures. The key message of this chapter is that social difference matters because it impacts both materially and symbolically on people's ability to engage with the idea of sustainable consumption. That means that people can be prevented from engaging because they do not have the resources to engage, or because they do not feel this is an agenda which aligns with their identity. If everyone is to have the opportunity to engage in sustainable consumption, as many would argue should be the case, we have to take social difference seriously.

Why think about social difference?

Some academics and practitioners have a tendency to treat consumers, citizens, or the public as a general entity, an amorphous mass of people who will react very similarly to any kind of intervention, irrespective of their backgrounds. There are two reasons why this is unhelpful. First, taking social difference into account allows us to design more effective interventions, and second there are justice implications associated with how people's needs affect their consumption.

Designing effective interventions

First, people's choices and habits are shaped by the categories they belong to or identify with. It is clear that a middle-aged couple will make different kinds of choices, and have different instincts about what they need and want, to a student in a shared house. Also that a middle-class consumer in the global North will have different energy needs (for e.g. warmth) than a middle-class consumer in the global South (for e.g. cooling). So at the very least, we must take social difference categories into account in order to properly understand what people are likely to do given certain social conditions.

The diversity of consumption patterns is not just down to these social or geographical categories, of course, as people might consume differently for all sorts of reasons. Figure 3.1 is taken from a UK-based study by Chappells and Medd (2008) and it shows what proportion of five contrasting households' overall water use was used for different purposes. Note that this does not say anything about the overall levels of water use in each household; rather, it explains how differently the water is used for different functions.

What immediately strikes you about Figure 3.1? Chappells and Medd were surprised by just how different these households' use profiles are. In this small sample of five households their toilet, bathing and washing practices must be very different.

The differences in the households' water-using practices brought out in Chappells and Medd's work are likely to be due to a number of factors. Some households will choose to use water in different ways, by, for instance, taking a bath rather than a shower. Some water-using practices will be deeply habitual and not really thought about, such as, for instance, putting underwear in the wash at

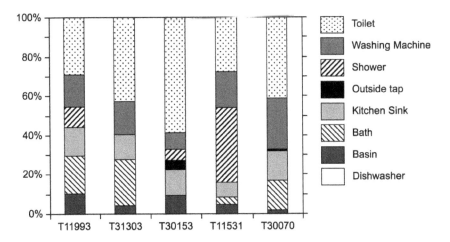

Figure 3.1 Five UK households' use of water for different purposes (from Chappells and Medd, 2008, reprinted by permission of Taylor & Francis Ltd)

the end of every day. Other practices will be driven by need. Health conditions, such as incontinence, require more regular washing of clothes and bodies, while pain can be eased by taking a warm bath.

Given that water is consumed in the context of very intimate practices (such as bathing or using the toilet), this is a highly sensitive area in which to intervene. Imagine the impact of a policy which taxed water based on each unit consumed. This could cause big problems for any poorer households represented in this diagram, as it might force them to change practices of cleanliness that would have serious impacts on their health and sense of identity. Other households, however, may just absorb the cost of the tax, and continue their water-use practices as they did previously, rendering the tax ineffective in curbing water wastage. As we will see later in the book, people's sense of identity, or their need to practice in a particular way for cultural reasons, will sometimes mean that they are prepared to take a financial hit in order to maintain their way of life. I hope this example makes clear that any intervention to promote sustainable consumption needs to be sensitive to the different needs and expectations of different types of people.

In the first instance, then, it is helpful to approach the topic of sustainable consumption with an eye on social difference because this will help us to create more socially sensitive, and by extension more successful, interventions. The topic of differing needs brings us to the second reason that it is important to think about social difference: social justice and equity issues.

Designing fair interventions

There are important ethical concerns, associated with the people's differing starting points, and as such their differing needs, that also require us to emphasise social difference. There are two key points here: first, that people's starting points (their geographical location, class, gender, ethnic origin, health, wealth, etc.) constrain their ability to engage in sustainable consumption, and second, that opportunities to engage in interventions sometimes exclude people who have specific characteristics.

The study of sustainable development has a strong and historic emphasis on the importance of addressing poverty and equity issues, which is not widely replicated in the sustainable consumption literature. The study of sustainable consumption tends to be concerned with the developed world, and to focus on wealthier demographics in the global North, where, as we saw in Chapter 2, much of the environmental impact is created. The field of environmental justice has repeatedly found that marginalised people (e.g. income poor, people of colour) live in low-quality environments (see, for instance, Agyeman, 2005) and we also know that those in the global South are more likely to suffer environmental impacts (Rees, 2008). Further, there is some evidence that marginalised people are more likely to bear the cost of environmental policy (Büchs et al., 2011). It is therefore ethically important to understand how poverty, and other forms of marginalisation and difference, structure people's ability to engage in different forms of consumption.

As well as understanding how the material world affects people's consumption possibilities, we also need to consider the barriers to inclusion that relate to identity. To give an example: poorer people might not have easy access to clean water through a tap and therefore must engage in different drinking practices to richer people, perhaps collecting water to drink, and paying a premium for this. These represent material barriers to sustainable water consumption (consumption that is not likely to make people ill). An identity-related barrier would include a household's reluctance to engage in sustainable consumption branded activities because these are 'not for the likes of us'. Below I will show that environmentalist identities in the global North are frequently associated with a particular type of middle-class identity. This can leave other groups feeling excluded from involvement in sustainable consumption, because this does not chime with their own sense of self.

In the next section, the importance of designing both effective and fair interventions by understanding social difference will be explored in relation to a series of specific 'differences' that seem to have an impact on people's ability to engage.

How does social difference connect with sustainable consumption?

So what do we know about how social difference connects with sustainable consumption? There is a substantial body of work on this topic, based on extensive qualitative and quantitative data. In this section, I will deal with a series of differences that have been reported to play a role in the nature of people's consumption patterns, and the resulting impacts on the environment. I start by looking at the relationship between income and environmental impact, then at how gender and disability structure people's consumption patterns. While I only discuss a small number of social differences here, this should give you a flavour of the ways in which consumption is structured by social context, as well as the impacts this has on what we can do to make consumption more sustainable. Studies on young people (Hume, 2010), and class (Anantharaman, 2014, 2016; Carfagna et al., 2014) are available, and in some cases expanded on in later chapters.

Income

One of the best-known correlations is between income and environmental impact. Numerous quantitative studies have shown that there is a strong correlation between how much you earn and the amount of carbon emissions that you produce (Druckman and Jackson, 2009; Büchs and Schnepf, 2013). This applies most starkly between nations, where if you plot (for instance) average carbon emissions against average GDP per capita of a nation, there is a clear correlation (see Figure 2.2). Within nations, this correlation also exists, with low-earning people on average producing less carbon emissions than high-earning people. A graph from one of these studies in the UK is shown in Figure 3.2.

Note that both axes have logarithmic scales here, which makes the correlation between income and CO_2 emissions look weaker than it is. Büchs and Schnepf's work in Figure 3.2 shows that not only do total CO_2 emissions per household increase as income increases, so do all the disaggregated elements of the carbon footprint, including transport, home and indirect emissions.

The implication from this research, and from the considerable body of work that confirms it in many nations of the global North, is that richer people are consuming considerably more, and contributing more substantially to the environmental impacts of these nations. Colleagues in the sustainable consumption research community have argued that both researchers and policy-makers need to give more attention to the rich (see studies such as Cohen, 2010). Certainly while the geographical focus of interest for sustainable consumption has tended to be the global North, we can see from the work linking CO_2 emissions in the UK with income that there are considerable differences between rich and poor households in the global North.

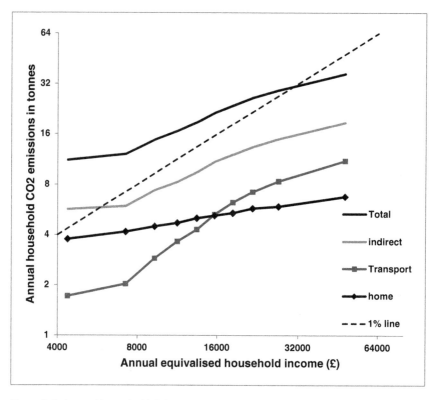

Figure 3.2 Annual household CO_2 emissions (by source) and their relationship to annual household income in the UK (reproduced from Büchs and Schnepf, 2013, with permission from the authors and under the terms of the CC BY license)

Why might such differences between rich and poor be important to take into account? When we think about asking (or even forcing) people to change their consumption patterns, we have to understand their differing starting points. Even in relatively wealthy nations, it may be the case that some people are consuming less of a resource than is sustainable. In their study of consumption in Lithuania in the period following the end of communism, Dagiliūtė and Juknys (2009) found that consumption of water and thermal energy reduced substantially as these industries were privatised, and households were charged for each unit of water/heat they used (see Figure 3.3). In 2006, average water consumption per person per day in Lithuania was 82 litres, compared to the World Health Organization's sanitary norms of 120 litres. Note also that despite a steady increase in some forms of consumption (personal cars, home appliances), other forms of consumption have persisted in staying rather low. This suggests that household consumption priorities shifted once costs of water and heat increased, and as a result they became under-consumers of these essential services, a form of unsustainable consumption.

Among the poorest people in the global North, under-consumption of a number of resources is widespread. This depends somewhat on the level of inequality in society: the gap between rich and poor, and the amount of redistribution that takes place through the tax system (Wilkinson and Pickett, 2009). In the UK, the poorest members of society are sometimes unable to access adequate warmth and other energy services, food and mobility (Lucas, 2012; Middlemiss and Gillard, 2015; Garthwaite, 2016). These forms of under-consumption can result in a range of social problems: the cold exacerbating asthma and heart complaints, children not being able to concentrate at school because they are hungry,

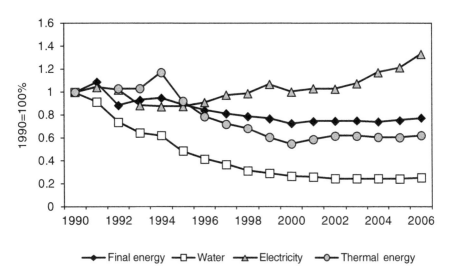

Figure 3.3 Change in consumption patterns in Lithuania between 1995 and 2006 (reproduced from Dagiliūtė and Juknys, 2008, with permission from the publisher, Kaunas University of Technology)

people not being able to access employment opportunities because they cannot travel to work. Frequently, poorer people suffer a number of these disadvantages at once, with impaired mobility, nutrition and warmth, for instance, leaving the poorest families still more desperate (Mattioli, 2014; Middlemiss, 2017). In other words, as well as being less substantial contributors to environmental problems, poor people in wealthy countries often suffer profound social and physical consequences of not being able to access resources. In thinking about sustainable consumption then, we must remember that consuming less is not good for people when it means they cannot meet their needs.

So it is clear that income plays an important role in structuring people's opportunities to consume. Which other social differences play a role? We can imagine that age, gender, ethnic origin, disability, religion, class, employment status, educational level, sexual orientation and geographical location could all have an impact on people's interest in ideas of sustainability, their existing practices, and their willingness or ability to make changes in their lives. There is not time to profile all of these here, instead I will focus on gender and disability, both of which have elicited interesting responses from thinkers in this field.

Gender

Gender is important to think about in relation to sustainable consumption, for two reasons: first, men and women tend to do different consumption work, with women still more likely to take responsibility for maintenance of the home and family. This means that men and women are differently affected by sustainable consumption policy. Second, in a world in which advertising and marketing pays considerable attention to gender, men and women are targeted differently, including targeting as sustainable consumers. This can have important impacts on people's understanding of themselves, and how what they do impacts on the environment and on other people.

The division of household labour between women and men has in most societies been skewed towards women taking on more responsibility for maintenance of the home and family, with men more likely to work outside of the home (Judkins and Presser, 2008). More recently, in the global North, the trend has been away from a 'male breadwinner' and towards an 'adult worker' model, where (in a heterosexual family context) both parents engage in paid work (Charles et al., 2008). Feminists note that for many women this has amounted to a 'triple shift' – caring for the home, the children and paid work.

Despite a shifting picture, women still do more hours of housework and less hours of paid work on average, and put more time into caring roles (looking after children or older people) (Domínguez-Folgueras, 2013; Druckman et al., 2012). Given that many of the practices we attempt to change in the name of sustainable consumption take place in the household (shopping, cooking, washing, cleaning), the implication is that greening household practices will, on average, have a greater impact on women than on men. Further, it is often the case that environmentally friendly household work is more labour intensive than ordinary household work, with, for instance, energy- or chemical-hungry appliances and practices replaced with someone's time.

Judkins and Presser's study on the division of labour in eco-friendly households in the US found that eco-friendly household work is indeed more labour intensive, and that women tend to do more of it. In the heterosexual households they studied they noted that 'Wives did more of this work and took primary responsibility for it' and noted that 'commitment to greater environmental sustainability in the home does not necessarily further equity in the marital relationship where domestic work is concerned' (Judkins and Presser, 2008, 937). There is a risk that ecologically conscious women take on more responsibility for home labour, and in doing so become further burdened by an unequal workload. Certainly Cairns and colleagues' study of Canadian 'eco-moms' found that women took on additional responsibilities associated with caring for the earth through caring for their children, and that in doing so they experienced difficulties in finding enough time to spend on, for instance, sourcing and preparing appropriately environmentally friendly foods for their children (Cairns et al., 2014). Swedish women were also frustrated by the amount of time that environmentally friendly household work takes up (Isenhour and Ardenfors, 2009).

Given that the burden of household work still falls disproportionately on women, any change to household practices needs to take into account impacts on gender equality. Dagmar Vinz's call for 'the development of sustainability strategies that no longer assume that unpaid care work provides the basis for an economy by serving as a "natural resource"' (2009, 165) is an important one. We need to be conscious of how women and men will be differently affected by sustainable consumption policy and practice, and as a result to ensure that damaging gender expectations and roles are not further entrenched in policy and practice.

Gender is important for sustainable consumption because it is being engaged by companies who want to sell things differently. Women are known to express more pro-environmental sentiments than men (Luchs and Mooradian, 2012), and marketers and advertisers have not hesitated to target women in campaigns encouraging ethical consumption. Companies are aware that 'Women are believed to make the majority of household consumption decisions, and are more likely than men to make decisions for pro-social and pro-environmental reasons' (MacGregor, 2016). This results in women being targeted because of their gender, sometimes in rather aggressive ways (ibid.).

Roberta Hawkins documents the targeting of mothers in the marketing of Derlea, a butter spread sold in Canada. The selling point here is that if you buy Derlea, the company donates some money towards providing malaria nets in Africa. The marketing message – 'First-ever Moms Helping Moms campaign mobilizes Canadian caregivers to help eradicate malaria in Africa' (Hawkins, 2012, 756) clearly positions the act of buying Derlea as gendered, and attempts to link women's interests across global North and South. Hawkins sees this as highly problematic: it suggests that only women (and indeed only mothers) have understanding and compassion, thereby marginalising non-mothers/men; it neglects (and indeed hides) the power differences between women in North and South by assuming that mothers have a shared understanding of life, and it individualises the solution to a health epidemic, by suggesting that buying butter is an effective means to solve malaria (ibid.). In effect, Derlea uses the idea of motherhood and the solidarity of women to sell a campaign which does nothing to address the inequalities between these women, and which also potentially reinforces gender stereotypes about caring that have further negative consequences.

Disability

Disability is another way in which people have constrained opportunities to participate in sustainable consumption, both from a material perspective and in relation to environmentalist identity. Deborah Fenney Salkeld, recently completed the first substantial study in this area (Fenney and Snell, 2011; Fenney Salkeld, 2016, 2017a, 2017b). I use this particular form of social difference as an example, because there are interesting insights from looking at sustainable consumption through a disability studies lens that are helpful to understanding how other forms of social difference impact on sustainable consumption. Before I continue, I should point out that disability is a very broad category, and people experiencing disability can have a wide range of life experiences, which may or may not have an impact on their engagement with sustainability.

Fenney Salkeld (2017a) approaches this topic using the social model of disability – an understanding of disability which contends that disability is not the property of an individual, instead it is a feature of a society which is not satisfactorily designed for people with impairments. In other words, disability exists as a result of the social fabric being designed for people without impairments, which this field sees as a result of unequal power relations between disabled and non-disabled people. This oppression of disabled people is called 'disablism', and the tendency to assume that non-disabled people's experiences are both 'normal' and 'desirable' is 'ableism' (ibid.). Fenney Salkeld (2016) notes that the individual model of disability (where disability is the property of the individual) is more commonplace than this social model, certainly in UK policy around disability rights.

The challenges that disabled people face in engaging with sustainability issues are on the one hand very similar to those living in poverty (because disabled people are on average poorer than non-disabled) (Fenney and Snell, 2011). On the other hand, disabled people may also have important needs which make sustainable consumption difficult. The most obvious of these would be that mobility-impaired people have to rely on motorised transport. Alongside such material world challenges, there are also challenges of identity and distinction. For instance, self-sufficiency is frequently seen as a life goal in the environmental movement. This can be problematic for people experiencing disability. One of Fenney Salkeld's respondents talks about her need for medication to treat her impairment: 'just eating lots of potatoes and homeopathy is not the substitute for this . . . the whole idea that natural is good, unnatural is bad, so basically you write off anyone who needs quote unquote "unnatural" support to live' (2017a, 513).

Fenney Salkeld notes that a discourse of strong sustainability is 'often linked to a kind of "heroic" vision of humanity as rugged and independent, as well as to a particular valorisation of the "natural"' (Fenney Salkeld, 2016, 453). See also Box 3.1, on the bike as an ableist symbol.

Fenney Salkeld notes multiple instances of disablism and ableism in sustainable consumption research and environmental policy (ibid.). In environmental policy, it seems that we either fail to recognise that a disabled constituency exists, or we see this constituency as merely vulnerable. As such, for instance, in UK sustainability policy, disabled people are referred to in terms of vulnerability (see English fuel poverty in Middlemiss, 2017) and needing protection from various environmental ills (Fenney Salkeld, 2016), this in direct contrast to the rational behaviour often expected from non-disabled people (ibid.). Having said that, all households are expected to 'do their bit' to meet government targets.

Box 3.1 The bike as ableist symbol

This advert from 2010 by Manchester Friends of the Earth (UK) suggests that anyone not travelling by bike is fat, and by implication lazy. The photo presents these options as if they are a matter of individual choice. Travelling by bike is often portrayed as a cornerstone of environmentalist identity in the UK (Horton, 2006), but, as Fenney points out, it is also an excluding practice. Effectively the bike is both a symbol of environmentalism and an ableist symbol, excluding and stigmatising those that cannot cycle, and distancing people with a disability from environmentalist identities (Fenney Salkeld, 2017a). One of Fenney Salkeld's participants experienced this as follows: 'there's a lot of people who cycle, who are very much into like physical fitness and all of that and have this kind of air of superiority about them because they're moving around on their own power' (ibid., 512–513).

Figure 3.4 Fat Lane (image courtesy of Creative Concern/Manchester Friends of the Earth; photography by Graeme Cooper, art direction by Mat Bend)

So what can we learn from disability studies here? As with other forms of social difference, we should be concerned about creating effective and fair interventions, and when we ignore disability, as Fenney Salkeld puts it: 'inaccessible solutions to environmental problems risk adding to disabled people's exclusion from participation, as well as threatening the success of these solutions' (2017a, 508).

Two insights from her work add depth to this analysis, however. The social model of disability might be a useful analogy, given that the way that society is organised fails to empower disabled people, we can also see that it fails to empower environmental lifestyles in the round. This suggests a more political analysis – challenging existing social structures rather than assuming that the individual is failing to take responsibility. We will return to these issues in later chapters. Further, the concept of 'ableism' or the privileging of non-disabled experiences, as well as the assumption that these are normal, encourages us to examine the kinds of subjects imagined by policy in a more critical way.

How do we explain and account for these differences?

There is no single body of academic work that directly addresses how to explain and account for the impacts of social difference on sustainable consumption, but there are plenty of places to turn for inspiration in related fields. In the study of sustainable consumption, a series of concepts are beginning to be engaged to think about how social difference can be better reflected in both thinking and decision-making. The first of these uses the concepts of identity, distinction and stigma to understand how consumption reflects and reinforces a range of identities. This body of work takes as its starting point that effective interventions in this field might need to consider how people feel and think about the idea of sustainable consumption, and how this sits with their various identities, as well as what material needs they have to engage in it. The second links into the broader literature on social and environmental justice, and considers the boundaries of responsibility of the individual, given their social context. This body of work tackles the issue of 'designing fair interventions' raised above.

Identity, distinction, stigma and class

The concepts of identity and distinction here are important because they allow us to see how people might be included in, or excluded from, sustainable consumption by virtue of their sense of self. In addition, by thinking about identity and distinction, we begin to understand how environmentalist identities are experienced by both environmentalists and others. The most important theoretical contributions here come from the leading sociologist Pierre Bourdieu in his text *Distinction* (1984), and many of the other authors here are drawing on his work. I will return to this discussion of identity and environmentalism in Chapter 9.

The concept of distinction relates to the idea of 'good taste'. Bourdieu argues that when we talk about good taste, we are really referring to markers of class

(Bourdieu, 1984). When we consume and practice, we do so in ways which display which particular class fraction we belong to. So, in each class fraction, it is considered good form to dress, eat, travel and have fun in particular ways. Further, the middle classes, who have more 'cultural capital' (meaning non-financial resources such as education) are the class fraction which determines what counts as 'good taste'. Bourdieu calls this domination of taste 'symbolic violence', since it allows the powerful middle classes to hold onto their power by having good taste – that is, by consuming in the 'right' way, and in doing so demeaning other forms of taste.

People engage in sustainable consumption in many ways, and can come from a range of class fractions. Writers in this area have argued, however, that sustainable consumers are predominantly middle class, and that being a sustainable consumer has positive effects on identity (Littler, 2011). This applies in many different national contexts. In Malaysia, for instance, Bryant and Goodman note (in relation to buying organic food) that 'the espousal of environmental causes through consumption is itself a prime means by which to boost one's standing in society' (2013, 53). They comment that this is a rather safe identity to espouse, in the sense that it has both personal benefits in showing one's good taste, and does not rock the boat politically. Dave Horton's characterisation of environmental activists from his studies in the UK is also a useful application of Bourdieu's work:

> Environmental activists distinguish themselves by the 'austerity of elective restriction', the 'self-imposed constraint' of 'asceticism', which is one strategy through which the dominated fractions of the dominant class demonstrate their freedom from 'brutish necessity' on the one hand and profligate 'luxury' on the other, and assert the distinctive power of their cultural capital.
>
> (Horton, 2003, 67)

Horton is arguing here that being a green activist is a means of distinction for people who belong to the dominant (i.e. middle) class, but who are a minority in that class (dominated). He is also saying that part of being green (or an activist) is to show how you are different from the poor ('brutish necessity') and the rest of the middle classes ('luxury'). In this case, consuming less is a way of communicating a particular identity.

This is echoed in Lindsay Carfagna and colleagues' work on US-based ethical consumers, in which they point out that these respondents are predominantly people with high cultural capital (Carfagna et al., 2014). They further explore how this class fraction relates to consumption, and how they differentiate themselves from their peers (the rest of the middle classes), expanding on Horton's notion of 'self-imposed aestheticism' above. Carfagna and colleagues talk about a new kind of materialism amongst ethical consumers, with an emphasis on the 'physicality of the goods and their connection to the earth' (ibid., 175). They also notice a preference for the local, which contrasts strongly to other high-cultural capital consumers, but that the local is treated in rather a cosmopolitan way. Finally, there is an embrace of manual labour in this group (growing your own, making food from scratch) which again contrasts with other high-cultural capital consumers, who tend to avoid association with manual work. It is important to note that these distinctions are not fixed however, and one of Carfagna and colleagues' claims, is that ethical consumers in the US amount to a new form of high-cultural capital consumer. Shirani and colleagues' work in the UK also suggests that there has been a shift in perceptions of green identities, and that they have become normalised, among middle-class consumers (Shirani et al., 2015). As one of their respondents put it: 'we move from being crackers, you know, crackpot kind of ex-hippies, to being mainstream without changing our stance whatsoever; it's merely the world changed around us' (ibid., 64)

By definition, distinction is about exclusion: creating identity around the differences between one class fraction and another. As such, environmentalist distinctions are likely to restrict some people's access to membership of environmentalist identities. This was perfectly expressed by a teenage interviewee we talked to in our work on fuel poverty (Middlemiss and Gillard, 2015). When asked 'What do you think an environmentally friendly person lives like?', her response was to pause, and then respond: 'Do we know anyone like that, mum?' My teenage respondent clearly does not see herself as 'environmentally friendly'. This brings us to our final concept of this section: stigma.

In an extensive review paper on the topic, Link and Phelan define stigma as 'labelling, stereotyping, separation, status loss, and discrimination' in the context of the exercise of power (2001, 367). In other words, stigma is about labelling people as different, linking these labelled people to negative stereotypes, making a separation between these labelled people and others, and these labelled people experiencing status loss and discrimination. We can see that distinction is likely to lead to stigma, as it is a means whereby groups of people are labelled by others as different. Note that stigma can be created both by the stigmatiser and the stigmatised.

So where could stigma exist in relation to sustainable consumer identities? First, environmentalists themselves have experienced stigma (Littler, 2009). One of Shirani and colleagues' respondents remembers his mother being embarrassed about him being an environmentalist: when this seemed like a rather deviant identity, it was one that was stigmatised (Shirani et al., 2015). More importantly for me though, there is widespread stigma against people who do not engage in these issues, or against people who 'only' engage in environmentalism for financial reasons. Given the connections of environmentalism with class discussed above, this includes people stigmatising the practices of the working classes, as ignorant (of environmental problems), or careless (neglecting the environment). This kind of stigma is an example of Bourdieu's 'symbolic violence'. It is also hugely problematic, because if we understand environmentalism in terms of distinction and identity, we can see that people are being deliberately excluded in symbolic terms, before being castigated for not wanting to be included. What Bourdieu teaches us is that these are not matters of choice: as a working-class person, you may not have the choice to engage in this agenda.

I will finish with Louise Reid and colleagues' discussion of the stigmas associated with renewable energy, which reveals the potential complexities associated with identity, distinction and stigma in relation to sustainable consumption (Reid et al., 2015). These authors point out that in the UK, renewable energy technology such as solar panels are frequently owned either by people who have middle-class environmentalist identities, or are installed on social housing developments. This could attract two forms of stigma: the stigma of being too middle class, or that of being too poor. In other words, potential recipients could feel that solar panels were 'too posh' if they did not belong to the environmentalist class fraction, and 'too desperate' if they live in social housing themselves. This example underlines how important it is to understand how issues of distinction play out in daily life. Certainly, by being aware of identity, distinction and stigma in both research and practice on sustainable consumption, we may be able to design more effective, and indeed fairer interventions.

Justice, citizenship and differentiated responsibility

Another useful theoretical input to thinking about fairer interventions, is the substantial literature on environmental justice. The primary focus of this literature is on the injustices caused by unequal access to environmental resources, in understanding who has had their rights (to clean environment and safe places to live) violated as a result of structural injustices. There is a strong connection between environmental justice studies in the US and the civil rights movement, with a recognition that people of colour are more likely to live in degraded and polluted places (Agyeman, 2005). In a sustainable consumption context, this literature is useful because it helps us think about what kind of injustices people might be exposed to.

The most obvious connection between consumption and justice here is through the environmentally harmful practices we engage in. For example, my use of a car to travel contributes to climate change, which is likely to cause a rise in sea levels affecting people in low-lying countries. This amounts to an injustice because I get all of the benefits of driving my car, while they incur all of the costs of my car driving. Shrader-Frechette characterises environmental injustice as follows: 'Environmental injustice occurs whenever some individual or group bears disproportionate environmental risks like those of hazardous waste dumps, or has unequal access to environmental goods like clean air, or has less opportunity to partake in environmental decision-making' (Shrader-Frechette, 2002, 3). While according to Büchs and colleagues:

> We might also add to this list: when someone does not have the opportunity to partake in environmental practices (because of material or symbolic barriers). People might also be affected by environmental injustice when they are more substantively affected by environmental policy.
>
> (Büchs et al., 2011)

Justice scholars commonly differentiate between procedural and distributive justice, hinted at in Shrader-Frechette's quote above (Bulkeley and Fuller, 2012; Walker and Day, 2012). Procedural justice means the opportunity to be involved in decision-making processes, and distributive justice – that is, the fairness of the distribution of resources. A third form of justice – recognition – is also important, and relates to the need to recognise people's exposure to injustice, and respect their circumstances (Walker and Day, 2012). In sustainable consumption research, policy and practice, the failure to recognise how social difference impacts people's ability to engage with the agenda could be considered a recognition injustice. We need to recognise that the world is not a level playing field, and that people have different capacities to act on sustainability (Middlemiss, 2010; Bulkeley and Fuller, 2012). Gordon Walker and Harriet Bulkeley (2006) observe this lack of interest in justice in work on sustainability as a whole. They attribute this to the over-emphasis on economy in a weak sustainability paradigm, and over-emphasis on environment in a strong sustainability paradigm, both of which neglect the social.

Given the focus on rights in much of the literature on environmental justice (for instance, the right to clean air, and to a fair distribution of natural resources), there is less consideration of responsibility, and how this might be affected by social difference (Middlemiss, 2010). In sustainable consumption, responsibility is an important and frequently discussed topic, and here we need to understand how the boundaries of responsibility are affected by social difference. There are multiple critiques in the literature of the tendency of this field to foreground the responsibility of the individual for making change (Maniates, 2001; Hobson, 2006; Middlemiss, 2010; Shove, 2010). The justice scholar Shrader-Frechette, suggests that 'To the degree that people have the ability to make a positive difference in such situations, therefore they are obliged to do so' (2002, 178).

This is a useful starting point for thinking about the intersection of justice and sustainable consumption, as it looks first to people's ability, which is clearly constrained by their circumstances. From our examples of income, gender and disability above, we could also add that constraining circumstances could be both material and symbolic.

Conclusion

At the end of this chapter, I hope it is clear to you that people have different capacities to act on sustainable consumption as a result of their social context. We have seen that by virtue of one's income, gender, disability, status, or class, one can have very different opportunities to engage in this issue. Other differences, which I have not focused on here, will also affect people's ability to engage in these issues. Taking social difference into account in both studying and acting on sustainable consumption is therefore highly important. If we ignore social difference in addressing sustainable consumption, people might be further marginalised or just ineffectively addressed by policy and practice. As Jo Littler puts it: 'exploitation can not only be addressed, and defeated, by consumption labelled as "ethical", but also produced through it' (2011, 36).

Some interesting further points arise from this body of work. First, it begs the question of which identities are compatible with environmentalism? My discussion of identity above would suggest that it is difficult to hold a working-class identity while also being an environmentalist. This is too hasty a conclusion, however. While we do know that many of the widely recognised forms of environmentalism correspond with middle-class identities, this does not preclude working-class environmentalisms existing or indeed emerging. Perhaps you are aware of such identities in your own culture?

Second, when we think about consumption levels, or how much stuff people need to live a decent life (a perpetual topic of comment by environmentalists), a social difference lens forces us to think more relatively. It is very difficult to talk about a blanket reduction in consumption, when we know that some people are consuming unhealthily small amounts of some resources. We do notice this in a global context (where we know that there is absolute poverty); however we tend to ignore it in the global North. A social difference agenda encourages us to see what people need as relative to their circumstances, and in doing so to understand that even basic needs can be difficult to prescribe. It also suggests that the distribution of resources is a centrally important theme in solving unsustainable consumption. In Chapter 12, I will discuss needs in more detail.

Further resources

Black Environment Network: www.ben-network.org.uk

References

AGYEMAN, J. 2005. *Sustainable Communities and the Challenge of Environmental Justice.* New York: NYU Press.
ANANTHARAMAN, M. 2014. Networked ecological citizenship, the new middle classes and the provisioning of sustainable waste management in Bangalore, India. *Journal of Cleaner Production*, 63, 173–183.
ANANTHARAMAN, M. 2016. Elite and ethical: The defensive distinctions of middle-class bicycling in Bangalore, India. *Journal of Consumer Culture*, 17, 864–886.
BOURDIEU, P. 1984. *Distinction: A Social Critique of the Judgement of Taste.* Cambridge, MA, Harvard University Press.
BRYANT, R. & GOODMAN, M. 2013. Peopling the practices of sustainable consumption: Eco-chic and the limits to the spaces of intention. *In*: BARENDREGT, B. & JAFFE, R. (eds) *Green Consumption: The Global Rise of Eco-Chic.* London: Bloomsbury.
BÜCHS, M. & SCHNEPF, S. V. 2013. Who emits most? Associations between socio-economic factors and UK households' home energy, transport, indirect and total CO_2 emissions. *Ecological Economics*, 90, 114–123.

BÜCHS, M., BARDSLEY, N. & DUWE, S. 2011. Who bears the brunt? Distributional effects of climate change mitigation policies. *Critical Social Policy*, doi:10.1177/02 61018310396036.

BULKELEY, H. & FULLER, S. 2012. *Low Carbon Communities and Social Justice* [Online]. Available: www.jrf.org.uk/sites/default/files/jrf/migrated/files/low-carbon-communities-summary.pdf [Accessed 21 December 2017].

CAIRNS, K., DE LAAT, K., JOHNSTON, J. & BAUMANN, S. 2014. The caring, committed eco-mom: Consumption ideals and lived realities of Toronto mothers. *In*: BARENDREGT, B. & JAFFE, R. (eds) *Green Consumption: The Global Rise of Eco-Chic*. London: Bloomsbury.

CARFAGNA, L. B., DUBOIS, E. A., FITZMAURICE, C., OUIMETTE, M. Y., SCHOR, J. B., WILLIS, M. & LAIDLEY, T. 2014. An emerging eco-habitus: The reconfiguration of high cultural capital practices among ethical consumers. *Journal of Consumer Culture*, 14, 158–178.

CHAPPELLS, H. & MEDD, W. 2008. What is fair? Tensions between sustainable and equitable domestic water consumption in England and Wales. *Local Environment*, 13, 725–741.

CHARLES, N., DAVIES, C. A. & HARRIS, C. 2008. *Families in Transition: Social Change, Family Formation and Kin Relationships*. Bristol, UK: Policy Press.

COHEN, M. J. 2010. Destination unknown: Pursuing sustainable mobility in the face of rival societal aspirations. *Research Policy*, 39, 459–470.

DAGILIŪTĖ, R. & JUKNYS, R. 2009. Sustainability of household consumption in Lithuania. *Environmental Research, Engineering & Management*, 47, 63–68.

DOMÍNGUEZ-FOLGUERAS, M. 2013. Is cohabitation more egalitarian? The division of household labor in five European countries. *Journal of Family Issues*, 34, 1623–1646.

DRUCKMAN, A. & JACKSON, T. 2009. The carbon footprint of UK households 1990–2004: A socio-economically disaggregated, quasi-multi-regional input–output model. *Ecological Economics*, 68, 2066–2077.

DRUCKMAN, A., BUCK, I., HAYWARD, B. & JACKSON, T. 2012. Time, gender and carbon: A study of the carbon implications of British adults' use of time. *Ecological Economics*, 84, 153–163.

FENNEY, D. & SNELL, C. 2011. Exceptions to the green rule? A literature investigation into the overlaps between the academic and UK policy fields of disability and the environment. *Local Environment*, 16, 251–264.

FENNEY SALKELD, D. 2016. Sustainable lifestyles for all? Disability equality, sustainability and the limitations of current UK policy. *Disability & Society*, 31, 447–464.

FENNEY SALKELD, D. 2017a. Ableism and disablism in the UK environmental movement. *Environmental Values*, 26, 503–522.

FENNEY SALKELD, D. 2017b. Environmental citizenship and disability equality: The need for an inclusive approach. *Environmental Politics*, 1–22.

GARTHWAITE, K. 2016. *Hunger Pains: Life Inside Foodbank Britain*. Bristol, UK: Policy Press.

HAWKINS, R. 2012. Shopping to save lives: Gender and environment theories meet ethical consumption. *Geoforum*, 43, 750–759.

HOBSON, K. 2006. Environmental responsibility and the possibilities of pragmatist-orientated research. *Social & Cultural Geography*, 7, 283–298.

HORTON, D. 2003. Green distinctions: The performance of identity among environmental activists. *The Sociological Review*, 51, 63–77.

HORTON, D. 2006. Demonstrating environmental citizenship? A study of everyday life among green activists. *In*: BELL, D. & DOBSON, A. (eds) *Environmental Citizenship.* Cambridge, MA: MIT Press.

HUME, M. 2010. Compassion without action: Examining the young consumers consumption and attitude to sustainable consumption. *Journal of World Business*, 45, 385–394.

ISENHOUR, C. & ARDENFORS, M. 2009. Gender and sustainable consumption: Policy implications. *International Journal of Innovation and Sustainable Development*, 4, 135–149.

JUDKINS, B. & PRESSER, L. 2008. Division of eco-friendly household labor and the marital relationship. *Journal of Social and Personal Relationships*, 25, 923–941.

LINK, B. G. & PHELAN, J. C. 2001. Conceptualizing stigma. *Annual Review of Sociology*, 27, 363–385.

LITTLER, J. 2009. *Radical Consumption*, Maidenhead, UK: Open University Press.

LITTLER, J. 2011. What's wrong with ethical consumption? *In*: LEWIS, T. & POTTER, E. (eds) *Ethical Consumption: A Critical Introduction.* Abingdon, UK: Routledge.

LUCAS, K. 2012. Transport and social exclusion: Where are we now? *Transport Policy*, 20, 105–113.

LUCHS, M. G. & MOORADIAN, T. A. 2012. Sex, personality, and sustainable consumer behaviour: Elucidating the gender effect. *Journal of Consumer Policy*, 35, 127–144.

MACGREGOR, S. 2016. Go ask 'Gladys': Why gender matters in sustainable consumption research. *Discover Society*. Available: https://discoversociety.org/2016/01/05/go-ask-gladys-why-gender-matters-in-energy-consumption-research/ [Accessed 29 March 2018].

MANIATES, M. F. 2001. Individualization: Plant a tree, buy a bike, save the world? *Global Environmental Politics*, 1, 31–52.

MATTIOLI, G. 2014. Where sustainable transport and social exclusion meet: Households without cars and car dependence in Great Britain. *Journal of Environmental Policy & Planning*, 16, 379–400.

MIDDLEMISS, L. K. 2010. Reframing individual responsibility for sustainable consumption: Lessons from environmental justice and ecological citizenship. *Environmental Values*, 19, 147–167.

MIDDLEMISS, L. 2017. A critical analysis of the new politics of fuel poverty in England. *Critical Social Policy*, 37, 425–443.

MIDDLEMISS, L. & GILLARD, R. 2015. Fuel poverty from the bottom-up: Characterising household energy vulnerability through the lived experience of the fuel poor. *Energy Research & Social Science*, 6, 146–154.

REES, W. E. 2008. Human nature, eco-footprints and environmental injustice. *Local Environment*, 13, 685–701.

REID, L., MCKEE, K. & CRAWFORD, J. 2015. Exploring the stigmatization of energy efficiency in the UK: An emerging research agenda. *Energy Research & Social Science*, 10, 141–149.

SHIRANI, F., BUTLER, C., HENWOOD, K., PARKHILL, K. & PIDGEON, N. 2015. 'I'm not a tree hugger, I'm just like you': Changing perceptions of sustainable lifestyles. *Environmental Politics*, 24, 57–74.

SHOVE, E. 2010. Beyond the ABC: Climate change policy and theories of social change. *Environment and Planning A*, 42, 1273–1285.

SHRADER-FRECHETTE, K. S. 2002. *Environmental Justice: Creating Equality, Reclaiming Democracy.* New York: Oxford University Press.

VINZ, D. 2009. Gender and sustainable consumption: A German environmental perspective. *European Journal of Women's Studies*, 16, 159–179.

WALKER, G. P. & BULKELEY, H. 2006. Geographies of environmental justice. *Geoforum*, 37, 655–659.

WALKER, G. & DAY, R. 2012. Fuel poverty as injustice: Integrating distribution, recognition and procedure in the struggle for affordable warmth. *Energy Policy*, 49, 69–75.

WILKINSON, R. & PICKETT, K. 2009. *The Spirit Level: Why Equality is Better for Everyone*. London: Penguin Books.

Part 2

Explaining sustainable consumption

4 'People don't understand'

One of the pet hates of my colleagues who teach environmental social sciences is the very common response that students make in their assignments when asked to come up with a solution to a complex environmental problem. Students see the problem as a lack of understanding: to paraphrase: 'if only people understood this problem, they would do what it takes to sort it out.' The response to such a lack of understanding is a vague call to 'increase education' on sustainable development issues.

If you have done this yourself, you are in good company. Indeed from the beginnings of the environmental movement, education has frequently been called upon as a solution to 'incorrect' behaviour. Policy-makers also frequently espouse the implicit theory that 'people just don't understand'. There is no need to take my word for it. Witness, for instance, the call for education in the *Brundtland Report*, one of the foundational documents of the modern environment movement: 'The changes in human attitudes that we call for depend on a vast campaign of education, debate, and public participation.' (World Commission on Environment and Development, 1987, 23).

More recently, in UK policy on sustainable consumption and production we can see a similar analysis of how change happens: 'Consumer buying decisions are often based on *incomplete information* as to the impacts of goods & services, and on *prices* which, as stated above, do not reflect the true costs of the product' (DEFRA, 2011; emphasis added).

In this way of thinking, consumers are expected to react to information, and therefore when information is incomplete, consumers can not react logically. Isenhour notes a similar instinct in Swedish environmental policy (Isenhour, 2010b, 2010a). Isenhour also points to Anthony Giddens's 'paradox' (2009) – that people will not respond to risk until they personally see its effects – as another example of an assumption that 'people don't understand' (Isenhour, 2010a). As you can see, calls for more education or for better information are widespread, historically, geographically and across sectors and disciplines.

In this chapter – the first of our 'stories' about sustainable consumption – I unpack the starting point that 'people don't understand', showing its failings and consider the potential and limits of education as a solution. I make two key points here: first, that sustainable consumption problems cannot be solved by education alone, and second, that calls for people to be 'educated' often cover up political motivations. Unlike the other chapters in this section, this story does not clearly originate in a discipline as such, although it is a common response from environmental scientists who have not perhaps thought about the complexities of the social world. In critiquing this point of view, I draw on insights from political science and science and technology studies, which result in a more nuanced understanding of the role of information.

Information-deficit model

Using the term 'information-deficit model' sounds rather grand, but this is not a sophisticated or complex theory. Instead it is an assumption that people don't understand and if they did, that they would do something about it. This is sometimes called the 'knowledge to action gap' (Markkula and Moisander, 2012). If we were to represent this idea in a diagram (see Figure 4.1), we would see a linear progression between knowledge (or science) and behaviour. The envisaged model of change here is that scientists inform policy-makers about the problem, policy-makers pass on that information to ordinary people, who change their behaviour as a result of being better informed.

This model of change is problematic in a number of ways, both because it ignores the politics that affect each of the steps in the model, as well as the multitude of other factors which might impact on each of these seemingly innocuous arrows. Let us take each of these in turn. First, there is unlikely to be a simple relationship between science and policy: there is limited evidence to show that science is merely translated directly into policy recommendations (Barr, 2003). In fact, the relationship between science and policy is embedded in the politics of the day. Which experts are listened to, and which expertise is used depends on what politicians and policy-makers see as appropriate, feasible, and politically tenable.

The information-deficit model also assumes that there is a simple relationship between government providing information about the issue in question, and people choosing to behave in 'appropriate' ways. There are several challenges here. People might object to the information provided, or to the behaviour that is deemed 'appropriate'. Informing people, or educating people, is not a simple matter of transferring values and beliefs from one set of people (government) to another (the general public). People are reflexive, critical and sometimes suspicious of the educator's motives, and rightly so! We will see in Chapters 7, 8 and 9 that people might be prevented from following government instruction by other drivers, including those instigated by government itself. People live in complex

Figure 4.1 Visual representation of the 'information-deficit model'

worlds, and many other factors impinge on why people behave in particular ways than just not having access to 'information'.

The information-deficit model does not explain change satisfactorily and is too easy to disprove. Let me try an experiment with you. Since you are reading this book, you are likely to be someone that is reasonably well educated on sustainable development issues. I certainly count myself among that number; indeed, anyone studying sustainability topics at degree level is in a highly educated minority. The likelihood is also that as part of this minority you have values that orient you towards caring for the environment. So my question for you is: do you live a sustainable life? Despite my education, values and efforts to reduce impact, my ecological footprint (see Chapter 2) is still twice the size of a sustainable one. While my education helps me to understand the impacts of my actions, and also allows me to understand ways in which I might mitigate these impacts, and my values predispose me towards acting on these issues, lots of other things get in the way of me behaving in a completely sustainable way.

Another problem with the story 'people don't understand' is that it is rather disrespectful of ordinary people, and encourages us to think of ordinary people as ignorant. Danny Miller sees this a symptomatic of a more substantial tendency of academics, and policy-makers: 'The single main problem with conventional writing about consumption is that it seems to consist largely of authors who wish to claim that they are deep by trying to show how everyone else is shallow' (Miller, 2012, 107).

It is a short step, indeed, between claiming that 'people don't understand' and claiming that 'people are stupid'. The environmental film *The Age of Stupid* reinforced this assumption (Armstrong, 2009). While in the film it is mainly the experts and the powerful who are being labelled stupid, it is a short step to assuming that anyone that does not behave 'correctly' is ignorant. Given that I am not ignorant, and that I still do not behave 'correctly', I think there is room for a bit more humility here.

In her eloquent critique of the information-deficit model, Kersty Hobson claims that this story has a more sinister role in international politics. In effect, she argues that the story that 'people don't understand' both fails to meaningfully address unsustainable consumption, and reinforces power differences between rich and poor countries: As she puts it:

> a discourse has been formed that does not threaten consumption as a form of practice but seeks to bind it to forms of knowledge – science, technology and efficiency – that embody the locus of power held by high-income countries in international relations.
>
> (Hobson, 2002, 99)

Effectively, Hobson is claiming that if we argue that 'people don't understand', global North governments can get away without doing very much, at the same time as asserting their dominance at a global scale. Hobson's argument is backed up by some empirical work on transport governance, which shows that transport planners working in local government in the UK use a language of choice and information when offering policy suggestions to elected officials, even though they do not really believe that such policies will have an impact (Marsden et al., 2014). The story that 'people don't understand' is a politically acceptable way of talking for transport planners: in effect, it traps them into using policies that they know are unlikely to be effective (ibid.).

The role of information in sustainable consumption

There is a risk that we take this critique too far, however. After all, if people know nothing about a problem, they are unlikely to be able to play a part in solving it. Clearly, having some understanding of a problem will often be an important start. In an extensive review paper on public understanding of climate change, Andrea Taylor and colleagues find that people often confuse different environmental problems, as well as their resulting effects (Taylor et al., 2014). So, for instance, people frequently confuse climate change with damage to the ozone layer. If we are to try to promote change based on people's values (see Chapter 6), and their commitment to environmental causes, this will be a challenge when people do not understand the core issues in the first place. This is not just a matter of educational achievement. In their study of university students at Plymouth University (UK), for instance, Cotton and colleagues find that even among highly educated students, studying at an institution that is recognised for its work on environmental issues, energy literacy (a form of environmental knowledge) was patchy (Cotton et al., 2015). They argue that in order to have effective energy literacy, people need to have knowledge of what you can do to change your consumption patterns, as well as what the problem is (ibid.). This tallies with other scholars' work on energy saving (Lorenzoni et al., 2007) and on environmental education (Jensen, 2002).

Taylor and colleagues also find that the relationship between climate change knowledge, attitudes and willingness to act is complex and that it is impossible to use one knowledge as a predictor of behaviour (Taylor et al., 2014). These authors reveal how people's self-perception, and their emotional reactions can have an impact on how they receive information. For instance, if people do not categorise themselves as 'vulnerable', they frequently will assume that something 'won't happen to me', despite being informed to the contrary. In looking at flood preparedness, Harries (2012) finds that some people who have previously experienced floods will ignore advice to take precautions, because they do not want to be reminded of the negative experiences they underwent. Clearly, neither providing information nor engaging in education has a straightforward connection with 'appropriate' or 'desired' behaviour.

While the link between providing information and behaviour change is often weak, there are ways in which information can be delivered which make 'informing people' a more effective strategy. Often this goes beyond merely providing information, and into combining information with persuasive techniques. For instance, Sutcliffe and colleagues used the ecological footprint as a means of explaining environmental impact to households (Sutcliffe et al., 2008). Alongside this information, they asked households to highlight any changes they intended to make, after their footprint was explained to them. They then revisited households two months later to find that many people had implemented these intended changes (ibid.). This study amounts to an intervention which combines informing people about their specific impact, then engaging them in target setting, and commitment to change. It is likely that change occurred as a result of the knowledge that the household's actions would be monitored when the researcher returned.

This also brings to mind the body of work on Ecoteams, a programme set up by the NGO Global Action Plan to promote collective action on environmental issues, which was subject to a number of academic studies (Hobson, 2002; Staats et al., 2004; Hargreaves et al., 2013a). The programme involves a small group of people discussing ideas around sustainable living collectively, and agreeing to self-monitor their waste, water, energy and transport practices. The process here is again a lot more involved than just 'providing information'; indeed, the information provided through the scheme tends to be subject to considerable scrutiny in the process of discussion. Some changes to behaviour are reported through this initiative, but they tend to be small, and either low cost or no cost (Hobson, 2002; Hargreaves et al., 2013a). Critically, though, people tend to make changes because they realise they can do things differently, not because they are better informed: in effect, the discussions about environmental problems and desired behaviours bring habits to the fore that previously would not have been thought about (Hobson, 2003; Middlemiss, 2011). There are also more problematic impacts of these schemes, however. For instance, being involved in Ecoteams frequently compounded feelings that these problems had 'little to do with them' and respondents were critical in their engagement: they realised they were being told to live differently while key institutions (government) were seemingly ignoring the same issues (Hobson, 2003).

As soon as we start digging into how information is actually used in context, we uncover more complex processes at play in people's understanding of the problem. Based on qualitative work about people's perception of energy information, Simcock and colleagues argue that the way people use information means that interventions would be more effective if they aimed at knowledge exchange rather than knowledge transfer (Simcock et al., 2014). In their study, as in the example of Ecoteams above, people engaged actively with information, rather than passively adopting it and the requisite behaviours. People also used a combination of expert and peer knowledge, and were more likely to take on new ideas if they were discussed (two-way) rather than lectured at. Critically, information on energy was seen as more relevant when it was talked about in the context of everyday lives, as opposed to in more abstract terms. This meant information being provided which was tailored to a specific household, rather than referring more generally to energy use.

A further challenge for people in making decisions about sustainable consumption is the sheer volume of information available, and the difficulties of processing this information in order to make a 'correct' choice. Witness the plethora of different labelling schemes that denote a product is in some way 'superior' ethically (see also Chapter 10 for a more extensive discussion of this). This amounts to an overload of information, leading to a need for people to process information and to make judgements about which types of information are important or reliable. Numerous studies have noted this challenge, in many contexts, from, for instance, large electronic equipment purchases (Young et al., 2004), to mothering ecologically (Cairns et al., 2014), to clothing (Markkula and Moisander, 2012). Markkula and Moisander's clothing example is especially rich because it shows just how aware clothing consumers are of the bigger picture. Their respondents understand that corporations want to make money as a first priority, and therefore feel that their own choices can only make a small difference. They are also affected by the dominant fashion discourse of 'fast fashion' which puts them into an 'aesthetic dilemma', meaning that they do not feel they can have both; as such they have to prioritise ethics over appearance, or vice versa. As these authors point out, the discourse of sustainable consumption is relatively weak, in the contemporary capitalist context, and any 'information' about the ethics of a product is subject to a fair amount of crowding out by other messages.

'People don't understand' in practice

Now that we have grasped the limits of the information-deficit model and had some indication of the role of information in sustainable consumption, it is interesting to think about where and how this story plays out in practice. What kinds of interventions are taken that assume that 'people don't understand'? In the following two sections, I will give examples of two types of intervention that have at their heart the provision of information to consumers. The first is the introduction of smart meters, which is becoming a common strategy in the global North, and has at its heart the belief that providing information to households through an electronic display will result in decreased energy consumption. The second is the phenomenon of green lifestyle TV which attempts to offer people information and motivation to green specific areas of their lifestyles.

Smart meters

The provision of smart meters by energy companies has become an increasingly popular strategy in the global North. In the UK, for instance, the government wants smart meters to be fitted in all homes from 2020 (DECC, 2009). The logic of providing smart meters for every household is partly connected with a more substantial smart grid infrastructure project, which allows information taken from household smart meters to be used by energy companies as a means of improving demand management.

However, there is an explicit role for the consumer here, who is anticipated to react rationally to information about their own energy use, provided in the electronic display associated with the smart meter, and adjust their behaviour accordingly (Strengers, 2011a, 2011b). As the UK Department of Energy and Climate Change (DECC) summarises, the meters are anticipated to 'provide consumers with real-time information on their electricity use to help them control consumption, save money and reduce emissions' (DECC, 2009, 7). There are several assumptions here: first, that people are able and willing to make rational trade-offs between the cost of energy and the needs they have for energy services. Second, that people are motivated by saving money, or by reducing emissions and waste. Third, that people are able to reduce their energy use as a result of this additional information. To spell this out, the provision of monitors is, for instance, expected to make people reduce their energy use at particular times of day, change their energy-using practices so as to reduce energy consumption, switch to more energy-efficient appliances, and to engage the whole household in the project of reducing energy consumption. Evidently the provision of information through smart meters will only work if these assumptions hold true. A final important assumption, is that reducing energy use is inevitably a good thing, which in the context of households experiencing fuel poverty, or health conditions affected by the cold, is not necessarily the case.

Overall, the introduction of smart meters is known to reduce energy use, with estimates ranging between 0–20 per cent reduction. The most extensive studies are a review paper of US studies suggesting between a 3 and 13 per cent reduction (an average of 7 per cent per cent) (Faruqui et al., 2010), and a UK base study of 60,000 households suggesting between a 0 and 3 per cent reduction (AECOM Limited, 2011). The wide range here shows how potential reductions in energy use are rather uncertain, and it is difficult to attribute change to any one specific driver. In the UK, for instance, household energy use has been reducing substantially in recent years (reduced by 25 per cent between 2005 and 2011) (Office for National Statistics, 2013) but these changes are likely to have a wide range of drivers (including, for instance, energy-efficiency changes in the home, and recession and associated austerity policy).

What is happening here is that a largely invisible form of consumption (energy) is being made visible by providing people with an in-house display (Hargreaves et al., 2013b). Elizabeth Shove points out that much of our consumption that has environmental impacts, particularly our consumption of energy and water, is inconspicuous; in other words, it is not something we think about very much, the very opposite of 'conspicuous consumption' (Shove, 2003). So smart meters are (at least temporarily) turning inconspicuous consumption conspicuous, making visible the cost impacts of every energy-consuming practice.

So how does the introduction of smart meters play out in people's daily lives? Is there a simple transfer of information happening here which results in now visible energy consumption being rationalised and reduced? We are fortunate in having access to two qualitative studies on the introduction of smart meters in the UK and Australia, which bring out some of the complexities of an intervention which aims to reduce the information deficit (Hargreaves et al., 2010, 2013b; Strengers, 2011b, 2011a). One of the most noticeable features of these two studies is the unforeseen consequences for households who are suddenly incredibly well informed about their own energy use. Households which are already experiencing financial difficulties, for instance, come to fear the smart meter, as it shows so clearly how much money they are spending. As one of Hargreaves and colleagues' respondents commented: 'She could kind of feel the money seeping out every time she had the boiler on. And to be honest beating herself up over it, you know. "I can't have it on because I'm wasting money, but I'm cold"' (respondent quote from Hargreaves et al., 2010, 6114).

In this context, knowledge creates both frustration, since people have limited control over the amount of money they have to spend on energy, and unhealthy behaviour, as people avoid using energy as a result of the new knowledge of how much it costs. Further, it can create tension within the household when the technology is used as a means of surveillance. Hargreaves reported an instance of a husband using the smart meter to monitor his wife's energy use, for instance (ibid.). Some of these tensions persisted, as Hargreaves found out when he returned twelve months later to the same respondents (Hargreaves et al., 2013b). We can see how such surveillance might become a means of enforcing a specific household member's ideas of how his or her family should behave, while also potentially providing an outlet for repressive or even abusive relationships. Jones and colleagues suggest that smart meters are 'part of the emerging everyday infrastructure of anxiety-induced behaviour regulation' (Jones et al., 2013, 152). This suggests that people's response to smart meters may be less rational than emotional, producing fear rather than logic.

In her Australian study, Yolande Strengers also found that respondents' reactions to information were not to merely change their behaviour. Indeed, in some instances, the smart meter became a legitimising technology: by further entrenching the status of specific energy consuming practices as non-negotiable (Strengers, 2011b). She found that respondents were aware of which appliances consumed a lot of energy, but used the knowledge they gained from the smart meter to justify their high consuming practices. As one respondent explained:

> I don't see the point because we're now aware of which appliances create red lights and they're all things that you need to use anyway so . . . it's not like you're going to say, 'I'm wasting, so let's do something about it'.
>
> (Respondent, quoted in ibid., 331)

Strengers points out that people are expected to react to smart meters by making small adjustments to their energy-hungry practices, rather than taking any more substantive measures. The quote from her data above suggests that is indeed how people respond. If smart meters are entrenching ideas of what is 'normal' and non-negotiable, as in the quote above, this is highly problematic, because ideas of what is 'normal' and 'necessary', which relate to such invisible consumption are actually quite changeable (Shove, 2003). This acceptance of 'normal' consumption was also noted in the longitudinal component of Hargreaves' study, with some respondents being defensive about their 'normal' use, in the light of other profligate consumers (Hargreaves et al., 2013b).

It is clear then that smart meters are not simply a means of transferring information from energy providers to energy consumers, resulting in a change in behaviour. While there is evidence of these technologies having an impact on overall energy use, they can also create problematic practices in the home – potentially resulting in either unhealthy levels of energy consumption, or reinforcing the convention that some energy use is non-negotiable.

Ethical lifestyle TV

Our second example of an attempt to provide information to consumers about ethical living is the rise of ethical lifestyle television since the beginning of the twenty-first century. This links into a more general profusion of food and interiors TV shows since the early 2000s. In shows about food, there has been an increasing emphasis on organic, free-range, locally sourced food, especially in shows led by celebrity chefs. Lifestyle shows which have an environmental slant focus on the challenges that 'ordinary' people face in going green. Tania Lewis sees this as part of the 'normalisation' of the ethical consumer: the fact that it has become more acceptable and commonplace to have concerns about the environmental and social impacts of consumption practices (Lewis, 2008). It is also rather paradoxical, that a medium that exists, according to Frances Bonner, to 'promote consumption as the vehicle to a fully realized identity' (2011, 231) should be engaging with environmental ideas that often promote consuming less. Indeed, Bonner finds that many of these shows promote 'consuming well instead of badly' rather than 'consuming less' (ibid., 235).

Lewis sees these shows as concerned with 'instructing people as to how to manage their everyday lives' (Lewis, 2008, 227), and as such they represent a distinctive form of information provision – showing people how to live sustainably or ethically, rather than telling people about environmental or social problems. Note that this is not just about TV programmes which tell you what to do: Bonner characterises lifestyle TV as acting as a 'cultural intermediary': effectively translating a certain way of being for the viewing public (Bonner, 2011). Jensen recommends that environmental education focus on visions and change strategies, as opposed to informing people about causes and effects, and lifestyle TV is an attempt to do this (Jensen, 2002). It also reveals the willingness of mass media outlets to engage in the politics of daily life through these kinds of behavioural recommendations.

Ethical lifestyle TV makes assumptions about people's interests in ethical consumption, and about what ethical consumption consists of. Clearly, media outlets are convinced that people are interested in attempting to live more ethically, otherwise such programmes would not be aired. There is also an assumption that people will watch these programmes and apply some of the lessons to their own lives. On lifestyle shows which document substantial changes that are unachievable for most (e.g. having your own water turbine), smaller, linked behaviour or technology changes are suggested that are more appropriate to most viewers. In food shows, there is an expectation that people will take on messages about organic, locally grown, free-range food.

Ethical lifestyle TV conceptualises ethical consumption as a set of choices made by individual viewers about their own consumption habits, which can be shaped by the information provided in such shows. As Lewis puts it, change here is conceived: 'in terms of personal self-control, self-management and informed choice' (Lewis, 2008, 235). In other words, the emphasis is on how information feeds into the daily life of the individual, and how information is used to make choices about daily life. Note that this is a profoundly individualised model of change, something I will discuss in greater detail in Chapter 5.

Ethical lifestyle TV also promotes rather superficial change. Given that most change recommendations are part of an individualised vision of how change can occur, they also have to be changes that are achievable within the daily lives of participants. The level of change recommended can come across as something like 'try not to buy things you don't need', or 'every little helps' (Lewis, 2008). Political campaigning, or attempts to change the broader social system are present (see, for instance, food presenter Hugh Fearnley-Whittingstall's *Big Fish Fight* in the UK), but more mundane recommendations to change small behaviours are more common (Bonner, 2011).

Note that another clear message being sent in ethical lifestyle shows is one of distinction (see Chapter 3). These shows appeal to middle-class (and often wealthy) identities (Lewis, 2008). Kitchens and houses are modern and open plan, often luxurious. Presenters invite us into their large gardens to show us their home-grown produce; in *Jamie at Home*, the celebrity chef Jamie Oliver introduces us to his gardener (Bonner, 2011). If anything, this further entrenches the practices of buying organic, locally produced, free-range food or the latest green technology as middle-class (or indeed upper-middle-class) pursuits. It also creates a sense that ethical consumption is a set of shopping opportunities – rather than an opportunity to reduce consumption.

Clearly, to see ethical lifestyle TV as a means of informing people is rather problematic, given this medium's history with selling consumption, rather than reducing it. For many people, however, this will be a central form of contact with the environmental movement, and as such has a potentially important influence on how people see sustainable behaviour. From the academic work here, it seems that sustainable consumption is being packaged as a particular type of identity: further entrenching the stereotypes of environmentalists as middle class and wealthy. An important lesson is that the way information is communicated will have an impact on how it is received.

Beyond the information-deficit model

Clearly in both these examples of interventions that use information, what is going on is more complex than the information-deficit model makes out.

When we look at how information works in everyday life, as in the smart meters example, we can see that it can have unintended social consequences, that its impact changes over time, and that it can reinforce ideas of what is normal, thereby further reinforcing unsustainable practices. In the ethical lifestyle TV example, we see that such communication positions ethical lifestyles for political and commercial ends. There is clearly not a simple relationship between policy, information and behaviour (Barr, 2003; Hobson, 2002, 2003). The actor in all of this – the 'ordinary person' – plays a reflexive role, as well as a role that is constrained by their life circumstances. We will see in Chapters 7, 8 and 9 how a number of disciplinary perspectives have added social and cultural depth, as well as politics to this analysis.

There are some useful insights to be had from theory on both the uptake of knowledge and information, and its political value here. First, we can usefully borrow from a seminal study by Brian Wynne about the public understanding of science (Wynne, 1992). In his case study about UK government relations with Cumbrian sheep farmers after Chernobyl, Wynne points out that farmers' willingness to believe and act on scientific information is not so much about their capacity to understand this information. Instead he finds that the public are more likely to listen to scientific messages when the authors of these messages inspire trust and credibility. Trust and credibility are in turn dependent on the social relationships, networks and identities of the various actors concerned. In other words, how we interpret a message depends on our relationship with the messenger. Indeed, we make judgements about the reliability of information, based on our ongoing relationships with the people who are giving out that information, as well as the conversations we have about that information within our networks, and our own knowledge of how things work.

If we apply these insights in the context of sustainable consumption, it suggests a rather different approach to the idea of providing information to promote behaviour change. We can see that we will need, on a case-by-case basis, to think about the relationships between the stakeholders doing the communicating, and those being communicated to. This could mean that in some cases it is inappropriate to communicate, due to a lack of trust or credibility. In other cases, it may be necessary to attempt to repair trust and credibility before communicating. Wynne's analysis, and the recommendation to think about how relationships impact on how information is communicated and received, is echoed in Simcock and colleagues' work on energy information outlined above (Simcock et al., 2014).

The second set of insights comes from a body of work on the political implications of a focus on providing information as a behaviour-change strategy. This work claims that providing information to provoke change is individualising: meaning that it encourages the people targeted to conceive of themselves as individuals responsible for making rational decisions based on the information that they receive (Middlemiss, 2014; Maniates, 2001). Individualising policies clearly assign the responsibility for sustainable consumption to the individual, rather than to governments, or to corporations, or to a combination of these stakeholders. It is fair to say that most attempts to produce change by informing people are based on this assumption: educate them and it is their responsibility to choose to behave correctly. You can read more about individualisation at the end of Chapter 5.

We can push a political analysis of individualising policy further. For instance, by attributing responsibility to the individual, and distancing it from other actors, Lewis argues that we are promoting a 'hegemonic culture of devolved self-governance' (Lewis, 2008). By this she means that if we only offer individualising interventions, people come to expect that change should only happen as a result of individuals exercising their responsibilities. The risk here is that by framing understanding as the problem, we constrain the type of solutions that are available. As Hobson puts it:

> does this form of sustainable consumption represent a glass ceiling . . . that constrains and limits the scope of possible engagements with the challenges of sustainability past those that are low or no-cost, small scale and 'stuff-focused', resulting in an exaggerated sense of the contributions that 'our bit' of reusing shopping bags and composting makes to overall sustainability?
>
> (Hobson, 2011, 194)

Certainly there is less room for more meaningful political action (political action that goes beyond individual behaviour change) in a world of individualised policy, a theme I will return to in Chapter 7. In addition, a focus on understanding completely avoids any discussion of the more structural determinants of practice: the infrastructure, culture, social norms, and materials that constrain the choices that we can make. I will return to these themes in Chapters 8 and 9.

Conclusion

At the end of this chapter, I hope that it is clear that the information-deficit model is an over-simplistic explanation of how people are likely to be persuaded to change. In our practical examples, for instance, we saw that providing information can have emotional consequences (smart meters), and is interpreted differently by people with different class backgrounds (ethical lifestyle TV). Indeed, Wynne would argue that information is always interpreted according to people's relationships with the provider of information, their identities, and their social networks, which place substantial constraints on their ability to generate trust and credibility (1992). There are two key messages I would like you to take from this chapter.

First, we should be suspicious of 'easy' solutions, given the complexity of the two examples I have elaborated above. Tom Hargreaves and colleagues' description of the daily reality of energy consumption based on their qualitative study gives us a sense of how complex a world we are encountering here, and therefore how limited a role a change in information might play. As they put it:

Our findings show that energy consumption in households involves multiple rationalities and logics, performed by multiple householders, often in complex and dynamic negotiations with one another, and in ways that change over time in response to different contextual forces.

(Hargreaves et al., 2013b, 132–133)

In the light of these kinds of findings, authors in this space argue that interventions need to be approached more systematically, to combine information provision with other resources and incentives, in order to make 'education' only one part of a bigger strategy (Markkula and Moisander, 2012).

Second, we ought also to be conscious that information is never apolitical, and we need to understand this in relation to both the producer of an intervention (who can hide behind an 'information' strategy as a means of avoiding action) and the consumer of one (who may be using consumption as a form of distinction). Kersty Hobson sees this strategy as wilfully ineffective: 'It does not threaten consumption but seeks to incorporate a new preference without impinging upon individuals' (supposedly) sacred and deeply entrenched lifestyles' (2002, 107).

Providing information, or educating people is certainly a very mild response to the kinds of environmental and social problems we saw in chapters 2 and 3. While it is important that people have a basic understanding of these problems, we should be suspicious of the motives of anyone who tries to give the impression that this is a strategy in and of itself.

Further resources

Manchester University's Sustainable Consumption institute on understandings of carbon footprinting of supermarket products: http://vimeo.com/2727318

References

AECOM LIMITED 2011. *Energy Demand Research Project: Final Analysis*. St Albans, UK: AECOM Limited.

ARMSTRONG, F. (director) 2009. *The Age of Stupid*.

BARR, S. 2003. Strategies for sustainability: Citizens and responsible environmental behaviour. *Area*, 35, 227–240.

BONNER, F. 2011. Lifestyle television: Gardening and the good life. *In*: LEWIS, T. & POTTER, E. (eds) *Ethical Consumption: A Critical Introduction*. London: Routledge.

CAIRNS, K., DE LAAT, K., JOHNSTON, J. & BAUMANN, S. 2014. The caring, committed eco-mom: Consumption ideals and lived realities of Toronto mothers. *In*: BARENDREGT, B. & JAFFE, R. (eds) *Green Consumption: The Global Rise of Eco-Chic*. London: Bloomsbury.

COTTON, D., MILLER, W., WINTER, J., BAILEY, I. & STERLING, S. 2015. Knowledge, agency and collective action as barriers to energy-saving behaviour. *Local Environment*, 21, 883–897.

DECC. 2009. *Smarter Grids: The Opportunity* [Online]. Department of Energy and Climate Change. Available: http://webarchive.nationalarchives.gov.uk/20091212081517/http://

www.decc.gov.uk/en/content/cms/what_we_do/uk_supply/network/smart_grid/smart_grid.aspx [Accessed 21 December 2017].

DEFRA. 2011. *Sustainable Consumption and Production Evidence Plan 2011/12* [Online]. Department for Environment, Food and Rural Affairs. Available: www.gov.uk/government/publications/sustainable-consumption-and-production-evidence-plan-2011-12 [Accessed 21 December 2017].

FARUQUI, A., SERGICI, S. & SHARIF, A. 2010. The impact of informational feedback on energy consumption – A survey of the experimental evidence. *Energy*, 35, 1598–1608.

GIDDENS, A. 2009. *The Politics of Climate Change*. Cambridge, UK, Wiley.

HARGREAVES, T., NYE, M. & BURGESS, J. 2010. Making energy visible: A qualitative field study of how householders interact with feedback from smart energy monitors. *Energy Policy*, 38, 6111–6119.

HARGREAVES, T., LONGHURST, N. & SEYFANG, G. 2013a. Up, down, round and round: Connecting regimes and practices in innovation for sustainability. *Environment and Planning A*, 45, 402–420.

HARGREAVES, T., NYE, M. & BURGESS, J. 2013b. Keeping energy visible? Exploring how householders interact with feedback from smart energy monitors in the longer term. *Energy Policy*, 52, 126–134.

HARRIES, T. 2012. The anticipated emotional consequences of adaptive behaviour – Impacts on the take-up of household flood-protection measures. *Environment and Planning A*, 44, 649–668.

HOBSON, K. 2002. Competing discourses of sustainable consumption: Does the 'rationalisation of lifestyles' make sense? *Environmental Politics*, 11, 95–120.

HOBSON, K. 2003. Thinking habits into action: The role of knowledge and process in questioning household consumption practices. *Local Environment*, 8, 95–112.

HOBSON, K. 2011. Environmental politics, green governmentality, and the possibility of a 'creative grammar' for domestic sustainable consumption. In: LANE, R. & GORMAN-MURRAY, A. (eds) *Material Geographies of Household Sustainability*. Farnham: Ashgate.

ISENHOUR, C. 2010a. Building sustainable societies: A Swedish case study on the limits of reflexive modernization. *American Ethnologist*, 37, 511–525.

ISENHOUR, C. 2010b. On conflicted Swedish consumers, the effort to stop shopping and neoliberal environmental governance. *Journal of Consumer Behaviour*, 9, 454–469.

JENSEN, B. B. 2002. Knowledge, action and pro-environmental behaviour. *Environmental Education Research*, 8, 325–334.

JONES, R., PYKETT, J. & WHITEHEAD, M. 2013. *Changing Behaviours: On the Rise of the Psychological State*. Cheltenham, UK: Edward Elgar.

LEWIS, T. 2008. Transforming citizens? Green politics and ethical consumption on lifestyle television. *Continuum*, 22, 227–240.

LORENZONI, I., NICHOLSON-COLE, S. & WHITMARSH, L. 2007. Barriers perceived to engaging with climate change among the UK public and their policy implications. *Global Environmental Change*, 17, 445–459.

MANIATES, M. F. 2001. Individualization: Plant a tree, buy a bike, save the world? *Global Environmental Politics*, 1, 31–52.

MARKKULA, A. & MOISANDER, J. 2012. Discursive confusion over sustainable consumption: A discursive perspective on the perplexity of marketplace knowledge. *Journal of Consumer Policy*, 35, 105–125.

MARSDEN, G., MULLEN, C., BACHE, I., BARTLE, I. & FLINDERS, M. 2014. Carbon reduction and travel behaviour: Discourses, disputes and contradictions in governance. *Transport Policy*, 35, 71–78.

MIDDLEMISS, L. 2011. The power of community: How community-based organisations stimulate sustainable lifestyles among participants. *Society and Natural Resources*, 24, 1157–1173.

MIDDLEMISS, L. 2014. Individualised or participatory? Exploring late-modern identity and sustainable development. *Environmental Politics*, 23, 929–946.

MILLER, D. 2012. *Consumption and its Consequences*. Cambridge, UK: Polity.

OFFICE FOR NATIONAL STATISTICS 2013. *Household Energy Consumption in England and Wales, 2005–11*. London: Office for National Statistics.

SHOVE, E. 2003. *Comfort, Cleanliness and Convenience: The Social Organization of Normality*. Oxford, UK: Berg Publishers.

SIMCOCK, N., MACGREGOR, S., CATNEY, P., DOBSON, A., ORMEROD, M., ROBINSON, Z., ROSS, S., ROYSTON, S. & HALL, S. M. 2014. Factors influencing perceptions of domestic energy information: Content, source and process. *Energy Policy*, 65, 455–464.

STAATS, H., HARLAND, P. & WILKE, H. A. M. 2004. Effecting durable change: A team approach to improve environmental behaviour in the household. *Environment and Behaviour*, 36, 341–367.

STRENGERS, Y. 2011a. Beyond demand management: Co-managing energy and water practices with Australian households. *Policy Studies*, 32, 35–58.

STRENGERS, Y. 2011b. Negotiating everyday life: The role of energy and water consumption feedback. *Journal of Consumer Culture*, 11, 319–338.

SUTCLIFFE, M., HOOPER, P. & HOWELL, R. 2008. Can eco-footprinting analysis be used successfully to encourage more sustainable behaviour at the household level? *Sustainable Development*, 16, 1–16.

TAYLOR, A. L., DESSAI, S. & DE BRUIN, W. B. 2014. Public perception of climate risk and adaptation in the UK: A review of the literature. *Climate Risk Management*, 4, 1–16.

WORLD COMMISSION ON ENVIRONMENT AND DEVELOPMENT 1987. *Our Common Future*. Oxford: Oxford University Press.

WYNNE, B. 1992. Misunderstood misunderstanding: Social identities and public uptake of science. *Public Understanding of Science*, 1, 281–304.

YOUNG, W., HWANG, K., MCDONALD, S. & OATES, C. 2004. Trade-offs by voluntary simplifiers in ethical decision-making. The Inter-Disciplinary CSR Research Conference, 22–23 October 2004, University of Nottingham, unpublished.

5   'People are selfish'

We now turn to one of the most powerful stories about human behaviour, which I summarise as 'people are selfish'. Many of the students I have taught over the years come to my class with this assumption. People are not always aware that this is an assumption, because the story is so widespread in society, and so engrained in the way that we tend to explain what people choose to do, that it is often presented as a 'truth' (Raworth, 2017, Chapter 3). Do you also tend to agree with the statement 'people are selfish'? Have you noticed before that you hold this assumption?

Once we notice the assumption that 'people are selfish' we start to see examples of it all around us. For instance, in the Anglo-Saxon world (US, UK, Australia, etc.), there is an expectation that people will try to reduce the tax that they pay as far as possible within the law. Recent global scandals around off-shore tax havens also suggest that as soon as they can afford to, the rich will find ways of avoiding paying tax altogether. This is a selfish act, because they benefit from all the services that tax revenues provide (transport services, education provision, health care) but they avoid paying for these services. To some extent, people have begun to see tax avoidance by the rich as normal, as evidence of our 'naturally selfish' tendencies.

An assumption of selfishness also lies behind many explanations of the problem of unsustainable consumption as well as the solution to this. Such assumptions are often rather oblique, implied rather than clearly stated. A nice example comes from Cindy Isenhour's work on Swedish consumers, where the leader of one of Sweden's largest environmental organisations explains how they think that people are motivated to act:

> We know that people make changes when they feel the effects of environmental problems closer to home. Then they will act . . . it becomes important to their welfare, to their family. But before people see those signs and feel damage, they won't do anything. Information campaigns though, they can help people to become aware of how these questions are affecting them in, I think, a more personal way.
>
> (Isenhour, 2010, 515)

This leader believes that people must feel personally threatened by environmental problems in order to take action, that ultimately people's selfishness must be engaged to provoke them to make change.

In this chapter I will challenge the idea that selfishness is a part of human nature. To do this, I will first look at the roots of this story in the rational choice model originating in economics. I will then outline critiques of rational choice, and work in the field of economics that has further advanced these ideas, including ecological and behavioural economics. I finish by profiling the work on individualisation, which deals with some similar ideas from a sociological perspective. By the end of the chapter, I hope you will be able to see that this story is too simple as a way to explain all the motivations of human beings. While sometimes, inevitably, people do act in their own interests, this does not work as a theory of all human behaviour.

Rational choice

A useful way in to thinking about rational choice is through the generic person that it conjures up: *homo economicus*. Economists imagine that this 'economic man' works in rational and self-interested ways: 'When faced with several courses of action, people usually do what they believe is likely to have the best overall outcome' (Elster, 1989, 22). So, people tend to make rational decisions based on the impact of the anticipated outcomes of those decisions on themselves. Critically, economists also believe that people will tend to 'maximise their own benefits', or 'satisfy their preferences' in decision-making (Paavola, 2001) – in other words, to make decisions in their own self-interests. This means that whenever *homo economicus* is required to make a choice, he/she will think about the possible outcomes of that choice, and pick the outcome that accrues the most benefits to him/herself. Note that economists do not believe that this kind of choice is made in a vacuum; indeed, as Jouni Paavola puts it, in rational choice, 'each consumer is understood to be interested only in her own welfare, to face choice alternatives that are given to her, and to try to do her best within the constraints set forth by her budget' (ibid., 229). For a history of the idea of *homo economicus*, see Kate Raworth's book *Doughnut Economics* (2017, chapter 3).

Before we move on from this description of *homo economicus*, we need to place this in the context of the broader discipline of economics. Rational Choice is a model to explain how people act, based in neo-classical economics. It does not, in itself claim that 'people are selfish', although that is an implication of 'maximising their own benefits'. However, given that maximising benefits can mean 'doing the thing that makes me happiest', it can also be used to explain altruistic or family-focused behaviours. So, for instance, you might explain people's donations to charity as a rational choice, given the positive impacts that this can have on people's sense of self. Note that in describing this act as a rational choice, we also turn it into one which could also be described as selfish.

Rational choice is a universal model of human behaviour, which tries to encompass all types of human response to social and physical circumstances. In other words, neo-classical economists explain all kinds of behaviours using this theory, and apply this theory to all human beings. Raworth (2017) argues that *homo economicus* has become both a powerful story about the way people behave, and a normative model of human behaviour: a standard to aspire to. While these were not the original intentions of the theory, the belief that 'people are selfish', and that selfishness is part of human nature is a very strong one in the contemporary world. This means that rational choice is often treated as a 'theory of everything', as well as an aspiration. Neo-classical economic thinking starts with the explicit *assumption* that people will act rationally and to maximise their benefits, out in the world this translates into a *belief* both that such assumptions always hold true, and that therefore selfish behaviour is somehow 'right'.

So, to take an example of how this plays out in the public domain, we turn to policy on sustainable consumption, which has sometimes espoused a theory of rational choice. This quote comes from the UK Environment Department: 'Ultimately the burden on the UK's environment is attributable to the choices and the actions of the consumers. To a great extent producers are, quite naturally, responding to meet the preferences of the consumers' (DETR, 1998, 4).

Here the language used is very much that of rational choice (and economics): the consumer has 'choice' which results in 'actions', the producers respond to meet consumer 'preferences'. Note the emphasis on individual choices by consumers here, and the way in which individual choices are conceived of as adding up to the 'burden' on the environment. In this way of thinking, any change in consumption, which is of course one of the objectives of sustainable consumption, is likely to come from individuals, making different consumption choices.

In the DETR quote above, the responsibility for sustainable consumption lies principally with the consumer, as Hobson points out (2006). Some economists take this logic even further, suggesting that buying things, and in doing so expressing one's preferences, is a form of voting (Dickinson and Carsky, 2005). In both these visions, the consumer holds the responsibility to act rationally, and this responsibility is the principle way in which politics and preferences can be expressed. Such an emphasis on the actions of individuals is particularly interesting in a government document – government being the clearest example of a collective actor.

So before we move on to look at the critiques of rational choice, I would first like to outline the full breadth of the assumptions inherent in this way of thinking. Note that these are also assumptions that hold true in the 'people are selfish' story with which we started. Rational choice assumes that:

1   Individual decision-making drives change: typically people who adopt rational choice see large-scale change as the result of the aggregation of lots of day-to-day individual decisions.
2   Behaviour is the result of rational thinking: the assumption here is that when people do things, they do them because they choose to (not instinctively, or as a result of social expectations).

3   People will make choices in their self-interest: while in economics it does not strictly follow that 'people are selfish by nature', this is a very common interpretation of this way of thinking. People (maybe including you) internalise this story and use it to explain all sorts of behaviour.

4   People bear responsibility for their behaviour: if you are making a decision about something, and choosing a particular outcome, you are responsible for the consequences of that decision.

Economics is not the only discipline that assumes rationality. We will see in Chapter 6 that some approaches to psychology also assume that people are choosing to make particular decisions. Psychologists are more likely to take into account elements of people's social context, however, and to consider any individual choices within context. Other disciplines (particularly sociology, see Chapter 8, and cultural studies, Chapter 9) would be highly critical of the idea that change happens as a result of adding up lots of small daily choices, as well as the idea that individuals are the main lever of change. In the next section, we look at some of the problems with this perspective, in order to understand why some economists, particularly those working on sustainable consumption, have chosen to move beyond this model.

Box 5.1 Applying rational choice in practice

If we want to harness people's rational responses, and encourage people to act in both their own self-interest and for the good of society, some of the most obvious ways of doing this are through financial measures. Some examples of this include:

- The Swedish government reducing VAT on repairs (in 2016): by reducing the tax on a type of expenditure, the government aims to make it more attractive for people to spend on repair than on buying new.
- Feed-in tariffs for renewable energy (many nations in Europe and beyond): by paying renewable energy consumers for energy that they generate, governments aim to make it more financially advantageous to invest in renewables.
- Reduced tax on efficient vehicles: if governments reduce forms of vehicle or road tax for efficient vehicles, while also increasing it for inefficient vehicles, it is more in people's interests to opt for an efficient car.

Note the language I use here – 'attractive', 'advantageous', 'in people's interests' – which all refers obliquely to the principles of rational choice: that people act in their own self-interest. Note also that we could use non-financial measures to encourage rational choice: through information (as in Chapter 4) or by appealing to people's values (as in Chapter 6).

Problems with rational choice

Some more detailed critiques of rational choice will emerge in later chapters of the book. Here I outline the key problems with the theory in order to allow a discussion of developments in economics beyond rational choice.

The most basic critique is that rational choice does not hold true in the real world:

> the key assumptions of the rational actor – that she has perfect knowledge and stable preferences, is selfish and makes calculations to identify an optimal decision that maximizes utility – are in contrast with empirical observations of how people actually make decisions concerning natural resource use.
>
> (Schlüter et al., 2017, 22)

This connects with another basic question: 'what is *the* rational choice?' In any given situation, it is difficult to understand which is the most rational choice an individual could take. Very often we can explain any outcome as 'rational' (or indeed as 'selfish'), if we try. For instance, we could say that it is selfish to choose to have children (with all the personal satisfaction and well-being that this entails) or to not have children (to allow oneself more time to focus on oneself). (Incidentally, I would not claim that either of these explanations are satisfactory given the complexity of these kinds of decisions.) In any case, it is clear that assuming that people will act rationally will not necessarily give us any predictive power over understanding how people behave. This ambiguity around what is rational was captured by Cindy Isenhour in her qualitative research on Swedish ethical consumers, where she found that people's interpretations of rationality differed substantially from the 'people are selfish' thesis:

> Whereas rationality is often conflated with the pursuit of individual self-interest, particularly in popular thought, many of the people who participated in my study argued that it was rational to take a long-term view, one based on social and generational equity, for the health of humans and the planet, regardless of personal cost.
>
> (Isenhour, 2010, 521)

This is an interpretation of rationality that is explicitly unselfish.

Second, rational choice only considers choices driven by rationality, as opposed to behaviours which are explicitly non-rational. For instance, as Shove (2003) pointed out in her classic text on the topic, people do not think about how much energy or water they are consuming when they take a shower. This means that this high energy- and water-using activity does not even register for most people, in their understandings of its economic cost or indeed in relation to its environmental impact. Many forms of consumption are habitual, even some which might at first glance seem to be rather more considered (see Chapter 8). For instance, people's uses of different travel modes are often connected to what they are in the habit of doing, and when people shop at the supermarket they are likely to consistently buy the same brands and products. There is also increasing interest in the role of behaviours that are driven by emotional responses (Sahakian, 2015; Russell et al., 2017). Clearly, non-rational behaviour cannot be explained by rational choice.

Third, those disciplines which are more inclined to think about structural restrictions to consumption would challenge the assumption in rational choice that people are actually *able* to choose. The concept of *agency* is useful here, which can be loosely defined as the capacity people have to act, and which tends to be invoked alongside the concept of *structure*, the social systems that shape individual actions. To take a simple example: if someone lives in a suburban location, their agency is limited by the physical design of their neighbourhood, which in a US context might have been designed with no walking infrastructure (sidewalks or pavements), and where residential areas have been located far away from shops and employers. In suburbia, walking and cycling to the shops and to work is not really an option for most people. They have had their agency curtailed by the physical design of their neighbourhood. As such, it makes little sense to describe suburban drivers as either 'rational' or 'selfish': this description fails to see that their rationality is structured by a series of choice sets available to them as a result of their context (Southerton et al., 2004).

Following on from this, many social science disciplines would challenge the idea that choices can be truly made by individuals. A wide range of social influences impact on people's lifestyles, and a variety of disciplines have addressed these. For instance, psychologists would point to the influence of subjective norms (what someone thinks other people expect of them) on people's behaviour (Bamberg and Möser, 2007). Anthropologists are more likely to point to the importance of the cultural context in which consumption takes place to understand consumption (Wilk, 2002; Miller, 2012). Sociologists think about how norms of comfort, cleanliness and convenience have impacted on consumption (Shove, 2003). Certainly if we focus on the individual making the decision, we are likely to miss much of the social context in which that decision was shaped.

Finally, it is also possible to make a moral critique of rational choice. There is a risk that by believing in *homo economicus* and by acting as if he exists, we bring him into being (Raworth, 2017). In sociology, the theory of individualisation suggests that we increasingly see ourselves as individuals, and understand the world from this perspective. Whether we also act as individuals is a matter of debate (Middlemiss, 2014). In a number of policy spheres, including that of sustainability, there is evidence, however, that treating people as if they will react selfishly does sometimes result in people taking more selfish choices (ibid.). This is referred to as policy 'individualising' the people it is aimed at, and discussed in more detail below. Clearly this is problematic, in a context in which we hope that we can persuade people to act for the good of others, the environment, and future generations. Would an individual maximising his or her own benefits also have positive impacts on the environment (Paavola, 2001)? Assuming that people act selfishly might result in more people actually acting selfishly, rather than in the interests of the earth, and distant others.

Developments in ecological economics

Ecological economics is a branch of economics established in the late twentieth century, which offers an alternative way of thinking about environmental problems. Typically characterised as advocating strong sustainability, it takes as a starting point the insight that the economy is embedded in nature, and indeed that the economy only exists because nature provides the essential materials and services that it requires (Røpke and Reisch, 2004). Inge Røpke and Lucia Reisch explain that the logic of ecological economics fits well with the idea of sustainable consumption. Ecological economists believe that the economy is so substantial that natural 'life support systems' are threatened. Given the interest in economic growth in this field, and the belief that economies cannot continue to grow without damaging these natural systems (covered in more detail in Chapter 13), there is also a strong focus on how problems of poverty can be solved, and issues of equity are central. Unsustainable consumption is seen by ecological economists as an appropriation of resources and waste sinks by the rich, to the detriment of the poor (ibid.).

Ecological economics is a very eclectic discipline. As we will see, ecological economists are not precious about their own discipline: while they set out with some assumptions from the discipline of economics, they are quick to revise these when evidence shows that an assumption does not adequately explain the real world: 'ecological economists happily tap into the knowledge provided by other fields dealing with consumption' (Røpke and Reisch, 2004, 6). This can make it difficult to say what counts as ecological economics and what does not. This inter-disciplinary approach can also alert authors to the tensions between disciplines. For instance, in her summary of practice approaches to sustainable consumption (see Chapter 8), Inge Røpke notes that rational choice explanations (which claim that people are mainly concerned with 'maximising their utility') conflict with these sociological theories: 'practice theory is at odds with any mono-causal explanations of people's willingness to consume ever more, whether this is based on optimization of utility, status competition or the presentation of self' (Røpke, 2009, 2496).

The inclusion of knowledge from other disciplines can also be quite challenging in a discipline which has a tradition of modelling behaviour (using quantitative methods to predict what people might do). The simple rules of rational choice, for instance, are much easier to model than theories which take into account multiple drivers of behaviour (Schlüter et al., 2017).

One of the main contributions of this field is to emphasise and overcome the limitations of rational choice theory, by challenging the idea that rationality is paramount, mainly through partnerships with other fields. At a minimum, this means expanding the idea of rationality to include all 'goal-oriented, intentional action' such that self-interest is only one of the possible drivers of rationality, alongside any number of other values (Paavola, 2001). Indeed, since people hold a number of different values, in particular, for our purposes, placing importance on nature and other people, they might sometimes make decisions that actually work against their own interests (ibid.). Jouni Paavola's thinking here combines ecological economics with insights from psychology (explored further in Chapter 6). Paavola and others emphasise the importance of social factors in shaping people's actions. As Nyborg and colleagues put it: even those that have environmental values take note of what their peers do, and what their peers do has an impact on their behaviour (Nyborg et al., 2006).

If we assume rationality, the actions we take can actually become counterproductive, when people are not motivated towards rational ends. For instance, Vatn (2005) talks about how people's rationales for why they act shape their response to policy. To take an example, in various countries, governments have tried to increase the number of people donating blood, by offering a financial incentive for people to donate. In theory, this should increase the number of donors because people will be motivated (by self-interest) to give their blood. In practice, paying for blood donation reduces the number of donors (ibid.). Why might this be? Imagine you are someone who regularly gives blood, when this new policy is introduced. How would you feel about this? Effectively, when we offer a financial reward to blood donors, we shift from an assumption that people will do this voluntarily to an assumption that people will only do this if rewarded. This means that current donors, are now being addressed as if they are self-interested, when they see themselves as altruistic. Taking money in exchange for donating blood feels a bit like selling one's body, when previously you gave your blood because you thought it was the right thing to do. When incentives are offered, this changes the way people make decisions about their actions (Bolderdijk and Steg, 2015).

Another bar to rationality is the role of consumption in signalling identity (Brekke and Howarth, 2006), a set of ideas that comes from cultural studies (see Chapter 9). Note that the idea of goods being consumed to display status is widespread (Paavola, 2001). Paavola talks about the value of signalling one's own difference through goods that one buys and owns, and points out that the more people do this, the less value there is in it (ibid.). For instance, if we all own a big car, there is less status acquired by owning one (having said that, it also perhaps makes it more challenging not to own a big car, as such ownership becomes a social norm). Brekke and Howarth find that people's possessions are signs both of success, and of the ability to spend wisely (2006). In a world in which production, incomes and consumption have increased, people have to spend more in order to reinforce their identities. To put this differently, in late modern society, more ownership of goods is required to allow us to appear in public without shame.

Ecological economists both challenge the assumptions inherent in economics, and partner with other disciplines in order to broaden the scope of economic research. This is clearly a critical and open-minded form of economics, which, while it wishes to reform economic thinking through examination of its key tenets, is also committed to remaining part of the discipline itself.

Developments in behavioural economics

Alongside these developments in ecological economics, another branch of this discipline, behavioural economics, has also engaged in thinking about environmental and sustainable consumption concerns. Behavioural economics contends that behaviour is not driven by rational choices; indeed, many behaviours we engage in are shaped by automatic processes or intuition, instead of deliberation and conscious thought (Kahneman, 2011). When we target people as rational beings (as, for instance, in Chapter 4), we only target some kinds of behaviour, and this body of work points out that there are gains to be had in targeting unconscious or non-rational behaviour (Lehner et al., 2016). Behavioural economics agrees with ecological economics that rationality is bounded: that there are limits to the power of the individual to decide rationally. It also draws on evidence that people are not always actively making decisions: they are frequently merely repeating their previous behaviour without thinking it through, or taking shortcuts by relying on habits (ibid.).

Policy based on behavioural economics is encapsulated in the term 'nudge', which became popular and influential when Thaler and Sunstein released a book on the topic in 2008. Nudge strategies are about changing people's behaviour by changing the environment in which they make choices, shaping the context in which they choose, without actively banning any particular behavioural outcome, or by changing the market. In their words: 'A nudge, as we will understand the term, is any aspect of the *choice architecture* that alters people's behavior in a predictable way without forbidding any options or significantly changing their economic incentives' (Thaler and Sunstein, 2008, 6; emphasis added).

Nudges amount to changes in the environment in which people make choices, as a way of pushing them towards 'correct' behaviour, rather than actively incentivising it or banning 'bad' choices. The kinds of techniques that nudge advocates, include the following (from among others, Ölander and Thøgersen, 2014; Lehner et al., 2016):

- **Social comparison**: where you compare people with nearby people and in doing so try to change what they think is 'normal'. This technique is used in utility bills, for instance, to compare people's consumption of energy or water to their neighbours' consumption, and in doing so make them think again about how much of a resource they use. Note that this assumes that people have a desire to be 'normal', and also takes the risk that people will increase their consumption if they are told that they consume less than others.
- **Defaults**: if the default is to opt out rather than opt in, more people are likely to do it. You may have heard this debate in relation to human organ donation: if we had to opt out of donating organs when we die it would be much easier to find enough organs for patients in need. In the environmental context, for instance, people might have to opt out of a 'green' energy tariff, or a smart grid trial, rather than opting in.
- **Anchoring**: if people have an idea that something is good, this can prevent them from changing their behaviour. So for instance, European Union energy-efficiency labelling rates appliances and buildings from A+++ to G. People buying a new appliance are likely to want to buy an A-rated appliance at a minimum, given that a B-rated appliance would seem like a sub-standard

product. Note that this is problematic from A+ upwards, as there is evidence to show that people anchor at A, and ignore the number of '+'s (Ölander and Thøgersen, 2014).

- **Changing physical environment**: if we change the physical environment, this can result in people behaving differently. Street design, for instance, can make people drive faster or slower depending on the cues given. It has also been found that reducing plate size can reduce food waste (Lehner et al., 2016).
- **Prompts**: these are reminders to people that they should be behaving in a different way. In environmental terms, this might include stickers to remind people to turn the lights off or an alarm when you leave the fridge door open. Prompts could also be in the form of feedback on energy consumption through bills, metering and displays.

Nudge techniques usually go beyond just providing information, and indeed beyond simplifying and framing information differently. However, often nudge strategies, such as the energy-efficiency labelling of buildings and appliances outlined above, are a mix of information (an account of the efficiency of a product) and a more deliberate attempt to get people to change their choices (the ranking of the efficiency of products, with the strong implication that lower-ranked products are not worth having) (Ölander and Thøgersen, 2014).

There is some suspicion of nudge strategies in the literature. Instinctively, I am drawn to the idea that this represents an 'easy fix' for government: a way of appearing to instigate change, while actually merely making small adjustments to the parameters of people's lives. Perhaps I am too cynical: Lehner and colleagues point out that nudges needs careful thought to ensure that they actually work (Lehner et al., 2016). The same authors also point out that when people are manipulated they become more suspicious of government. Further there is a risk that these measures are unfair: it is possible that people who can identify a nudge will not be as susceptible, and therefore have more choice as to whether they respond (ibid.). Having said that, people are generally accepting of nudge-type interventions that already take place across a number of European countries (UK, Germany, France, Italy) (Reisch and Sunstein, 2016).

Nudge is characterised as a form of liberal paternalism: a 'policy approach that preserves freedom of choice (i.e. libertarianism), but encourages the public sector to steer people in directions that will promote their own welfare (i.e. paternalism)' (Lehner et al., 2016, 175). This is a very particular flavour of politics – one that is comfortable with steering people's behaviour, potentially without their knowledge, but not with more targeted regulatory or financial strategies (for instance, banning or taxing behaviours to discourage them). While nudge represents a more gentle approach in some ways, still allowing for people to make choices, it is also rather invisible, which begs the questions whether it is offering choice at all. Further, by not engaging with people through deliberation, this strategy misses an opportunity to engage the public in thinking about sustainable consumption, an approach which might backfire in the long run when other strategies are employed (Lehner et al., 2016).

Critical assessments of behavioural economics also object to its individualising logic. Nudge assumes that people can be manipulated as individuals to make 'better' choices, understanding people's daily lives as governable without their knowledge. Jones and colleagues accuse behavioural economics of replacing the idea of *homo economicus* with 'citizen fool'; in other words, by rejecting the assumption of rationality this way of thinking treats people as if they are stupid, and infinitely manipulable (Jones et al., 2013). Given its emphasis on instinc-tive behaviour, nudge fails to engage people as social beings (Hobson, 2013), or indeed as environmental citizens (Lehner et al., 2016). Individualisation, as a broader critique of rational thinking, is the theme of my next section.

Individualisation

In all the chapters of this section of the book, I finish with a critical analysis of the perspective I have just profiled. In this chapter, the critical commentary started fairly early on, in the 'problems with rational choice' section. Writing about 'people are selfish' is challenging because it is such a widespread (often uncritical) belief, and yet the academic literature on sustainable consumption has mostly moved on from this assumption. Nevertheless, as a student of this topic, you may not yet have had the chance to think through these critiques.

So what critical points are there left to make about the 'people are selfish' starting point? There is a broader social critique, the idea of individualisation, which is a frequent point of discussion in relation to sustainable consumption (Maniates, 2001; Middlemiss, 2014). In Michael Maniates's work on this topic, he recounts the experience of teaching sustainability to students in the US, and points out how students often turn to their own lives when asked for solutions to sustainability problems. By this I mean that if you ask people what they think is the solution to the problem, they respond with 'well, perhaps I could avoid flying this year', or 'I'll try to turn the tap off when I brush my teeth.' This amounts to an individualised understanding of how change can happen, or what policy is appropriate: people think that they are the only source of a solution, and take the responsibility for change on themselves.

This kind of individualisation of responsibility is rather problematic, given the complexity of sustainability problems, as it suggests a straightforward solu-tion, which ultimately is too small to make enough of a difference. Sarah Marie Hall comments on how solutions to the 2008 financial crisis were individualised:

> at the onset of the recent financial crisis, consumers were situated as being doubly responsible; simultaneously blamed for a culture of debt, borrowing and spending on credit, while at the same time urged to consume to lift the economy out of crisis.
>
> (Hall, 2015, 141)

Clearly these messages are both illogical ('spend less! No, spend more!') and unlikely to create a meaningful solution. They also represent a different kind of relationship between government and citizen: where citizen (rather than government) is supposed to take the lead in sorting out major social problems (Lewis and Potter, 2011). Jo Littler (2009) argues that individuals, in such an understanding, perpetuate and endorse a neo-liberal system by engaging with this narrative of responsibility.

There is another aspect of individualisation that is important, however. Social theory suggests that in contemporary life we actually see ourselves as individual beings, rather than as social beings. Norbert Elias calls this image of human beings 'homo clausus', or the cloistered human being, who exists on his own without reference to the wider world (Elias, 2000). In this understanding, categories such as gender, ethnicity, class and status are increasingly irrelevant, as people do not feel solidarity to each other in relation to these categories. George Monbiot, the British environmental activist, takes this as a starting point in his recent writing, where he paints a picture of the world as full of disjointed individuals, and proposes a new politics to remedy this social and environmental 'wreckage' (Monbiot, 2017). This starting point poses some important challenges to the idea of sustainable consumption (Middlemiss, 2014; Raworth, 2017). We tend to see the solution to sustainability problems more generally as being collective: that we all have to work together to ensure the planet survives (see Chapter 11 for more on this). If we are really more and more individualised, how will we come together to produce solutions to collective problems?

Fortunately, the evidence on individualisation suggests a much less bleak picture than Monbiot's 'wreckage' makes out. Indeed, feminists, for instance, would argue that the story of individualisation neglects to consider the caring work that people continue to do in raising children and looking after older people (Middlemiss, 2014). Recent scandals around sexual harassment suggest some solidarity among women in response to predatory behaviour, and environmental activists are often committed to abstract others (such as future generations or people impacted by climate change in other countries, see Chapter 7). It is probably the case that people experience and perpetuate individualisation in some aspects of their lives, and act altruistically in others, consistent with sociological understandings of the 'reflexive' consumer (Beck and Beck-Gernsheim, 2002). This can lead to a rather muddled understanding of what people do and why – because they act differently in different roles and with different goals.

Ali Browne finds such a muddle in the water industry. In this context, the dominant way of thinking about consumers is complicated: 'people' are lots of things, mostly rooted in ideas of rationality, but amounting to a whole lot more than just 'selfish':

'People' are characterized as *rational* (i.e., they can easily change their behavior related to resource use); they are also *irrational* (their behavior deviates from the rational course of action as a result of issues such as insufficient information or lack of skills/capability); they are *resource focused* (they make resource use decisions based on the environment such as knowledge of water supplies or energy consumption/carbon emissions); they are *economically focused* (they make resource use decisions based on economics and costs of water and energy or other products); they are *technologically focused* (they are interested, engaged, and savvy with technologies); and they are *responsive* (to technology, to cost, to information provision, to what other people pay or consume).

(Browne, 2015, 416; original emphasis)

At a minimum, then, we should avoid attempting to characterise people's motivations so narrowly. Clearly not everyone is selfish, all of the time, and by attempting to create such a theory of everything, we neglect the wide range of motivations and drivers that impact on human life. We also need to be alert to the possible consequences of this kind of thinking: that by believing 'people are selfish' we create policy and practice that encourages selfish action. These are high-risk strategies in the context of sustainable consumption, where any substantive change is likely to need a collective effort (see Chapter 11).

Conclusions

While economists working on sustainable consumption have largely left behind the assumption that 'people are selfish', this story is a very powerful one in the public discourse about human nature. As such, it is hugely important for you, as a student of this topic, and as someone who may shape the field in the future, to understand the flaws in the way that the story of *homo economicus* has been adopted in the public domain. Understanding all of human behaviour as rooted in self-interest is over-simplistic; clearly people are affected by a range of motivations. The theory itself is ineffective given that it does not help us understand what to do about sustainable consumption. Finally, the idea of human nature as selfish potentially works against idea of sustainability: the more we repeat this as a 'truth', the more likely people are to believe that it is desirable to act in their own interests, rather than in the interests of humanity or the environment (Middlemiss, 2014).

Ecological and behavioural economists have presented important counter-narratives in recent years, which move away from the assumption of rationality. Partnerships with other disciplines have been key to these developments, and ecological economics is an especially open-minded discipline in this context. If we are to take a critical approach to understanding these developments, it is essential to understand where they come from, and to understand the assumptions on which they are based. While neither of these newer bodies of literature would start with 'people are selfish', other elements of rational choice, for instance, the idea that change happens through the aggregation of individual actions, remain. As we will see, the more structurally oriented disciplines (sociology in Chapter 8, and cultural studies in Chapter 9) see social change as amounting to more than just the sum of the parts.

References

BAMBERG, S. & MÖSER, G. 2007. Twenty years after Hines, Hungerford, and Tomera: A new meta-analysis of psycho-social determinants of pro-environmental behaviour. *Journal of Environmental Psychology*, 27, 14–25.

BECK, U. & BECK-GERNSHEIM, E. 2002. *Individualization: Institutionalized Individualism and its Social and Political Consequences*. London: Sage Publications.

BOLDERDIJK, J. W. & STEG, L. 2015. Promoting sustainable consumption: The risks of using financial incentives. *In*: REISCH, L. & THØGERSEN, J. (eds) *Handbook of Research on Sustainable Consumption*. Cheltenham, UK: Edward Elgar.

BREKKE, K. A. & HOWARTH, R. B. 2006. Two alternative economic models of why enough will never be enough. *In*: JACKSON, T. (ed.) *The Earthscan Reader in Sustainable Consumption*. London: Earthscan.

BROWNE, A. L. 2015. Insights from the everyday: Implications of reframing the governance of water supply and demand from 'people' to 'practice'. *Wiley Interdisciplinary Reviews: Water*, 2, 415–424.

DETR (DEPARTMENT OF ENVIRONMENT, TRANSPORT AND THE REGIONS) 1998. *Consumer Products and the Environment*. London: Her Majesty's Stationery Office.

DICKINSON, R. A. & CARSKY, M. L. 2005. The consumer as economic voter. *In*: HARRISON, R., NEWHOLM, T. & SHAW, D. (eds) *The Ethical Consumer*. London: Sage Publications.

ELIAS, N. 2000. *The Civilizing Process: Sociogenetic and Psychogenetic Investigations*. Hoboken, NJ: Wiley-Blackwell.

ELSTER, J. 1989. *Nuts and Bolts for the Social Sciences*. Cambridge, UK: Cambridge University Press.

HALL, S. M. 2015. Everyday ethics of consumption in the austere city. *Geography Compass*, 9, 140–151.

HOBSON, K. 2006. Environmental responsibility and the possibilities of pragmatist-orientated research. *Social & Cultural Geography*, 7, 283–298.

HOBSON, K. 2013. 'Weak' or 'strong' sustainable consumption? Efficiency, degrowth, and the 10-Year Framework of Programmes. *Environment and Planning C: Government and Policy*, 31, 1082–1098.

ISENHOUR, C. 2010. Building sustainable societies: A Swedish case study on the limits of reflexive modernization. *American Ethnologist*, 37, 511–525.

JONES, R., PYKETT, J. & WHITEHEAD, M. 2013. *Changing Behaviours: On the Rise of the Psychological State*. Cheltenham, UK: Edward Elgar.

KAHNEMAN, D. 2011. *Thinking, Fast and Slow*. London: Macmillan.

LEHNER, M., MONT, O. & HEISKANEN, E. 2016. Nudging – A promising tool for sustainable consumption behaviour? *Journal of Cleaner Production*, 134, 166–177.

LEWIS, T. & POTTER, E. 2011. Introducing ethical consumption. *In*: LEWIS, T. & POTTER, E. (eds) *Ethical Consumption: A Critical Introduction*. Abingdon, UK: Routledge.

LITTLER, J. 2009. *Radical Consumption*. Maidenhead: Open University Press.

MANIATES, M. F. 2001. Individualization: Plant a tree, buy a bike, save the world? *Global Environmental Politics*, 1, 31–52.

MIDDLEMISS, L. 2014. Individualised or participatory? Exploring late-modern identity and sustainable development. *Environmental Politics*, 23, 929–946.

MILLER, D. 2012. *Consumption and its Consequences*. Cambridge, UK: Polity.

MONBIOT, G. 2017. *Out of the Wreckage: A New Politics for an Age of Crisis.* London: Verso Books.

NYBORG, K., HOWARTH, R. B. & BREKKE, K. A. 2006. Green consumers and public policy: On socially contingent moral motivation. *Resource and Energy Economics,* 28, 351–366.

ÖLANDER, F. & THØGERSEN, J. 2014. Informing versus nudging in environmental policy. *Journal of Consumer Policy,* 37, 341–356.

PAAVOLA, J. 2001. Towards sustainable consumption? Economics and ethical concerns for the environment in consumer choices. *Review of Social Economy,* 59, 227–248.

RAWORTH, K. 2017. *Doughnut Economics: Seven Ways to Think Like a Twenty-First Century Economist.* London: Random House.

REISCH, L. A. & SUNSTEIN, C. R. 2016. Do Europeans like nudges? *Judgement and Decision Making,* 11, 310–325.

RØPKE, I. 2009. Theories of practice: New inspiration for ecological economic studies on consumption. *Ecological Economics,* 68, 2490–2497.

RØPKE, I. & REISCH, L. A. 2004. The place of consumption in ecological economics. *In:* REISCH, L. A. & RØPKE, I. (eds) *The Ecological Economics of Consumption.* Cheltenham, UK: Edward Elgar.

RUSSELL, S. V., YOUNG, C. W., UNSWORTH, K. L. & ROBINSON, C. 2017. Bringing habits and emotions into food waste behaviour. *Resources, Conservation and Recycling,* 125, 107–114.

SAHAKIAN, M. 2015. Getting emotional: Historic and current changes in food consumption practices viewed through the lens of cultural theories. *In:* HUDDART KENNEDY, E., COHEN, M. & KROGMAN, N. (eds) *Putting Sustainability into Practice: Applications and Advances in Research on Sustainable Consumption.* Cheltenham, UK: Edward Elgar.

SCHLÜTER, M., BAEZA, A., DRESSLER, G., FRANK, K., GROENEVELD, J., JAGER, W., JANSSEN, M. A., MCALLISTER, R. R., MÜLLER, B. & ORACH, K. 2017. A framework for mapping and comparing behavioural theories in models of social-ecological systems. *Ecological Economics,* 131, 21–35.

SHOVE, E. 2003. *Comfort, Cleanliness and Convenience: The Social Organization of Normality.* Oxford, UK: Berg Publishers.

SOUTHERTON, D., WARDE, A. & HAND, M. 2004. The limited autonomy of the consumer: Implications for sustainable consumption. *In:* SOUTHERTON, D., CHAPPELLS, H. & VAN VLIET, B. (eds) *Sustainable Consumption: The Implications of Changing Infrastructures of Provision.* Cheltenham, UK: Edward Elgar.

THALER, R. & SUNSTEIN, C. 2008. *Nudge: Improving Decisions About Health, Wealth, and Happiness.* New Haven, CT: Yale University Press.

VATN, A. 2005. Rationality, institutions and environmental policy. *Ecological Economics,* 55, 203–217.

WILK, R. 2002. Consumption, human needs, and global environmental change. *Global Environmental Change,* 12, 5–13.

6   'It's all about values'

In this chapter, we start with the received opinion that if people have pro-environmental values they will consume more sustainably. In doing so, we encounter the discipline of psychology, as well as the sub-discipline of social psychology. After economists, psychologists were the second social science discipline to become active in thinking about sustainable consumption. The main focus here is on how the things that people think are important affect the way that they behave. I am using the word 'values' in the title here to encompass all the judgements that people make about how important things are. In practice, this could refer to people's specific attitudes towards a behaviour they are being asked to engage in, or a broader set of values towards the environment and other people.

You are already getting a taste of the kind of terminology that psychologists use in talking about environmental issues. First, the term 'sustainable consumption' is not widespread; instead, the main concept here is 'pro-environmental behaviour' or 'environmentally significant behaviour' (Stern, 2000), meaning any behaviour that has (positive) consequences for the environment. I will define both 'attitudes' and 'values' more precisely below; for now, attitudes refer to specific thoughts about something, whereas values reflect a general orientation towards a topic (for e.g. the environment). Most of the concepts used by psychologists relate to the specific thoughts and feelings people have about engaging with pro-environmental behaviour. As a result, in this chapter we will mostly be thinking about what happens in people's heads (as opposed to what happens in society or in the material world) and how people's thoughts and feelings impact on what they end up doing. Of course, people's thoughts and feelings are influenced socially, by their peers, by general notions of acceptability, etc.

While the discipline of psychology addresses this in a highly systematic way, the idea that values influence behaviour is also a very strong story in the public sphere, and frequently used to justify policy and practice. The argument is frequently made that change can only happen if people make decisions informed by their values. As the chapter goes on, we will see how these ideas play out in public policy, which often leaves behind the rigours of the discipline, instead envisaging a more general relationship between how people think and feel, and what they do. Both the rigorous disciplinary version of this relationship, and the looser public policy version, have attracted criticism for focusing too closely on the individual as the locus of change, and in doing so implying that individuals acting responsibly are paramount in addressing environmental problems. The chapter concludes with a detailed summary of these critiques.

Psychological explanations of change

Psychologists active in this field tend to work with predominantly quantitative data, and to be looking for correlations and causal relationships between a defined set of variables. As a result, this is a relatively homogeneous field, in comparison to some of the others we will encounter. Psychological theories are universal theories – theories that can be applied in a number of contexts, and are frequently developed for more general use, to look at a wide range of social problems (other than environment). Theories are often tested and confirmed by bringing together a defined set of concepts, and testing the relationships between these concepts in an empirical setting. These theories attempt to explain the universal truths of human behaviour, by showing what needs to happen/exist in order for a certain type of outcome to occur. As a result, it is also possible to generalise across studies: when many psychologists use the same kinds of models, based on the same variables (sometimes even measured in the same way), you can look across a number of studies to understand the relationships between variables in a more general sense (see, for instance, Hines et al., 1987; Bamberg and Möser, 2007). Note also that these models aim to be predictive: given the logic here is to map the kinds of variables that influence how people act, the objective is to be able to predict how they will act according to the nature of the 'input' variables. There are some similarities here to economic theories, which try to predict how people will act based on prices, for example.

I will start by introducing two of the models used by environmental psychologists, and explain their logic. Note that this short summary is by no means comprehensive! I have picked two theories that feature prominently in the literature in order to give you a sense of this field. Many other approaches exist, and are exerting some influence (for instance, Gatersleben et al., 2002; Thøgersen, 2005; Kahan, 2012). Psychology models tend to look a lot like flow diagrams, to be read from left to right, with a series of interlinked concepts showing how various inputs (attitudes, norms, values, etc.) result in the output: frequently 'pro-environmental behaviour'. After presenting two of these models, I will also discuss some of the 'meta-theoretical' models that have emerged from the cross-study generalisations that have been attempted in this field. This section will end with a discussion of the attitude-behaviour or value-action gap.

Theory of planned behaviour (TPB)

The theory of planned behaviour is a general theory about how people are likely to act; it was proposed by Ajzen (1991), and is used extensively in environmental psychology. This is a theory based on rational choice, in the sense that it conceives of someone deciding whether to enact a particular behaviour or not, based on their rational evaluation of the consequences of taking that decision. Unlike in economic theory, the main elements that are understood to affect behaviour are to do with people's values.

Ajzen identifies three main elements (shown in Figure 6.1) that will influence people's intention to behave in a certain way, and their behaviour itself (ibid.):

1   People's *attitudes towards the behaviour* are their beliefs about whether the behaviour is a good idea or not. Such attitudes can of course be influenced by social and personal factors.
2   A *subjective norm* is what you think is normal given what other people think or do, and therefore reflects what you think you are likely to get away with socially.
3   *Perceived behavioural control (PBC)* is a person's belief as to how easy or difficult the behaviour will be to actually undertake (note that the dotted line between PBC and behaviour shows that psychologists think PBC has both a direct and indirect influence on behaviour).

Note that while this model essentially describes something happening in someone's head (I might have a positive attitude to the behaviour, an impression that such a behaviour is normal, and a feeling that I can do it), there is a 'social' input

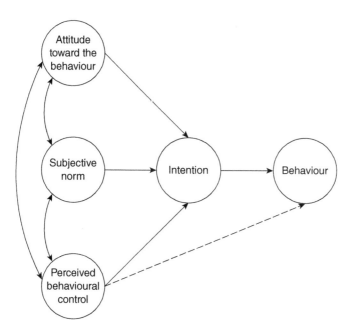

Figure 6.1 The theory of planned behaviour (reprinted from Ajzen, 1991, with permission from Elsevier)

here also. After all, all three elements might be affected by what people around me think and do.

Value-belief-norm (VBN) theory

Paul Stern and his colleagues provide an alternative explanatory model, which is also widely used. Stern makes explicit that a range of behaviour types can potentially impact on the environment (Stern, 2000). This includes daily consumption behaviours, but also environmental activism, support for government policy such as tacit agreement with government initiatives, and the influence that people exercise in other spheres of their lives, such as the workplace (ibid.). He and his colleagues also document how a range of value-related factors impact on people's intention to perform 'environmentally significant behaviours'. This includes people's values, beliefs and norms, as detailed in Figure 6.2.

To be a little more precise about the range of factors influencing people's intention to behave:

1   *Values* are people's overall orientation (i.e. are they sensitive towards the needs of the environment and others or not).
2   *Beliefs* are people's understanding of the problem, including their perspective on environment and their understanding of the consequences of their actions.
3   *Personal norms* are people's feeling of responsibility for taking environmental action.

There are similarities and differences between this model and the theory of planned behaviour detailed above. For instance, you can see that 'perceived behavioural control' and 'perceived ability to reduce threat' are fairly similar. The main difference here is that Stern's model has a broader perspective: while Ajzen focuses on the person's thoughts about a particular behaviour, Stern also takes into account the general orientation of that person towards environmental issues (their values), as well as their understanding of environmental issues

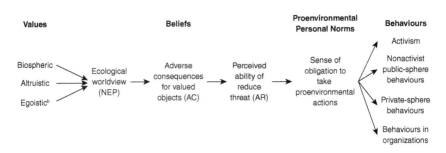

Figure 6.2 The value-belief-norm theory (from Stern, 2000; reproduced with permission from Wiley)

(NEP and AC in the diagram). Note that all of these factors indicate people's predisposition towards pro-environmental behaviour, and cannot be used as a simple predictive tool.

Meta-theoretical models

Given that psychologists believe it is possible to find general truths about the way that humans think and behave, there is also a strand of work in environmental psychology which brings together findings collected under different theoretical traditions. I call this 'meta-theory' because it is 'higher order' theory – theory built on bringing several other theories together. The most systematic attempt at this is Hines, Hungerford and Tomera's paper (1987), followed by Bamberg and Möser's summary of research (2007) from the intervening twenty years. These studies produce even more general statements about which variables impact on people's behaviour because they bring together multiple empirical studies which were designed around the theoretical models I introduced above.

Out of these meta-theoretical projects come some more interesting insights for sustainable consumption. Bamberg and Möser draw on all the research based in the theory of planned behaviour and the norm activation model (see Schwartz, 1977) within a 20-year time frame. From a values perspective, Bamberg and Möser are able to draw out very general lessons about how behavioural intention is structured by a number of values or attitude-driven questions:

> the intention to perform a pro-environmental behavioural option can be described as a weighted balance of information concerning the three questions 'How many positive/negative personal consequences would result from choosing this pro-environmental option compared to other options?', 'How difficult would be the performance of the pro-environmental option compared to other options?' and 'Are there reasons indicating a moral obligation for performing the pro-environmental option?'
>
> (Bamberg and Möser, 2007, 21)

The novelty here, is that Bamberg and Möser are able to say that on average each of these questions (which refer to the variables of attitude, perceived behavioural control and moral norm in turn) predicts a similar proportion of people's intention to behave. From this, they judge that these variables have equal importance. Note that while these three central concepts have equal weighting in terms of predicting behavioural intention, together they only predict 52 per cent of variance of intention, and this in itself only predicts 27 per cent of variance in behaviour. In other words, the predictive models the psychologists are aiming at are not incredibly successful when averaged out in this way.

Perhaps averaging out studies over many locations and behaviour types is less helpful than thinking about where each model makes the most sense. Indeed, further integrative research has shown that different models are better at predicting different things (Steg and Vlek, 2009). For instance, Steg and Vlek find that the value-belief-norm theory is good at predicting low-cost environmental behaviour, whereas the theory of planned behaviour is better at predicting high-cost environmental behaviour (ibid.). Clayton and colleagues (2015) provide a diagrammatic explanation (Figure 6.3) of how instinctive, or habitual behaviour (discussed in more detail below) is more likely to be influenced by infrastructure, incentives and feedback – all of which might require the kinds of intervention governments are comfortable with, whereas conscious decisions are more clearly linked to what might be broadly categorised as 'values' – things that people think about the world, and attachments that they have.

Intentions, behaviours and gaps

While some of the diagrams above can look quite simple (attitude, leading to intention, leading to behaviour), psychologists have found a complex picture in their combined efforts to understand this field. For example, Birgitta Gatersleben and her colleagues found that when they measured overall environmental impact of households in the Netherlands, the households that engaged in pro-environmental behaviour, and declared pro-environmental attitudes, tended to have a larger environmental impact than those that did not (Gatersleben et al., 2002). Overall environmental impact was more likely to be influenced by household size and income than it was values (ibid.). This suggests that if we focus on explicitly 'pro-environmental behaviour', we may not be looking at the most environmentally detrimental actions of a household, an argument taken on

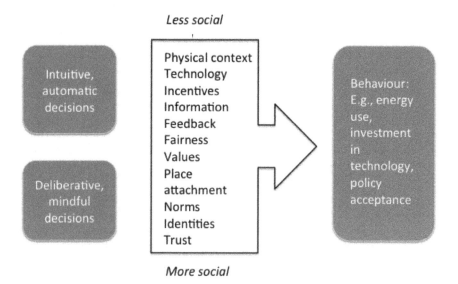

Figure 6.3 Influences on climate-related behaviour (from Clayton et al, 2015; reprinted by permission from *Nature Climate Change*)

forcefully by the sociologist Elizabeth Shove (2003), as we will see in Chapter 8. Further, in her studies of environmental activists, educators and professionals, Rachel Howell notes that these people are often motivated as much by pro-social values as they are by pro-environmental ones (Howell 2013; Howell and Allen, 2017). If people are equally motivated by pro-social values, should we be taking a broader outlook on values also?

One of the key problems with this body of work, or, to be fair, the public tendency to assume that values produce behaviour, is the complicated relationship between these two concepts. For instance, the two models discussed above focus on understanding how values and attitudes impact on people's intention to behave, rather than their behaviour itself. The gap between intention and behaviour is often quite substantial. Psychologists know this, and put it down to a range of factors. As Stern eloquently summarises:

> Many environmentally significant behaviors are matters of personal habit or household routine (e.g., the setting of thermostats or the brand of paper towels purchased) and are rarely considered at all. Others are highly constrained by income or infrastructure (e.g., reinsulating homes, using public transport). For others, environmental factors are only minor influences on major actions (e.g., choosing an engine size option in a new automobile, deciding whether to centrally air condition a home), or the environmental effects are unknown to the consumer (e.g., choosing between products that have different environmental impacts from their manufacturing processes).
>
> (Stern, 2000, 415)

This distance between how people think and what they do is also referred to as the attitude-behaviour gap or the value-action gap. As well as the challenges Stern outlines above (habit, financial/infrastructural constraints, knowledge), we might also add:

- People could hold attitudes that result in conflicting behaviours (e.g. love for travel, and care for the environment) (Young et al., 2009).
- People's attitudes could be determined by their behaviour (e.g. it becomes hard to hold pro-environmental values when you are a 'petrol-head') (Phipps et al., 2013).
- Non-rational (or as psychologists would say 'affective') drivers also might interfere with people's values and beliefs (e.g. negative emotions increasing food waste) (Young et al., 2017).

Stern's resulting categorisation of four causal influences on behaviour includes:

1   Attitudes/values
2   Context (includes a long list of factors external to the individual)
3   Personal capability (skills and knowledge to engage in behaviour)
4   Habit.

This paints a complex picture of decision-making which is also apparent in more recent work (for instance, Young et al., 2009; Zhao et al., 2014). Indeed, Stern (2000) notes that each of these causal factors might have a smaller or larger impact on behaviour depending on what that behaviour is.

While Stern clearly recognises some of the challenges of putting so much emphasis on values or attitudes, it is intriguing that many psychologists have remained wedded to the values orientation of the central models in their field. Indeed, Steg and Vlek (2009) point out the limited attention paid to contextual factors (also called 'situational factors', and tending to encompass anything that is not psychological) and to habit in this body of work. Some attempt to explain when and why values translate into action (when the gap is overcome), for instance, when people feel responsible and act on that responsibility (Luchs et al., 2015). There have been attempts by both psychologists and interdisciplinarians to move beyond an internal focus on values, as we will see. We will also see that the focus on attitudes is a rather easy one for those implementing change: it represents a softer target for government or industry than harder goals of major infrastructural change, or even taxation.

Some advances in research

In the previous section I introduced some of the central ways in which psychologists explain why people behave in the ways they do. We also got some sense of the limits of these models, and the potential for further development by incorporating further concepts and variables. Here I will give some examples of further work that has attempted to broaden the scope of psychological enquiry, by understanding non-rational drivers of behaviour (habits), by understanding how people's behaviour is structured by larger, more social ideas (identity), and by understanding how people's perception of the problem and its distance from themselves (risk).

Habits

If behaviour was mainly determined by values, you might expect to see some overlap between behaviours: as someone changes one behaviour, they might then continue to transform others which require the same kind of value orientation. Thøgersen and Ölander (2003) call this idea 'spill-over' of behaviours (from one category to another), but find that this only happens to a moderate degree, and some behaviour categories (e.g. transport) are not affected by spill-over at all. This suggests that people's daily decisions are not only governed by their values, and also that other drivers are impacting on what they do. The importance of habit in structuring behaviour is a more general concern of the discipline of psychology. Daniel Kahneman's *Thinking, Fast and Slow* is a useful popular introduction to this more general field (2011).

In the environmental sphere, a number of authors have complemented thinking about values, by including habits as a driver of behaviour. Ölander and

Thøgersen's 'Motivation, Opportunity, Ability' model (1995) brings in 'ability' variables, which relate to people having the 'task knowledge' and acquiring habits. These authors find that people become more confident to take on unfamiliar behaviour, and more competent at it, once they have experience of it (ibid.). As people learn new behaviours, in this case regarding recycling, they find that 'Until the habits of source separation are well ingrained, there is a high risk of sorting failures as a consequence of "the force of (old) habit"' (ibid., 364). The suggestion here is that actually doing something makes a difference to how people feel about it: behaviour is influencing attitude.

Marcus Phipps and colleagues use insights from Albert Bandura about the cyclical relationship between society and individual to expand on this vision of a mutual relationship between attitudes and behaviour (Phipps et al., 2013). They explain how our current behaviour impacts on the potential for future behaviours, but also on our attitudes towards that future behaviour. They use a case study of a community toy library in New Zealand: a service that allows you to borrow toys, so as to try them out, or to avoid having to buy them. By using the library, parents get some unexpected benefits: getting to know other likeminded people in the community, teaching children the value of sharing and using toys responsibly, using the toy library to reduce the numbers of toys they buy, and helping children to build a different kind of relationship with the market. We can see how all of these things might change the opportunities on offer to those children in the future, as well as their ability to engage in different kinds of consumption (in particular, with the sharing economy). Further, Phipps and colleagues noted that 'sharing' behaviours spilled over for those involved, resulting in people joining book clubs, engaging in clothes swapping, car sharing and more (ibid.).

Identity

Another concept that helps to explain groups of behaviours, is that of identity. Lorraine Whitmarsh and Saffron O'Neill (2010) find that if people self-identify as 'pro-environmental', this is a better predictor of behaviour than the New Economic Paradigm (NEP), a common means of measuring environmental values. There are some interesting parallels here with the work of anthropologists, who, as we will see, also have interests in how identity impacts on people's consumption (see Chapter 9). Birgitta Gatersleben and her colleagues have shown that there is a strong relationship between identities, values and behaviours, and suggest that identities may be a broader category than values (Gatersleben et al., 2014). In other words, people's identity as a motorist, or parent, for example, could help to structure the kinds of values that they hold, and, in turn, how they behave.

Gatersleben and colleagues identify a number of consumer identities that have positive impacts on people's pro-environment behaviour, in particular frugal and moral identities (ibid.). Frugality is all about avoiding waste, and those with frugal identities will avoid both wasting money and all other resources. Moral identities connect more clearly to the values described more generally in this field. This work is particularly interesting because it shows, as is frequently argued by anthropologists and sociologists, that people have multiple consumer identities which are apparent in different contexts, and that are sometimes conflicting (see also Murtagh et al., 2012a). It also shows that two different people might engage in the same behaviour for completely different reasons, in connection with their consumer identity.

In a study of travel mode choice, Niamh Murtagh and colleagues (2012b) found that not only did people's self-identity impact on how they travel, but that if you threaten people's self-identity, this creates even greater resistance to change. In an experiment where participants were shown stories about hypothetical interventions in their area, they found that if a (self-identified) motorist was faced with a punitive initiative to reduce car use, they were more likely to resist change than if they were faced with a more encouraging initiative. Further, people were less resistant to change if they had some experience of alternative modes (walking, public transport) and therefore could integrate this into their self-identity: 'Through walking at least sometimes, individuals may begin to see themselves as "someone who walks", and this identity then may guide subsequent behaviour' (ibid., 324).

Risk perception

As well as being interested in how values translate into consumption behaviour, psychologists have also had a longstanding interest in how people's understandings of the world, result in them having concerns for the environment. This work links back to Chapter 4, but tends to have a particular concern with the translation of understanding into values. Recent work on psychological distance, or 'the extent to which an object is removed from the self' (Newell et al., 2014, 453), fits into this mould. Researchers have found that people particularly experience psychological distance in relation to global environmental problems (ibid.), for instance, many people feel a distance from the problem of (and indeed solution to) climate change (Spence et al., 2012). Alexa Spence and colleagues characterise 'psychological distance' to climate change as having four dimensions, which I have paraphrased here as the beliefs people hold:

- Temporal ('climate change will happen in the future')
- Social ('climate change will happen to someone else')
- Geographical ('climate change will happen somewhere else')
- Uncertainty ('climate change may not happen at all')

Spence and colleagues' research found that when people have a low sense of psychological distance (i.e. they think that climate change is a problem they will most likely face personally and imminently), they will also have a higher level of concern and preparedness to act. However, this is not a simple relationship: if people think that developing countries will be highly impacted by climate change (social psychological distance), they are also more prepared to act. These studies suggest that it would make sense to try and reduce the psychological distance that people experience in this regard, as a means of promoting more sustainable behaviour. We can imagine doing this by communicating differently about the problem – for instance, by communicating about climate change in relation to people's locality.

Lorraine Whitmarsh (2008) conducted some research on people with direct experience of flooding or air pollution (in the South of England), in order to establish whether such direct experience affects people's understanding of risk. This is relevant to our understanding of psychological distance, as it deliberately singles out those who 'should' feel lower distance, given the risks they have been exposed to. Intriguingly, those who had experienced flooding had very similar understandings, values and behavioural responses to climate change as non-victims. Victims of flooding see climate change and flooding as separate issues, generally attributing flooding to poor water management or recent development. On the other hand, those who had experienced air pollution tended to have higher pro-environmental values, and as a result were more likely to take action personally. The fact that air pollution is a continuous state, and that flooding tends to be a one-off event may be relevant here. Intriguingly, more recent research suggests that flood victims do experience a decrease in psychological distance, and as a result are more likely to perceive themselves as vulnerable, to take climate change more seriously, and to support government action on mitigation and adaptation (Demski et al., 2017). These different studies suggest that reducing psychological distance may require different approaches in different contexts, and that psychological distance changes over time.

Psychology in policy

Environmental psychology is a field which has become highly influential in sustainable consumption policy. In the UK, for instance, psychological insights were central in crafting the 'Framework for Pro-environmental Behaviour' in 2008 (more details below). This is likely to be for a number of reasons. Psychological theories seem to be more approachable for a lay person than those in some other fields (e.g. sociology), but they also add depth to the simplicity of economic theory. Given the focus on values, psychological insights are also easier to implement; values are a relatively soft target, and as such, policy implications are less controversial. Psychological insights are not going to result in a radical reshaping of infrastructure, or society more generally. As a result, and as you will see in the critique below, approaches that rely on changing attitudes or values are sometimes accused of being rather ineffective, as a way of allowing governments to 'look busy' while not actually investing very much.

In addition, the received opinion that 'it's all about values' has an important role. This means that there are a range of interpretations of psychological evidence in the public domain, some of which are based as much on a gut feeling that it would all work out 'if people just valued the right things' as they are on formal psychological research. When we look at attempts to implement psychological ideas in policy, we must be aware that these are not always 'pure' applications – they are influenced by non-theoretical insights, by politics, and by ideas of feasibility (see Marsden et al., 2014 for a discussion of this point with regards to transport policy).

I begin here by looking at the academic work on policy, which outlines how government should intervene in public life, and the types of intervention that psychologists think that government should make. I then give an example of a government intervention that is highly influenced by psychological thinking. Note here that this is not a 'pure' example of psychological theory in action: it is a partial implementations of this theory, complicated by politics in a world in which some things are too controversial to be said or done.

Evidence for policy

Psychologists themselves have characterised and evaluated the potential for policy to draw on their theory. Linda Steg and her team in Groningen in the Netherlands have been central in this effort. They characterise their approach as follows:

> we argue that promoting behaviour change is more effective when one (1) carefully selects the behaviours to be changed to improve environmental quality, (2) examines which factors cause those behaviours, (3) applies well-tuned interventions to change relevant behaviours and their antecedents, and (4) systematically evaluates the effects of these interventions on the behaviours themselves, their antecedents, on environmental quality and human quality of life.
>
> (Steg and Vlek, 2009, 309)

Note that this reads as a rather common-sense approach; however, there are some clear assumptions that need unpicking here. For instance, with the first point, the authors assume both that behaviours are best targeted as individual entities, and that there is some logic as to why a specific behaviour might be selected for attention. The second point assumes that each behaviour is affected by different factors. The third point assumes that behaviours can be changed by interventions. None of these seem terribly controversial, but you will see as the book progresses that other disciplinary approaches would disagree that these assumptions hold true.

The type of policy that comes out of psychological thinking typically targets the individual, and in particular the individual's way of thinking. This could include informing people about 'appropriate' behaviour, persuading people to change their attitudes, providing role models of 'good behaviour' (ibid.). Often psychologists think about 'antecedent strategies' or strategies that lead to change (for example getting people to commit to a target) or 'consequence strategies', strategies that result in some kind of response (for example positive feedback on change) (Abrahamse et al., 2005). Policy might involve trying to change the cost, or even people's perceptions of the 'cost' of a behaviour (Steg et al., 2014).

It might also involve attempts to ensure people's values are better reflected in the decisions they make (i.e. that they prioritise environmental values in decision making) (Steg et al., 2014). This work also can be outward looking, with structural policies aimed at changing the costs and benefits of behaviour, or providing infrastructure (Steg and Vlek, 2009).

DEFRA's framework for pro-environmental behaviour, in the UK

In 2008, the Department for Environment, Food and Rural Affairs (DEFRA) in the UK released a 'Framework for Pro-environmental Behaviour', the culmination of a programme to introduce psychological perspectives into environmental governance (DEFRA, 2008). Under the centre-left New Labour government, the department had begun hiring psychologists to work alongside the natural scientists and economists already on the staff. A key thinker in sustainable consumption, academic Tim Jackson (see, for instance, Jackson, 2006), who is actually more accurately defined as an environmental social scientist, was also influential in this government department at the time, and was enthusiastic about psychological insights.

The end result is not a purely psychological approach – far from it. However, there are strong connections with the discipline in the way that DEFRA understood the problem of 'behaviour change'. DEFRA's explanation of how different behaviours are more or less easy to achieve (from its perspective as government) is telling:

> there are some behaviour goals to which the door is relatively open, as most people are already willing to act and have a high ability to do so . . . The more challenging behaviour goals are either those where there is low ability and low willingness to act . . . or those where willingness is low although people acknowledge that they could act.
>
> (DEFRA, 2008)

Note that DEFRA concentrates on ordinary people here, as the target of policy. This chimes well with psychological insights. Further, DEFRA characterises its goals based on people's willingness and ability to engage with them. There are strong connections here to ideas of perceived behavioural control (ability), moral norm and attitudes (willingness) (Ajzen, 1991). The use of 'willingness', suggests that people are assumed to be aware of what is asked of them and as a result, someone having pro-environmental values would be quite important. The insights from the field that I have highlighted on habit and context (or 'situational factors') above are also loosely incorporated here, in the idea of 'ability'. You might not have the ability if you do not live in the right kind of place for instance.

So what kind of action would logically stem from the quote above? We can imagine interventions designed to persuade people to change their ways, or to persuade them of their ability to change. These amount to very soft policy measures, in comparison to the harder approach that an economist would promote (control of the market, taxation) or, as we will see, the more systemic approaches in Chapters 8 and 13. Nevertheless they are not beyond controversy. For instance, governments can be concerned about the risks of 'telling their citizens what to do'. Persuading people to change their daily lives might be seen as too intrusive on the part of the state. Jones and colleagues' interviews with DEFRA employees about the increase in psychological influence on government thinking show some concern about the role of the state. In this quote from one of their interviewees:

> We are not out to tell people they've got the wrong values. That's not right. They have their values for whatever reason they have their values, but working from there, actually, can we still get to an end point that is good for everybody?
>
> (Interview with DEFRA employee, in Jones et al., 2013, 155)

Note that the framework for pro-environmental behaviour is also heavily influenced by ideas of social marketing. Briefly, this involves categorising consumers into types (or market segments) who then can be approached in different ways. This is not exactly a psychological approach: it defines, for instance 'waste watchers' as a market segment that is characterised by wanting to avoid wasting things (attitude), but also by socio-demographic boundaries (typically older people, who are not very wealthy).

Critiques

I have hinted throughout that this starting point – 'it's all about values' – and the psychological work that underpins it, has attracted some criticism. The critiques from all sides revolve around the centrality of the concept of values in this way of thinking, a concept which authors see as fractured (Cherrier, 2007), reductionist and politically contentious (Rose, 1996), or irrelevant (Shove et al., 2012). Further, the impact of placing values so centrally is to individualise thinking around political solutions (Maniates, 2001; Middlemiss, 2014) and to paint the individual as chiefly concerned with 'disciplining' themselves into 'good' behaviour (Isin, 2004), both of which have political implications, as discussed in Chapter 5. It also represents a way in which government can avoid meaningful engagement in change, by shifting both the responsibility and the solution for environmental problems to the individual, and their failure to engage in 'correct' values and behaviours.

The geographer Hélène Cherrier (2007) notes that it is difficult to point to what is 'good' or 'ethical' in a postmodern world, since traditional values are set to one side, and it is therefore less clear to people what might be the 'right' thing to do. This is a familiar story in my life also: I have had so many conversations about which particular behavioural choice is 'right' given the complexity of the environmental consequences of our actions (for instance: should I buy local milk, organic milk, or no milk at all?). Perhaps an ethical compass provides new direction in this context, as a new means of navigation to replace traditional values, and Cherrier finds some evidence of this. However, the transience of values in a postmodern world, the possibility of values transforming, and the complexity of behavioural impacts, mean that we cannot rely on these as a predictive guide to people's behaviour.

One of the challenges to this body of work relates to its tendency to see the individual as key, and their thought processes as central to any understanding of social change. We have talked about individualisation in Chapter 5, and the same sorts of concerns arise here. By focusing on the individual and their thinking, we imply that this is the appropriate locus of change, the appropriate focus for policy-makers interested in making an impact (Middlemiss, 2014). Critical scholars label this approach to change as 'neuro-liberal', and point out that in this vision or 'narrative' of change, the individual is understood to be a 'neurotic citizen' concerned with disciplining their own behaviour according to their values (Isin, 2004; Jones et al., 2013). Nikolas Rose would argue that governments tend to paint a uniform picture of their 'neurotic citizens', to assume that all citizens react in this way, and as a result to understand policy as needing to address such a citizen (Rose, 1996). A cynical analysis of a focus on values, and on the 'neurotic citizen' would argue that this is a deliberate attempt to get people to be more self-obsessed, in order to detract from more substantial social and political change.

There is a possibility of understanding values in a more political way. Barnett and colleagues, and others, are inclined to see ethical consumerism (as covered in detail in Chapter 7) as a context in which values are mobilised politically, by groups of people, to express their politics through behaviour in their daily lives (Barnett et al., 2010). Ethical consumerism amounts to 'the outcome of organised efforts by a variety of collective actors to practically rearticulate the ordinary ethical dispositions of everyday consumption' (ibid., 19).

On the other hand, as we will also see in Chapter 8, some writers taking a practice perspective have summarily dismissed the very notion of the importance of values. As Elizabeth Shove points out in response to the body of work by DEFRA (introduced here as the 'Framework for Pro-environmental Behaviour' above): 'Strategies of this kind assume that a raft of "behaviours", including driving, eating, washing and so on, are essentially similar in that the "choices" people make about them reflect their environmental commitments, whether these be strong or weak' (Shove et al., 2012, 142).

Shove and others writing in this field focus on inconspicuous consumption: acts of consumption that are hidden, frequently habitual, and that do not rely on any conscious environmental commitment or values.

Conclusions

This chapter tackled the received opinion that 'it's all about values'. We started with the idea that if people held 'correct' environmental values, and then expressed these values through their behaviour, this could resolve the problems associated with unsustainable consumption. In order to understand the concept of values more rigorously, I have drawn on the discipline of psychology, which also places values at the centre of the analysis. Psychologists have studied a wide range of pro-environmental behaviours, using a fairly narrow set of concepts, most of which are connected to what is happening in people's heads, as opposed to people's habits, or the contexts that people inhabit. Despite this rather narrow set of concepts, psychologists are aware that the relationship between values (or attitudes) and behaviour is not a simple one, and in many cases they are reaching out for ways to add to such a simplistic explanation of change.

As we will see in the next chapter, not everyone would agree that values are centrally important. However, we should be careful not to dismiss values out of hand. The very presence of sustainable consumption on the political agenda, at international, national and local scales, is down, after all, to the formation of a pro-environmental set of values in response to emerging scientific information about environmental risk. To be simplistic, the expression of values about environmental and ethical problems in political life is fundamental to even beginning to tackle this issue. There are numerous ways of understanding how values are engaged in sustainable consumption, however, and a simple understanding of individuals as actors performing their values through their daily lives, misses the bigger picture of individuals contributing to a politics of sustainable consumption through their values. More of this in Chapter 7, when we get to grips with political approaches to this topic, and in Chapter 13 which looks at the possibilities for more radical change, often inspired by environmental values.

References

ABRAHAMSE, W., STEG, L., VLEK, C. & ROTHENGATTER, T. 2005. A review of intervention studies aimed at household energy conservation. *Journal of Environmental Psychology*, 25, 273–291.

AJZEN, I. 1991. The theory of planned behavior. *Organizational Behavior and Human Decision Processes*, 50, 179–211.

BAMBERG, S. & MÖSER, G. 2007. Twenty years after Hines, Hungerford, and Tomera: A new meta-analysis of psycho-social determinants of pro-environmental behaviour. *Journal of Environmental Psychology*, 27, 14–25.

BARNETT, C., CLOKE, P., CLARKE, N. & MALPASS, A. 2010. *Globalizing Responsibility: The Political Rationalities of Ethical Consumption*. Indianapolis, IN: Wiley.

CHERRIER, H. 2007. Ethical consumption practices: Co-production of self-expression and social recognition. *Journal of Consumer Behaviour*, 6, 321–335.

CLAYTON, S., DEVINE-WRIGHT, P., STERN, P. C., WHITMARSH, L., CARRICO, A., STEG, L., SWIM, J. & BONNES, M. 2015. Psychological research and global climate change. *Nature Climate Change*, 5, 640.

DEFRA. 2008. *A Framework for Pro-environmental Behaviours* [Online]. Available: www. gov.uk/government/uploads/system/uploads/attachment_data/file/69277/pb13574-behaviours-report-080110.pdf [Accessed 21 December 2017].

DEMSKI, C., CAPSTICK, S., PIDGEON, N., SPOSATO, R. G. & SPENCE, A. 2017. Experience of extreme weather affects climate change mitigation and adaptation responses. *Climatic Change*, 140, 149–164.

GATERSLEBEN, B., MURTAGH, N. & ABRAHAMSE, W. 2014. Values, identity and pro-environmental behaviour. *Contemporary Social Science*, 9, 374–392.

GATERSLEBEN, B., STEG, L. & VLEK, C. 2002. Measurement and determinants of environmentally significant consumer behavior. *Environment and Behavior*, 34, 335–362.

GATERSLEBEN, B., MURTAGH, N., CHERRY, M. & WATKINS, M. 2017. Moral, wasteful, frugal, or thrifty? Identifying consumer identities to understand and manage pro-environmental behavior. *Environment and Behavior*, 1–26.

HINES, J. M., HUNGERFORD, H. R. & TOMERA, A. N. 1987. Analysis and synthesis of research on responsible environmental behavior: A meta-analysis. *Journal of Environmental Education*, 18, 1–8.

HOWELL, R. A. 2013. It's not (just) 'the environment, stupid!' Values, motivations, and routes to engagement of people adopting lower-carbon lifestyles. *Global Environmental Change*, 23, 281–290.

HOWELL, R. & ALLEN, S. 2017. People and planet: Values, motivations and formative influences of individuals acting to mitigate climate change. *Environmental Values*, 26, 131–155.

ISIN, E. F. 2004. The neurotic citizen. *Citizenship Studies*, 8, 217–235.

JACKSON, T. (ed.) 2006. *The Earthscan Reader in Sustainable Consumption*. London: Earthscan.

JONES, R., PYKETT, J. & WHITEHEAD, M. 2013. *Changing Behaviours: On the Rise of the Psychological State*. Cheltenham, UK: Edward Elgar.

KAHAN, D. M. 2012. Cultural cognition as a conception of the cultural theory of risk. In: ROESER, S., HILLERBRAND, R., SANDIN, P. & PETERSON, M. (eds) *Handbook of Risk Theory*. Dordrecht: Springer.

KAHNEMAN, D. 2011. *Thinking, Fast and Slow*. London: Macmillan.

LUCHS, M. G., PHIPPS, M. & HILL, T. 2015. Exploring consumer responsibility for sustainable consumption. *Journal of Marketing Management*, 31, 1449–1471.

MANIATES, M. F. 2001. Individualization: Plant a tree, buy a bike, save the world? *Global Environmental Politics*, 1, 31–52.

MARSDEN, G., MULLEN, C., BACHE, I., BARTLE, I. & FLINDERS, M. 2014. Carbon reduction and travel behaviour: Discourses, disputes and contradictions in governance. *Transport Policy*, 35, 71–78.

MIDDLEMISS, L. 2014. Individualised or participatory? Exploring late-modern identity and sustainable development. *Environmental Politics*, 23, 929–946.

MURTAGH, N., GATERSLEBEN, B. & UZZELL, D. 2012a. Multiple identities and travel mode choice for regular journeys. *Transportation Research Part F: Traffic Psychology and Behaviour*, 15, 514–524.

MURTAGH, N., GATERSLEBEN, B. & UZZELL, D. 2012b. Self-identity threat and resistance to change: Evidence from regular travel behaviour. *Journal of Environmental Psychology*, 32, 318–326.

NEWELL, B. R., MCDONALD, R. I., BREWER, M. & HAYES, B. K. 2014. The psychology of environmental decisions. *Annual Review of Environment and Resources*, 39, 443–467.

ÖLANDER, F. & THØGERSEN, J. 1995. Understanding of consumer behaviour as a prerequisite for environmental protection. *Journal of Consumer Policy*, 18, 345–385.

PHIPPS, M., OZANNE, L. K., LUCHS, M. G., SUBRAHMANYAN, S., KAPITAN, S., CATLIN, J. R., GAU, R., NAYLOR, R. W., ROSE, R. L. & SIMPSON, B. 2013.

Understanding the inherent complexity of sustainable consumption: A social cognitive framework. *Journal of Business Research*, 66, 1227–1234.

ROSE, N. 1996. Identity, genealogy, history. In: HALL, S. & DU GAY, P. (eds) *Questions of Cultural Identity*. London: Sage Publications.

SCHWARTZ, S. H. 1977. Normative influences on altruism. *Advances in Experimental Social Psychology*, 10, 221–279.

SHOVE, E. 2003. *Comfort, Cleanliness and Convenience: The Social Organization of Normality*. Oxford, UK: Berg Publishers.

SHOVE, E., PANTZAR, M. & WATSON, M. 2012. *The Dynamics of Social Practice: Everyday Life and How It Changes*. Thousand Oaks, CA: Sage Publications.

SPENCE, A., POORTINGA, W. & PIDGEON, N. 2012. The psychological distance of climate change. *Risk Analysis*, 32, 957–972.

STEG, L. & VLEK, C. 2009. Encouraging pro-environmental behaviour: An integrative review and research agenda. *Journal of Environmental Psychology*, 29, 309–317.

STEG, L., BOLDERDIJK, J. W., KEIZER, K. & PERLAVICIUTE, G. 2014. An integrated framework for encouraging pro-environmental behaviour: The role of values, situational factors and goals. *Journal of Environmental Psychology*, 38, 104–115.

STERN, P. 2000. Towards a coherent theory of environmentally significant behaviour. *Journal of Social Issues*, 56, 407–424.

THØGERSEN, J. 2005. How may consumer policy empower consumers for sustainable lifestyles? *Journal of Consumer Policy*, 28, 143–177.

THØGERSEN, J. & ÖLANDER, F. 2003. Spillover of environment-friendly consumer behaviour. *Journal of Environmental Psychology*, 23, 225–236.

WHITMARSH, L. 2008. Are flood victims more concerned about climate change than other people? The role of direct experience in risk perception and behavioural response. *Journal of Risk Research*, 11, 351–374.

WHITMARSH, L. & O'NEILL, S. 2010. Green identity, green living? The role of pro-environmental self-identity in determining consistency across diverse pro-environmental behaviours. *Journal of Environmental Psychology*, 30, 305–314.

YOUNG, C., HWANG, K., MCDONALD, S. & OATES, C. 2009. Sustainable consumption: Green consumer behaviour when purchasing products. *Sustainable Development*, 18, 20–31.

YOUNG, C. W., RUSSELL, S. V., ROBINSON, C. A. & CHINTAKAYALA, P. K. 2017. Sustainable retailing – Influencing consumer behaviour on food waste. *Business Strategy and the Environment*, 27, 1–15.

ZHAO, H.-H., GAO, Q., WU, Y.-P., WANG, Y. & ZHU, X.-D. 2014. What affects green consumer behavior in China? A case study from Qingdao. *Journal of Cleaner Production*, 63, 143–151.

7 'The personal is political'

In this chapter, I will cover the 'micro-politics' of sustainable consumption, looking at explanations of shopping, consumption and consumerism which explicitly engage with the politics of these acts. There are connections between these 'micro-politics' and the macro-level critiques of the political and economic systems of our age, a topic which I will cover in more detail in Chapter 13 ('Revolution or evolution'). By politics here, I mean the ways in which power is exercised through daily practices which relate to sustainable consumption (for good or ill), as well as the potential connections between consumption and citizenship.

You may have heard of the phrase 'the personal is political' before in relation to the feminist movement. Indeed, part of the politicisation of the role of women in society is about understanding how women's daily lives amount to a performance of bigger political ideas. In the 1960s, this slogan was used to point out that women's work in the home had an impact on their position and status in society. I chose 'the personal is political' as a chapter title because in the context of sustainable consumption, we also find that how people live their daily lives has an impact on broader political considerations at a societal level. As we will see, there are also some feminist points to be made about the politics of sustainable consumption, a topic also alluded to in Chapter 3.

Before we dig into the literature, I'd like to introduce a typology from Spaargaren and Oosterveer (2010) which I find useful in thinking about political action on sustainable consumption matters. These authors propose three roles for citizen-consumers in environmental problems – environmental citizenship, political consumerism and life(style) politics – and point out how these roles engage different greening practices of consumption. The three roles are defined as follows:

- Environmental citizenship: 'refers primarily to the participation of citizens in and their orientations towards political discourses on sustainable development' (ibid., 5).
- Political consumerism: the consumer 'uses his or her buying power not just to satisfy needs but to reveal to the providers of products and services their specific ethical and political preferences as consumers' (ibid., 6).
- Life(style) politics: 'the ways in which (groups of) individuals at some points in time – are made to reflect on their everyday lives and the narratives attached to it' (ibid., 10).

Spaargaren and Oosterveer's typology is useful because it reminds us that politics is present in all sorts of contexts in which citizen-consumers operate. We might crudely characterise the definitions above as citizen-consumers acting in the public domain, the market, and in their personal lives.

In this chapter I will deal with two of Spaargaren and Oosterveer's types directly: ecological citizenship and political consumerism (both explained below). Another consideration of politics that I raise here, is the politics inherent in action on sustainability itself. Here we find instances of people being excluded from such action by relationships of power, as we have seen in Chapter 3, and will explore further in Chapter 11.

Note that many of the contributions within this field come from political science or political theory. These include contributions that are entirely theoretical, and others that are based on empirical data. There is also an emerging interest in the politics of sustainable consumption from anthropologists, sociologists and human geographers working in this area. The politics of sustainable consumption is therefore a multi-disciplinary part of this field.

Environmental/ecological citizenship

In the simplest sense, a political approach to sustainable consumption is important because it reminds us of the tensions between lives lived by the wealthy, and lives lived by the poor, whether on a local, national, or global scale. As we have seen in Chapter 2, extensive evidence exists to show that the richer people get, the more they consume. Further, the more people consume, the larger impact they have both on poorer people, and on the environment. The concept of environmental or ecological citizenship is useful here, and frequently called upon by scholars working on the politics of daily life in relation to the environment. Note that 'environmental' and 'ecological' are used rather interchangeably in the literature. Here I will use 'environmental' or 'ecological', according to the preference of the author concerned.

Dobson (2003) characterises an ecological citizen as someone who is committed to the common good (not acting on self-interest in contrast to Chapter 5) and who accepts responsibility for their environmental impact, while claiming some environmental rights. The ecological citizen is mainly concerned with fulfilling their responsibilities to reduce impacts on the environment, as opposed to claiming their citizenly rights (such as voting, accessing natural resources, etc.) (ibid.). Ecological citizens practice citizenship in their everyday lives (just as feminists do). Ecological citizenship aims to ensure a fair distribution of resources across the borders of the nation state. Note that this conception of ecological citizenship is theoretical, and amounts to an idea of what an ecological citizen could be. It is useful because it shows us how environmental issues require us to think differently about the nature of citizenship.

My students sometimes find it hard to understand the value of this vision of an ecological citizen. Perhaps this is because it does not offer any specific solutions, instead being of value in describing an ideal or a goal for citizenship.

Gill Seyfang explains Dobson's concept of the ecological citizen as 'a descriptive rather than explanatory concept, a normative model of how an environmental ethic could be derived' (2006, 388). Such a normative model could be used to highlight how widespread conceptions of citizenship, and indeed how real-life practices of citizenship differ from this model. It also brings to the fore issues of justice and distribution of resources in discussions of sustainability (Seyfang, 2005). We might use it to investigate, as Seyfang has (2006, 2009), where environmental citizenly practice is emerging, and what support mechanisms might exist to encourage citizenly practices.

There have been a number of critical responses to such a model of an ecological citizen, mainly based around the need for a more contextualised and politicised vision of the citizen (Hobson, 2002; Scerri, 2009; Middlemiss, 2010; Scerri and Magee, 2012). Kersty Hobson, for instance, points out that while this concept moves away from a neo-liberal conceptualisation of people as consumers with freedom to choose, it still individualises environmental solutions, as 'an environmental citizen is someone who has internalised information about environmental problems, creating a sense of personal responsibility and duty that is then expressed through consumption and community actions' (Hobson, 2002, 102).

Environmental citizenship ideas are built on similar foundations to the ideas that underpin the arguments in Chapter 4 ('people don't understand'). Andy Scerri also sees the dominant understanding of citizenship in western democracies as a form of 'stakeholder citizenship', which 'emphasises self-responsibility and atomistic voluntarism as if these were sufficient for a society to come to grips with the ecological problem' (Scerri, 2009, 475). Scerri and Magee argue that Dobson's grounding of justice in virtue 'does not necessarily foster political obligations' (2012, 400). By individualising and responsibilising environmental issues, we risk diffusing political responses and fail to take seriously political environmental campaigns about the lack of corporate or government commitment to sustainability, for instance (Scerri, 2009). Hobson (2013) emphasises the importance of understanding what kinds of citizen are being made in the service of environmental citizenship. There is a risk that Dobson's ecological citizen is a rather compliant figure, who merely fulfils his individual obligations without contesting the bigger political picture.

These critiques lead us to some interesting developments of the idea of ecological citizenship by authors drawing on empirical data. Anneleen Kenis (2016), for instance, observes contrasting practices and politics of citizenship in her study of Transition Towns and Climate Justice Action in Belgium. Transition Towns initiatives (see Chapter 11 for an introduction to these) practice a communitarian form of citizenship: members have a rather traditional idea of the 'common good' (based on a 'back to the land' ethic) and promote dialogue and consensus in decision-making, rather than debate. In contrast, the form of citizenship engaged by Climate Justice Action is more confrontational: the idea of the common good also exists, but it is constructed by the group through a debating process. By avoiding conflict, and seeking consensus, Transition Towns is potentially silencing dissenting voices and homogenising its activities.

A further body of work draws on studies of environmental citizens to argue for the need for a more conducive cultural environment for the practice of environmental citizenship (Horton, 2006; Evans, 2011; Huddart Kennedy, 2011). David Evans (2011) documents how environmental citizenship is only one of the priorities people have (alongside, for instance, parenting, good health and being a good consumer), and that integrating this into their lives is not easy, because environmental citizenship practices are not so culturally embedded as are these other priorities. Dave Horton (2006) finds that environmental citizenship practices are embedded in a culture of environmentalism, through green spaces, networks, and materials, and that to promote good environmental citizenship, we must also facilitate this culture of environmentalism. Emily Huddart Kennedy (2011) documents how collective engagement with these ideas in Canada, through neighbourhood networks, enables participants to conceive of their action as contributing to social change, rather than merely to reducing individual impact.

Shopping practice as politics

The idea of citizenship is only one way in which political concepts have been used to understand consumption's intersection with environmental and ethical issues. A number of authors have begun to explain everyday life, especially people's shopping practices, as political acts. Nick Clarke (2008) argues that we are seeing a shift from 'ethical' to 'political' explanations of consumption. The former (ethical) involves thinking about how consumers take a moral perspective on their consumption choices; the latter (political) involves understanding consumption as embedded in the political world, organised and mobilized by social movements, and used as a tool to address policy-makers and politicians (ibid.). Note that there are a range of opinions on how successful political consumption can be, and to what extent this movement represents a renewed engagement in civic life, or corporate greenwash capturing well-intentioned consumers. There is also evidence that consumers of ethical products (in this case, fair trade) see themselves as part of a broader politics, rather than just ethical agents making informed decisions (Clarke et al., 2007).

Michele Micheletti (2003) has a positive interpretation of the role of the consumer. Micheletti uses the term 'political consumerism' to mean a way of practicing politics through acts of consumption in daily life. She sees political consumerism as an opportunity to address politics through products (ibid.). Political consumerism marks a shift away from the dominant consumerist focus on self-interest (as profiled in Chapter 5), and towards an idea of consumption which is about producing a collective good (Johnston, 2008). As another group of influential writers in this field explain it: 'The emergence and growth of contemporary ethical consumption is, we propose, indicative of distinctive forms of political mobilization and representation, and of new modes of civic involvement and citizenly participation' (Barnett et al., 2010, 1).

These authors reject the idea that political participation is declining, or that shopping is apolitical, and propose that ethical consumption acts are in themselves a collective and political response to environmental and social problems. When consumers boycott, buycott, or campaign on ethical issues, they are engaging in a form of collective and political action appropriate to a capitalist and consumerist world. As corporations increasingly act as 'private governments', which due to globalisation are difficult to hold to account (Micheletti, 2003), conventional spaces for political action are less influential, and international spaces are often completely closed. Micheletti sees the role of political consumerism as reclaiming the space of consumption as an appropriate space for politics (ibid.).

There is clearly a parallel with feminist concepts of 'the personal as political' here. Feminists understand everyday life as highly gendered, and try to understand how social change might be instigated in the everyday, by men and women sharing paid and unpaid work, for instance. In the context of ethical consumption, there is a similar commitment to translating politics into everyday life: 'Ethical consumption campaigning seeks to embed altruistic, humanitarian, solidaristic and environmental commitments into the rhythms and routines of everyday life' (Barnett et al., 2010, 13).

Writers in this field tend to blur the distinction between people acting in citizen or consumer roles. Rather than setting up the citizen and the consumer as opposing concepts, and claiming that people act in different ways as citizen and consumer, this body of work merges the two concepts, in the 'citizen-consumer'. A citizen-consumer is a citizen who chooses to express their values through consumption. The philosopher Kate Soper describes citizen-consumers as 'individuals whose consumer practices and conceptualizations of the "good life" are inextricably linked to their "citizen" concerns for environmental preservation and sustainability' (2004, 113). The idea that we act as citizen-consumers therefore has the effect of eroding the division between the public and private sphere. It also reveals how political values are engaged in a series of daily practices: buying for political, ethical, social reasons; exercising self-restraint and self-sacrifice, and displaying solidarity with others. As a citizen-consumer, someone would engage in shopping differently by using 'everyday foods as leverage points to generate reflexivity, encouraging consumers to think critically, buy more selectively, and seek out information on the environmental and social costs involved in their daily meals' (Johnston, 2008).

Micheletti (2003) argues that this represents both an ethical engagement in shopping, resulting in less harmful shopping practices, but also a renewal of democracy, with more practices of daily life being included in political action. There are some parallels to Dobson's idea of an ecological citizen profiled above here, although the work on citizen-consumers places more emphasis on the act of shopping as a political act.

This concept of the citizen-consumer is not without its critics. At the very least, we need to ask as Barnett and colleagues do, if this amounts to a 'new form of political agency' or 'shift away from active citizenship', meaning a shift away from the more familiar acts of citizenship such as voting, and holding politicians to account (Barnett et al., 2010). There is also a lack of clarity as to how these two roles intersect: how do citizen-consumers balance these two roles? Josée Johnston (2008) addresses this question in her study of Whole Foods Market, a high-end and self-consciously ethical supermarket chain in the US. In this case study, she finds that the role of consumer, rather than that of the citizen, tends to be prioritised in the way that products are presented and sold. In Whole Foods, there are three contradictions between citizen and consumer roles: consumer choice is prioritised above citizenly behaviour by Whole Foods every time (people can opt out of the 'good' choices but still feel 'good' about themselves by shopping at Whole Foods); Whole Foods denies the importance of class in their customer base, which leads both to a lack of questions about who has access to 'good' food, and a reinforcement of class differences (Whole Foods frames ethical consumers as making better choices, rather than being better resourced), and Whole Foods sells consumption as a form of environmental conservation when in real terms the increased choice they offer reduces environmental good (ibid.).

Johnston produced Table 7.1 drawing on her work at Whole Foods, and her reading of the literature, which summarises how the roles of consumerism and citizenship differ (ibid.). Note that 'political economy' here means the political, economic and social system that prevails in each vision of the world. 'Political ecology' here means the way that the political economy intersects with the environment. Johnston does not intend in this table to show consumerism and citizenship as two completely distinct things, but instead to show that they 'represent two very different explanatory frameworks and normative ends – ends that are not easily reconciled in the citizen-consumer hybrid' (ibid., 248). In other words, we have to remain critical of the idea of political consumerism, because the concepts of consumerism and citizenship come from very different worldviews, and as such have some important contradictions. A citizen-consumer is to some extent a contradiction in terms.

Clearly we must approach the idea of the citizen-consumer critically; otherwise we fail to challenge two problems related to this concept. First, the tendency to characterise individuals as market actors, and to conceive of their power to change the world through this lens (as consumers rather than as citizens).

Table 7.1 Consumerism versus citizenship (from Johnson, 2008; reprinted by permission from Springer, *Theory and Society*)

	Consumerism: maximizing individual interest	*Citizenship: collective responsibilities to a social and ecological commons*
Culture	Prioritise individual choice and variety	Limiting individual choice and variety; collective solutions
Political economy	Consumer markets valued; social status through consumption	Equitable access and empowerment for all social classes; markets restricted
Political ecology	Conservation through consumption	Reduce consumption; re-evaluate wants and needs

Second, the problems associated with a capitalist, consumerist society which relies on the unsustainable exploitation of the environment and other people to provide wealth for the few. These systemic issues are dealt with in more detail in Chapter 13. The key impact of thinking about these issues politically, however, is that we begin to see solutions in this light also. As Nick Clarke puts it: 'It changes the question from how many ethical products must be sold before, say, development is achieved, to how many ethical products must be sold before legislators are persuaded to act in such areas as trade or labour conditions' (2008, 1878).

Researching and acting on consumption politically requires us then to maintain a critical outlook, focusing on systemic issues rather than an ethical one which is more likely to focus on micro-behaviour.

Some examples of political consumer action

I have become a little bogged down in ideas here, and I would like to move into thinking about how these ideas play out in real life. Of course, the study of consumption is long-standing, and it has frequently been concerned with political and moral questions (Clarke, 2008). There is also a long history of consumer activism, frequently associated with a broader political events, including, for instance, the US boycotting British produce during the American Civil War in the 1860s (Lewis and Potter, 2011), Gandhi encouraging his compatriots to 'buy Indian' to make a stand against imperial Britain (Littler, 2011), and boycotts of South African products during the apartheid era. Lang and Gabriel (2005) argue that since the 1980s we have entered a new phase of consumer activism, which they call 'alternative consumption'. While previously the focus was on making the market safer for individual consumers, improving workers' rights, or on supporting broader political movements, in this new phase, the central concern is the damage caused by collective consumption patterns, to the environment and to other people (ibid.).

This shift in consumer activism from the 1980s onward is frequently explained by the rise of corporate power, and the need to change political tactics to account for this. Naomi Klein's *No Logo* (2001) is a key text in this movement: she argues that the centrality of the brand in contemporary life makes it easier to hold corporations to account, and as such amounts to an easy way to leverage political power. This can result in a range of action types, including boycotting, buycotting and direct action. Below I give three examples of consumer activism from around the world, drawn from my reading of case studies from other authors.

Killer Coke, US

Robert Foster (2014) documents the 'Killer Coke' campaign which emerged in the United States in the early 2000s, after a union leader was killed in a bottling plant in Colombia. An activist set up the campaign to explicitly boycott the Coca-Cola brand, resulting in lots of university campuses in the US banning

Coca-Cola products from sale in student unions. Given the ubiquity of global brands, boycotts can, as Foster puts it: 'provide a vehicle for creating large geographically dispersed publics' (ibid., 28). While not all activists will share a single perspective on a product, this kind of campaign is relatively easy to mobilise especially in the age of the Internet. Coca-Cola's response has been to partner with its critics, starting in 2004, and more 'aggressively' since 2007 (ibid.). Large corporations such as Coca-Cola increasingly seek out partnerships with large NGOs (in this case, WWF), in order to attempt to address the concerns that are raised (ibid.). While this kind of partnership goes some way towards addressing the issues that are raised in such boycotts, partnerships tend to exclude smaller NGOs, and those with more radical visions (for instance, those who are not convinced that corporates can effectively deliver development).

Consuming sustainably in Malaysia

Bryant and Goodman (2013) document the emerging sustainable consumption market in George Town, Malaysia (population 400,000). Malaysia is a nation with a prospering middle class, and George Town has a handful of organic food shops, in a context in which there is no organic food in supermarkets. The marketing focus here is on organic consumption as healthy living, and the organic food shops sell expensive foodstuffs to relatively wealthy middle-class consumers. The decor and products in the shops are clearly aimed at the middle classes, and mirror similar shops in the global North, being located in US-style shopping malls, and offering reading material on personal well-being. Bryant and Goodman see this emerging market as a reaction to concerns about environmental problems, as well as responding to a sense that Malaysians must 'do something': 'alternative shopping is tantamount to a detox politics that cleanses the nation's environmental behaviour through the example of personal cleansing' (ibid., 51). The authors note that this is a non-confrontational politics, which suits Malaysia's leaders, as well as the middle-class consumers using these shops, as it focuses on personal lives as opposed to the broader politics of income distribution or environmental issues.

Young people in Brazil

Livia Barbosa and colleagues' study of political consumerism among young people in Brazil reminds us of the importance of understanding cultural context when studying these issues (Barbosa et al., 2014). In Brazil, young people are not particularly engaged in political consumerism. This starts with a suspicion of the very idea of engaging with politics through shopping:

> There are doubts about the potential of the consumer-citizen to bring about changes and also about the value of this form of participation. The individualistic way of trying to provoke change is seen as inadequate and collective initiatives are considered better and more adequate.
>
> (Barbosa et al., 2014, 99)

Barbosa and colleagues offer three explanations for this suspicion of political consumerism among the young in Brazil. First, that Brazilian social movements are active on political issues in consumption, and are seen to be rather successful at this, and as such there is less of a perceived need for individual action. Second, that individuality in Brazil is understood as a need for equality and collective action in order to allow all to thrive, and there is less sense that individuals need to differentiate themselves politically through consumption. Individual action is therefore only perceived as effective if it is a part of collective action. Third, young people live with family a lot longer, so they are less likely to need to make consumption decisions.

Power relations and sustainable consumption

So I have profiled the concepts of environmental/ecological citizenship and political consumerism, and shown some examples of what that might mean in practice in different parts of the world. So far the focus has mainly been on the citizen, or citizen-consumer, their actions in daily life (shopping, other environmentally impactful acts), and how these relate to broader politics of our late capitalist society. In this section, I broaden the discussion to think about how relations of power play out in sustainable consumption research and practice.

In a recent call to the sustainable consumption research community, Doris Fuchs and colleagues particularly emphasised the tendency to ignore issues of power in this literature, which they see as central to the politics of sustainability:

> This work of creating conditions that initiate and accommodate real net reductions in consumption in planned and just ways is thus inextricably tied up with questions of power – the power to initiate change in service of sustainability and long-term human prosperity, and the power to blunt such changes by entrenched interests and institutions.
>
> (Fuchs et al., 2016, 299)

This quote brings to mind power as it is exercised at national, corporate, or global scale with relation to sustainability. Further, it also suggests power to prevent 'change in service of sustainability', bringing to mind Trump pulling out of the Paris agreement in 2017, big corporates funding climate change denial lobbies, and international negotiations resulting in rather lacklustre outcomes reflective of the politics of the parties involved. I will tackle these more systemic power issues in Chapter 13.

There is also an emergent body of the literature which looks at how power is exercised at a more local level in the specific context of sustainability policies and projects. This more local understanding of power and politics in sustainability is where we will focus our attentions here. Thinking about power and politics at a local scale has grown out of qualitative research on sustainability initiatives, where researchers have noticed a series of tensions in these projects which relate to a politics associated with the social groupings that people belong to – for instance, class, gender, ethnicity, place, or age. This body of work is important because it reveals the tensions within the kinds of sustainability projects which risk being thought of as 'good' social initiatives that make 'good' environmental changes. In a sense, this new literature holds sustainability projects to account socially, asking questions such as who benefits and who loses from these projects, who is permitted to join, and how are others excluded, either deliberately or otherwise. In doing so, this literature attempts to give marginalised actors a voice, and to show where action on sustainability is potentially marginalising less powerful actors. It also shows which actors tend to benefit from sustainability initiatives, and to show how they both benefit, and reinforce social inequalities in doing so.

One of the critical questions I started out with in the Introduction to this book is the question of 'who is the subject' being invoked here: what kind of person are we thinking of when we think about a 'sustainable consumer', 'ecological citizen', or 'citizen-consumer'? Kim Humphery claims that a vision of a 'citizen-consumer' often produces both stereotypical and contradictory subjects, with the western consumer being understood as 'both a mindless purveyor of consumerism, and at the very same time, as a potential agent of individual, social and cultural change' (2010, 95–96). As he points out, this betrays rather muddled understandings of the power of the individual: a belief that the individual (or individuals acting collectively) has the power to reform market structures, alongside an assumption that people who do not engage in ethical consumption are 'dupes of the market', and have no agency.

This critique brings to mind the work on individualisation profiled in Chapter 5, which shows how thinking about the individual as the locus of change in the context of sustainable consumption is problematic. Not only that, but Humphery and others have pointed out that the subjects evoked by the anti-consumerist movement, particularly the active agent of social and cultural change, is someone who would need to have access to a range of resources to be able to perform this function (Littler, 2009; Humphery, 2010; Middlemiss, 2010). Jo Littler profiles the book by Body Shop founder Anita Roddick, *Take It Personally* (2001), and points out that 'The personalized identity politics of this anti-consumerist text engenders an over-investment in individual agency, in which a series of mainly middle-class individuals are awarded the task of remoulding consumption' (Littler, 2009, 78).

In other words, much anti-consumerist thought is individualising, and assumes that actors have access to a range of personal resources. The people being positioned as active participants in this story are very commonly painted as 'universal' subjects, but in reality are more likely to be privileged: whether through their class, gender, able-bodied, or ethnicity status (see Chapter 2). The people positioned as 'dupes of the market' are also much more likely to be under-privileged, and this represents an even more problematic take on the 'stupidity' (see Chapter 4) of those unable to participate. Clearly, some 'citizen-consumers' will be able to participate fully in environmental action and others will not have access to opportunities to engage.

In a case study of Zero-Waste projects based in new middle-class communities in Bangalore, India, Manisha Anantharaman (2014) untangles how the power inequalities between residents and servants manifest themselves in project design and outcome. Critically, while these projects allow middle-class residents to identify themselves as 'green', they actually rely on the labour of the poor to achieve any form of waste reduction – in this case, household servants, and waste sorters employed by the community. As a result, these schemes may have positive environmental outcomes, but they also 'replicate these cultures of servitude' (ibid., 182). In other words, they do nothing to challenge the vast inequalities in India, and the resulting presence of a class of people who have no choice but to engage in this kind of work. Drawing on this case, Anantharaman takes the idea of 'ecological citizenship' to task, pointing out that by focusing so intently on the responsibilities of consumers to green their daily lives, this theory risks further marginalising those ecological 'creditors', those that have relatively low-impact lives. Their exclusion from the theory, apart from as victims, also suggests that they do not have a defined role to play, or indeed any agency in relation to their own future.

There are echoes of work on community and consumption in a western context here (as featured in Chapter 11), where authors have found that these initiatives are frequently led and populated by middle-class volunteers (Taylor Aiken et al., 2017), thus reinforcing the connection between environmentalism and middle-class identities. Understanding these less tangible outcomes of sustainable consumption projects through a political lens is essential; if we fail to notice these ongoing inequalities, and to notice the reinforcement of such inequalities and resulting identities through environmental action, we are failing to appreciate the social impact of such action.

The domination of community action on sustainable consumption by middle-class volunteers is not a coincidence; neither is their tendency to set the tone of the debate. In India, as indeed elsewhere, middle-class people are typically better resourced in terms of their connections to people in positions of power, their ability to raise funds, and their access to the law and the media to promote their cause: 'the elite positions of new middle class individuals, and their access to social, economic and cultural capital enable them to be effective networked ecological citizens who can affect cultural and institutional change' (Anantharaman, 2014, 181).

The risk is that when we see such action transform the nature of waste management in Bangalore, we assume that individuals have access to resources more generally. Such assumptions are very common. In Yvonne Braun and Assitan Traore's work on plastic bags in Mali (2015), they report on the Prime Minister of Mali's suggestion that the solution to the widespread use of plastic bags in shopping (and resulting littering and pollution), is that 'Women simply need to go back to the woven shopping baskets and to paper packaging for groceries sold on the market.' As Braun and Traore point out, asking for individual consumer action, or even coordinated political action from women in Mali is highly problematic, when women have a lower social status, are locked into particular actions through history of decision-making and operate in a context of political failure to implement waste policy which exacerbates the littering situation (ibid.).

Recent work by authors studying environmental activists in the US and Canada has shown how they deliberately frame their work as apolitical, based in everyday life rather than in ideas or ideologies (Lorenzen, 2014), indeed sometimes even avoiding mentioning the environmentalist nature of their work altogether in order not to 'turn people off' (Huddart Kennedy, 2016). In these cases, activists are trying to avoid the 'environment' as a political object, to show the personal, health, or social benefits in engaging in something, which happens to have environmental benefits too. This amounts to an appeal to the consumer rather than the citizen: rather than telling doom-and-gloom stories about environmental disaster and the necessity for action, to talk about the opportunities that environmental practices hold for people (more of this in Chapter 12). This is rather a departure from the idea that 'the personal is political', my premise for this chapter. Hopefully, I have shown how such an apolitical framing is deeply problematic. After all, we live in a highly unequal world, and we also exploit the environment in a highly unequal way. As we saw in Chapters 2 and 3, environmental exploitation results in social, economic and human impacts which are far more likely to affect disadvantaged people.

Conclusions

In this chapter, I have profiled an interest in the connection between politics and people's personal lives. Ideas of ecological/environmental citizenship, political consumerism, and the citizen-consumer have been used to think about how people's daily actions might be imbued with politics, and might in turn have an impact on the politics (or indeed political economy) of contemporary life. Given that citizens belong to a collective entity, these ways of thinking suggest a more collective approach to addressing sustainable consumption, which I will return to in Chapter 11, especially in contrast to the economic and psychological perspectives we have seen so far (in Chapters 5 and 6). I also documented a new body of work that reveals the power relations inherent in environmentalist action – that shows how the political is personal in environmental activism.

'The personal is political' suggests that we need to think critically and carefully about politics and engagement in environmental action. Two key points here:

- While political consumerism brings the concepts of citizen and consumer closer together, there are also risks inherent in framing sustainable consumption as political activism. There is a risk of greenwash here, which I revisit in Chapter 10. It is sometimes difficult to differentiate superficial and meaningful political commitment to environmental change, and the blurring of the lines between citizen and consumer is a challenge here. On the other hand, consumer identities, practices and politics, are very much part of everyday life in the twenty-first century, and our field has the potential to make interesting contributions in thinking about the boundary between citizen and consumer.

- In this spirit of the feminist movement, which has (sometimes!) expressed its solidarity with other social and civil rights movements, it is important that we are self-critical about the environmental movement's impact on power relations. This includes taking note of the risk of reproducing power inequalities and excluding marginalised groups from environmental action, as a result of the power relations inherent in the action itself (as also covered in Chapter 2).

I return to politics in Chapter 13, 'Revolution or evolution?', where I consider some of the more macro-level thinking about the potential for progressive change.

Further resources

Personal change does not equal social change: orionmagazine.org/article/forget-shorter-showers/

References

ANANTHARAMAN, M. 2014. Networked ecological citizenship, the new middle classes and the provisioning of sustainable waste management in Bangalore, India. *Journal of Cleaner Production*, 63, 173–183.

BARBOSA, L., PORTILHO, F., WILKINSON, J. & DUBEUX, V. 2014. Trust, participation and political consumerism among Brazilian youth. *Journal of Cleaner Production*, 63, 93–101.

BARNETT, C., CLOKE, P., CLARKE, N. & MALPASS, A. 2010. *Globalizing Responsibility: The Political Rationalities of Ethical Consumption*. Indianapolis, IN: Wiley.

BRAUN, Y. A. & TRAORE, A. S. 2015. Plastic bags, pollution, and identity: Women and the gendering of globalization and environmental responsibility in Mali. *Gender & Society*, 29, 863–887.

BRYANT, R. & GOODMAN, M. 2013. Peopling the practices of sustainable consumption: Eco-chic and the limits to the spaces of intention. In: BARENDREGT, B. & JAFFE, R. (eds) *Green Consumption: The Global Rise of Eco-Chic*. London: Bloomsbury.

CLARKE, N. 2008. From ethical consumerism to political consumption. *Geography Compass*, 2, 1870–1884.

CLARKE, N., BARNETT, C., CLOKE, P. & MALPASS, A. 2007. The political rationalities of fair-trade consumption in the United Kingdom. *Politics & Society*, 35, 583–607.

DOBSON, A. 2003. *Citizenship and the Environment*. Oxford, UK: Oxford University Press.

EVANS, D. 2011. Consuming conventions: Sustainable consumption, ecological citizenship and the worlds of worth. *Journal of Rural Studies*, 27, 109–115.

FOSTER, R. J. 2014. Adversaries into partners? Brand Coca-Cola and the politics of consumer-citizenship. In: BARENDREGT, B. & JAFFE, R. (eds) *Green Consumption: The Global Rise of Eco-Chic*. London: Bloomsbury.

FUCHS, D., DI GIULIO, A., GLAAB, K., LOREK, S., MANIATES, M., PRINCEN, T. & RØPKE, I. 2016. Power: The missing element in sustainable consumption and absolute reductions research and action. *Journal of Cleaner Production*, 132, 298–307.

HOBSON, K. 2002. Competing discourses of sustainable consumption: Does the 'rationalisation of lifestyles' make sense? *Environmental Politics*, 11, 95–120.

HOBSON, K. 2013. On the making of the environmental citizen. *Environmental Politics*, 22, 56–72.

HORTON, D. 2006. Demonstrating environmental citizenship? A study of everyday life among green activists. *In:* BELL, D. & DOBSON, A. (eds) *Environmental citizenship.* Cambridge, MA: MIT Press.

HUDDART KENNEDY, E. 2011. Rethinking ecological citizenship: The role of neighbourhood networks in cultural change. *Environmental Politics,* 20, 843–860.

HUDDART KENNEDY, E. 2016. Environmental evaporation: The invisibility of environmental concern in food system change. *Environmental Sociology,* 2, 18–28.

HUMPHERY, K. 2010. *Excess: Anti-Consumerism in the West.* Cambridge, UK: Polity.

JOHNSTON, J. 2008. The citizen-consumer hybrid: Ideological tensions and the case of Whole Foods Market. *Theory and Society,* 37, 229–270.

KENIS, A. 2016. Ecological citizenship and democracy: Communitarian versus agonistic perspectives. *Environmental Politics,* 25, 949–970.

KLEIN, N. 2001. *No Logo.* London: Harper Collins.

LANG, T. & GABRIEL, Y. 2005. A brief history of consumer activism. *In:* HARRISON, R., NEWHOLM, T. & SHAW, D. (eds) *The Ethical Consumer.* London: Sage Publications.

LEWIS, T. & POTTER, E. 2011. Introducing ethical consumption. *In:* LEWIS, T. & POTTER, E. (ed.) *Ethical Consumption: A Critical Introduction.* Abingdon, UK: Routledge.

LITTLER, J. 2009. *Radical Consumption.* Maidenhead, UK: Open University Press.

LITTLER, J. 2011. What's wrong with ethical consumption? *In:* LEWIS, T. & POTTER, E. (eds) *Ethical Consumption: A Critical Introduction.* Abingdon, UK: Routledge.

LORENZEN, J. A. 2014. Convincing people to go green: Managing strategic action by minimising political talk. *Environmental Politics,* 23, 454–472.

MICHELETTI, M. 2003. *Political Virtue and Shopping: Individuals, Consumerism, and Collective Action.* New York: Palgrave Macmillan.

MIDDLEMISS, L. 2010. Reframing individual responsibility for sustainable consumption: Lessons from environmental justice and ecological citizenship. *Environmental Values,* 19, 147–167.

RODDICK, A. 2001. *Take It Personally.* Red Wheel/Weiser Online.

SCERRI, A. 2009. Paradoxes of increased individuation and public awareness of environmental issues. *Environmental Politics,* 18, 467–485.

SCERRI, A. & MAGEE, L. 2012. Green householders, stakeholder citizenship and sustainability. *Environmental Politics,* 21, 387–411.

SEYFANG, G. 2005. Shopping for sustainability: Can sustainable consumption promote ecological citizenship? *Environmental Politics,* 14, 290–306.

SEYFANG, G. 2006. Ecological citizenship and sustainable consumption: Examining local food networks. *Journal of Rural Studies,* 22, 385–395.

SEYFANG, G. 2009. *The New Economics of Sustainable Consumption: Seeds of Change.* Basingstoke, UK: Palgrave Macmillan.

SOPER, K. 2004. Rethinking the 'good life': The consumer as citizen. *Capitalism, Nature and Socialism,* 15, 111–116.

SPAARGAREN, G. & OOSTERVEER, P. 2010. Citizen-consumers as change agents in globalizing modernity: The case of sustainable consumption. *Sustainability,* 2, 1887–1908.

TAYLOR AIKEN, G., MIDDLEMISS, L., SALLU, S. & HAUXWELL-BALDWIN, R. 2017. Researching climate change and community in neoliberal contexts: an emerging critical approach. *Wiley Interdisciplinary Reviews: Climate Change,* 8 (4).

8 'We don't have a choice'

As in most of the chapters in this section, we start with a rather simple observation about how change happens: 'we don't have a choice'. In its basic form, this perspective sounds rather deterministic, but as we will see, it actually reflects a sophisticated attempt to move away from explanations of change which focus on the individual (as in Chapters 5 and 6). From this perspective, which originates in the discipline of sociology, the types of behaviours people engage in from day to day are not chosen by individuals, or dependent on their attitudes to the world. Instead people act because of the social, technical and infrastructural conditions that they inhabit, and their daily practices are structured by (and impact on) these conditions.

A landmark text in this way of thinking is Elisabeth Shove's book *Comfort, Cleanliness and Convenience* (2003), which marked a radical departure in the study of sustainable consumption, from explanations of change which prioritise the individual (agency) rather than more structural drivers. Shove took examples of 'inconspicuous' consumption practices (consumption that uses resources in an invisible way, such as showering or laundering) and tracked their development historically, providing an explanation of how such practices have changed over time, and the drivers of such change. Since then, many academics have followed suit, and produced detailed histories of particular practices. More recent work in this field has also looked to make links from these insights to policy on sustainable consumption. This body of work is often referred to as 'practice theory' or a 'practice approach'.

Thinking back to the introductory chapter to this book, we could characterise this as a perspective that sees consumption as 'embedded' in the social, technical and infrastructural conditions that people inhabit. Geels and colleagues would call this a 'configurative' approach, which understands how people act in relation to (for instance) the technologies they use, financial markets, and the cultural meanings of consumption (Geels et al., 2015). From a sociological point of view, the idea that 'what people do is shaped by their social context (and vice versa)' is not new; this is one of the fundamental starting points of the discipline. In many ways, the engagement of sociological thinking in sustainable consumption studies has been more eye-opening for the disciplines that tend to focus on individuals and their behaviour (economics, psychology), than it has for sociology itself.

To date, the individualistic disciplines have had considerably more purchase in the policy world, and people working from a practice perspective would like their ideas to have more traction (Shove, 2010a; Southerton et al., 2004). Writers from this sociological perspective are highly critical of individualistic approaches, and often see the two bodies of work as incompatible. This is because they have a very different understanding of how the world works. If you believe that people's attitudes and choices will have a minimal influence on what they do, and that people's practices (their 'doings') and the context of these practices (the infrastructure and technology that exists, the social norms they are influenced by) are very important, you are unlikely to have a lot of time for explanations or policy solutions that prioritise the former (Shove, 2010a).

Before I begin, it is worth noting that this is a wide-ranging interest among sociologists, and that I am presenting a rather simple picture of the field in the interests of communicating the main ideas to you as a student. If you would like to understand the complexities of this field in more detail, Dan Welch and Alan Warde (2015) do an excellent job of mapping the various scholarly communities working on this topic.

Understanding practices

To start off, we need to get to grips with the idea of 'practices'. It is helpful to define these in opposition to the idea of behaviour which can be approximately defined as 'what people do'. In economics (Chapter 5) and psychology (Chapter 6), this might be further defined as 'what people choose to do' or 'what people's values lead them to do'. Practices are different because while they describe 'doings', they do so in a deeper manner by linking these to social and cultural norms, infrastructures and things. A practice therefore consists of what is being done, as well as the social world that makes that an appropriate action, and the material world which enables that action to take place. Practices might include bathing (getting oneself clean), laundering (cleaning one's clothes), cooking, working, or travelling.

Given this perspective is such an embedded one, you can imagine that in explaining practices, we also have to explain the social and material worlds in which they occur. When we understand practices as actions embedded in social and material worlds, we are also more likely to investigate particular types of action – for instance habits, 'inconspicuous consumption', or things people do regularly rather than one-off behaviours.

It helps to think about this through an example. I have chosen that of bathing, inspired by Shove's chapter on the topic (2003, Chapter 6). I would like you to think about how you keep your body clean. Here are some questions to start you off:

1   Do you regularly take a bath (say more than once a week)?
2   Do you shower regularly (daily or more)?
3   Do you wash yourself alone or with other people present?

The chances are, if you live in one of the most developed nations, you shower alone and daily or more without thinking very much about either the need for this, or the consequences of it. Indeed a recent study showed that 28 per cent of people surveyed in the UK took seven or more showers a week (Browne et al., 2015). Certainly over the years I have taught at the University of Leeds, the majority of my class has described their bathing practices as characterised by regular showering, with the occasional wallow in a bath. The idea of taking just one bath a week (and no showering in between) is also seen as somewhat disgusting by the millennial generation, despite the fact that their parents probably grew up in such a regime.

What is the significance of these insights? First, bathing practices are culturally and historically specific. It has not always been the case that people shower daily, and other practices of bathing persist in various parts of the world. For instance, in Roman times, washing was a collective and social activity, not something people did alone (Shove, 2003). Shove also reports on people's accounts of showering in the 1700s, when being 'wet all over at once' was an alien experience (ibid.). The practice of daily showering is relatively new, and geographically specific, becoming gradually established in the global North from the 1980s onwards.

One of the ways in which culture impacts on practice is through people's expectations of normality, expectations that are constructed through social interaction. So, for instance, if you live in a daily showering culture, and you choose not to shower daily, you will smell different to other people and that smell will not be seen as 'normal'. It may be more difficult for you to establish and maintain relationships with other people. These means that the things that people do – their practices – are constructed socially, that they are strongly influenced by collective ideas of normality. Note that none of this is usually talked about so explicitly: you are unlikely to be told that you 'smell' by someone else; instead we have a collective and tacit understanding of what level of body smell is acceptable in different contexts.

Second, bathing practices are deeply habitual. This means that they have become so ingrained in our daily lives that we do not really think about them. If you are in your twenties, and if you live in a developed nation, you were probably brought up showering daily, and you probably see this as a 'normal' way of keeping clean. You are unlikely to actively think about why you shower daily, the implications of showering daily, or the possibility of changing your bathing practices, because this is a habitual activity, that is a taken-for-granted part of daily life. This means that despite the fact that daily showering is a relatively new custom, we tend to understand it as set in stone, and find it hard to see how it might change in order to meet sustainability goals.

Habitual forms of consumption are interesting environmentally, because they are often highly inconspicuous. How many of us know how many kilowatts of energy it takes for us to have a shower, or how many litres of water, never mind the financial or environmental cost of these resources? On the other hand, we are very likely to know the cost of a cup of coffee, and to consider the ethical implications of how that coffee was grown.

Third, these practices are possible because of the infrastructures that have evolved, and the various material objects we interact with in daily life. Showering depends on clean running water being piped into our houses, and 'dirty' soapy water being piped away and treated. It also depends on gas or electricity networks to heat the water. Showering depends on a shower being installed (a relatively recent technology).

So practices are temporally, geographically and culturally specific, are often habitual, and are part of the interaction between infrastructure, technology and norms. Understanding practices involves understanding the social, cultural and material context of people's actions, in contrast to more individualistic models which are more likely to attempt to understand the individual's state of mind and its influence on behaviour. There is an emphasis on understanding actions in everyday life here, but in practice approaches, the 'doing' of the practice is merely a window into a deeper understanding of how that 'doing' is connected with social rules, infrastructures, and systems (Kennedy et al., 2015).

From individual to social

So, practice scholars claim that the central argument of the body of work which focuses on the individual as the locus of change is misleading. As Shove puts it, this work 'misses the point that much consumption is customary, governed by collective *norms*, and undertaken in a world of *things* and *socio-technical systems* that have stabilizing effects on routines and habits' (2003, 9, emphasis added).

In other words, much of what we do is determined by our collective expectations of how things should be – the technology, infrastructure, culture and social systems that we inhabit – not by individual attitudes (psychology), or for financial reasons (economics). Shove has been forthright in building a strong rebuttal of the theories in these other disciplines (Shove, 2010a). Shove also points out that customary consumption, consumption governed by habit or consumption that is inconspicuous (that we do not actively think about), has a substantial impact on the environment, and that by focusing on conscious consumption choices (e.g. conspicuous consumption, or 'ethical' choices) we risk missing some of the picture (Shove, 2010b).

Just as in other fields, we have some key concepts that help to explain how practices are made up, and how change in practice might happen. Practice approaches are diverse, and different authors draw on a range of different concepts. For your sake, as newcomers to these ideas, I will simplify somewhat by focusing on a recent contribution from Shove, Pantzar and Watson, which is influential in the field (Shove et al., 2012). In this work, change is not seen as a linear process, from input to outcomes, but rather, as a constant interaction between three elements: materials, competences and meanings. These are defined as follows:

- Materials – including things, technologies, tangible physical entities, and the stuff of which objects are made;
- Competences – which encompasses skill, know-how and technique, and
- Meanings – in which we include symbolic meanings, ideas and aspirations (ibid., 2012, 14).

We can see that this approach puts considerable emphasis on how the physical world (through material) and the social world (through meanings and competences) shape how people act, as well as how the sum of competences in society enable these elements to be coordinated in a practice. As one element changes, the other elements are affected by that change and they also adapt to this new reality. Shove and her colleagues draw on the idea of 'co-evolution' here, which reflects a systemic understanding of how practices are produced, where the way that one element changes impacts on the way another adapts.

A study from Brazil by Livia Barbosa and Letitia Veloso (2014) might help to bring some life to these ideas. They report on practices of cleanliness, cooking and eating in Brazil, in the context of a household transitioning from being working class to middle class. One of the ways of signifying this transition is to own a large number of appliances – including those that relate to food preparation, such as refrigerators and fridge-freezers. This means new objects coming into the home, objects that rely on a connection to the electricity grid. These objects also have an important cultural significance: to show that a household can afford them. Brazilian food preparation expectations, however, lead to an intriguing outcome. Culturally, the expectation is that food should be bought and cooked from fresh ingredients on a daily basis. There is a stigma associated with using leftovers, which relates to the importance in Brazilian culture of a daily fresh meal. This is also associated with norms of cleanliness which consider such food unclean. As a result, refrigerators are often left entirely empty, since leftovers are thrown away, and food is bought on the day.

Box 8.1 Some useful practice concepts

A number of concepts are useful to explain how norms, things and socio-technical systems impact on what people do:

- **Lock in:** used to explain how people's practices are constrained by the technologies they use, by their expectations, or by their circumstances. The temperature of a home could be seen to be locked in by a combination of bodily needs (Wallenborn and Wilhite, 2014), cultural expectations, and building standards (Shove, 2003).
- **Choice sets:** refers to how people's decisions are limited by their resources, and the norms and structures that they inhabit (Levett et al., 2003). For instance, suburban neighbourhoods are frequently designed for car use, making it difficult to walk or cycle.

To engage in the language of the three elements here, we can see that in Brazil there is a strong set of meanings associated with producing a 'good' meal (ingredients for which must be freshly bought and made) which results in a rather wasteful use of materials, including objects (the fridge) and the electricity needed to power it. Another strong cultural meaning is that associated with the transition from working to middle class: the need to own and run the 'signifiers' of middle -class life (electrical appliances). The competences that households hold in relation to food preparation are mismatched with the materials that households own, as a result of a transition to the middle classes. This is perhaps an example of a practice in transition: where the seemingly illogical ownership of a material can be explained by the conflict between two different sets of meanings, and the associated competences. In the process, a substantial amount of resources (the fridge and the electricity) are being used rather wastefully.

So how might we anticipate change in this context? How do we reduce this kind of waste? Unlike some of the more linear explanations of change, practice explanations do not attempt to predict change. Having said that, they *do* allow us to imagine a range of potential futures, and then think of ways in which these might be encouraged. For instance, in the Brazilian case, we could attempt to change the meaning of appliance ownership, or leftover food. More on this below, under 'translating theory to policy'.

To finish off here, we need to point out the radically different position of the individual in this way of understanding the world. When we discuss sustainable consumption using Shove and colleagues' three elements (2012), for instance, there is very limited time spent on thinking about the individual involved in engaging in practices. This is in stark contrast to psychological or economic approaches, where efforts focus entirely on explaining how the individual behaves; in this approach, the individual can disappear from view entirely. This can be quite disconcerting. Shove characterises practices as existing almost independently of people: practices have their own trajectories, they recruit 'practitioners', indeed they almost as have agency in themselves (Shove, 2010b). Other writers in this field are more likely to see the individual as the 'intersection' of practices (Warde, 2005).

Taking a practice approach to sustainable consumption

In this section, I will profile a number of interesting studies that engage with ideas of sustainable consumption through a practice lens. This section is by no means exhaustive: there are lots of examples of interesting research projects that have used practice approaches to this topic. Here, I would like to give you a flavour of the range of understandings that come from scholars experimenting with these ideas through their empirical work. Note that this is my summary of each of these people's work, and you can follow up each one in detail in the referenced paper.

What counts as clean in Melbourne?

Tullia Jack has used novel methods in her work to explore what people think of being clean, and how far people are prepared to experiment with being dirty (Jack, 2013). Jack asked a diverse group of volunteers from Melbourne, Australia to wear a pair of jeans most days for three months without washing them. After they committed to the experiment, they joined a Facebook group to discuss their experiences, and she also interviewed them at the end of the three months.

This seemed at the outset to be a very challenging assignment, and the people that signed up felt rather apprehensive. People did not find it very difficult once they stopped washing their jeans, however, and almost all of the participants stuck to the brief. Indeed, people began to develop new practices of cleanliness, such as turning their jeans inside out every night to air them. Jack found that 'the expectation of not washing was more repulsive than the actuality, hinting that there may be a perception barrier to changing practices' (ibid., 412).

This work is particularly interesting because it suggests that it is possible to challenge the conventions that structure our everyday lives: the expectations of cleanliness, the habit of washing clothing when only slightly dirty, the need for 'clean' smelling clothes. It seems that habitual practices are not beyond influence, and the awareness and reflection created by Jack's intervention among her respondents led to an acceptance of a rather radical life change.

Changing meanings of cycling in Bangalore

Taking a practice approach, Manisha Anantharaman's (2016) study of cycling in Bangalore, India is another fruitful application of this way of thinking. Anantharaman shows how an emerging trend among middle-class residents to cycle in the city is shifting the meaning of the practice of cycling. In India, the car is a powerful symbol of middle-class respectability, and being able to afford a car is therefore a mark of status. Cyclists, on the other hand, tend to come from poorer demographics, and cycle because they have no alternative.

Changing the meaning of the practice of cycling involves turning it into something that is acceptable for middle-class professionals to engage in. This involves having expensive equipment: western bikes, clothing and accessories, to make clear that, while you are engaging in the practice of cycling, you are not in the same category as a 'livelihood cyclist'. Anantharaman calls these 'defensive distinctions', ways in which people set themselves apart in order to legitimise previously unacceptable practices, and to distinguish themselves from other practitioners (the poor). This is nicely captured by a quote from one of her respondents:

It helps that these bicycles are expensive . . . people can think of them as an upgrade and not as beneath them . . . there are some people who are buying their first bicycle now, instead of their first car but they will do that only if it is expensive and if people around them know that they can buy a car if they want to (Nikhil, 29).

(Ibid., 9)

One of the ways in which this kind of practice becomes legitimate is by its practitioners making claims to be motivated environmentally to ride a bike. Anantharaman sees this as a justification which allows them to change the meaning of the practice to a virtuous environmental act, rather than the necessity for someone who cannot afford a car.

In making such a defensive distinction between middle-class and livelihood cyclists, and in promoting the new meanings associated with environmentalism, Anantharaman points out that this new practice of cycling is problematic, given that it is 'othering' the poor (or setting the poor apart as different):

This othering is especially problematic in a political context where the government is highly receptive to the needs of middle-class communities, but has a record of marginalizing the urban poor. Furthermore, it deepens the stigma associated with poor cycling identities.

(Ibid., 15)

Anantharaman's study is one of the few pieces of work in this area that addresses power and inequality, something that tends to be lacking in this body of work.

Understanding practices at a nation scale (UK)

Perhaps given the starting point of this body of work, in Shove's detailed and historical account of a number of inconspicuous consumption practices, much of the later work done in this area also draws on either historical or qualitative data. Ali Browne and colleagues' extensive quantitative study of water using practices in the UK is a notable and interesting exception (Browne et al., 2015). Drawing on an extensive survey with southern English water users (n=1802), they use the data to understand what clusters of bathing practices exist within the population. This is a deliberate tactic to avoid creating an 'averaged consumer' or even types of water-using consumer, both common strategies in the water industry and in social psychological research.

Some interesting and important findings emerge. First, they assumed in designing their survey that most people would shower once a day at most, but they found that a sizeable proportion of their respondents showered more than seven times a week (28 per cent). This is has a high environmental impact, and suggests that we may be underestimating the amount of body cleaning going on. Some of the practice clusters that the authors identified are also very revealing. For instance, there were two clusters of practices that involved low-frequency showering, shown below:

Two findings here are particularly interesting: first, that these low-frequency groups are mostly made up of people over 45, thus it is possible that these are

Table 8.1 Low-frequency clusters of practice (adapted from Browne et al., 2015)

Practice cluster	% of sample	Frequency	Demographic of practitioners
Low-frequency showering	12%	about 4 times a week	typically older people (mostly over 45)
Low-frequency bathing	7%	about 4 times a week	typically older people

both minority and dying practices. Second, that these low-frequency practices were most commonly engaged in by people who were not particularly interested in environmental issues. These people were not abstaining for environmental reasons (ibid.).

Practice and change

Those taking a practice approach have only relatively recently engaged with questions of deliberate change – questions of how society might be changed to reduce the negative environmental and social impacts of some forms of consumption. This area of study is all about change, as understood over time, and in relation to changing infrastructures, norms and practices. It is sometimes difficult to see where agency can be exercised, however. While this work does offer a fascinating story of how and why practice changes, it begs the question 'how one might intervene in this process?' Even among its chief proponents there is some doubt as to whether it is either possible or useful to attempt to steer practices in particular directions (Shove and Walker, 2010; Evans et al., 2012). There is, however, a recognition that if we start with a practice approach, we see the problem of sustainable consumption very differently, and as a result we come up with different kinds of solution (Shove, 2011). This raises the possibility of using practice approaches to offer new perspectives on interventions (Strengers et al., 2015).

Despite the challenges in turning evidence on practice into specific policy outcomes, the intentions of these authors, as expressed by Shove, are radical. As she puts it, in the context of environmental problems:

> relevant societal innovation is that in which contemporary rules of the game are eroded; in which the status quo is called into question; and in which more sustainable regimes of technologies, routines, forms of know-how, conventions, markets and expectations take hold across all domains of daily life.
> (Shove, 2010a, 1278)

In other words, when we look at problems holistically, as we must through a practice lens, and understand action as only a symptom of what lies underneath, any change we anticipate must be transformative. Change also must be programmatic, or systematic: it must address multiple practices at once, and attempt to understand how the elements of practices can be simultaneously targeted by multiple policies (Evans et al., 2012). While this appeals strongly to me as someone who has worked on environmental issues for a long time (and seen relatively little progress in addressing these), it is also a rather difficult sell politically. Practice scholars know this, and they recognise that even producing evidence on how practices evolve is contentious for people in power. Part of the challenge for a practice approach is that it seems radical in the context of the status quo: 'policy makers fund and legitimise lines of enquiry which generate results which they can handle and which are consequently defined as "concrete, achievable and manageable"' (Shove, 2010a, 1281).

One of the clear contributions of this approach to thinking about reducing the impacts of consumption, is to emphasise the importance of context, whether social, material, infrastructural, or cultural, on the shaping of people's daily lives. At its most basic, this involves looking to the 'system of provision' in a specific context: the geography (for e.g. urban sprawl, topography), infrastructure (for e.g. availability of public transport or bike networks, piped gas and water), and materials (e.g. access to a car, widespread presence of showering technology) available to a group of inhabitants (Vliet et al., 2005). Again in rather basic terms, it is possible to say that people can only live the lives that their systems of provision allow, and that 'grey' systems will not produce 'green' consumers (Spaargaren, 2000). In relatively early work in this vein, Gert Spaargaren claimed that 'When there is a high level – both in quantitative and qualitative respects – of green provisioning, people are more or less brought into a position in which the greening of their corresponding lifestyle segment becomes a feasible option' (2003, 690).

While greening systems of provision does not inevitably result in greener practices, material and infrastructural contexts have a substantial effect on shaping the way people live their lives. A context such as suburbia, for instance, affects how people move around: very often suburban neighbourhoods are designed for car users, not walkers or cyclists, and situated a substantial distance away from amenities and workplaces. The level of cycle infrastructure provision in some northern European countries, such as the Netherlands or Denmark, is tied to extremely high levels of cycling rates. In my home county of West Yorkshire in the UK, a project called 'Warm Zone' in Kirklees aimed to insulate lofts and cavity walls of all houses in the metropolitan area between 2007 and 2010 (irrespective of income); this resulted in over 51,000 households having some form of treatment, reducing carbon emissions of the city region by an estimated 39,000 tonnes of CO_2 per year (Kirklees Council, 2010).

Evidently this type of infrastructural initiative can have transformative impacts. However, those working in this area advocate a more subtle and holistic approach. At the heart of this way of thinking is a truly co-evolutionary vision of how the world works, which would argue that systems of provision amount to more than just 'context'; indeed, we have seen above that context is not separate from practices but is an integrated part of it (Shove, 2010a). One way of achieving a more holistic approach is to focus on the everyday practice as a central management object, as opposed to the resources that are used by practices. Yolande Strengers (2011) calls this 'co-management of every day practices' and points out that the value of seeing the world through a practice lens is that you understand how everything is intimately connected, rather than attempting to deal with problems that are separated out into silos of production or consumption, behaviour or infrastructure. Strengers points out that:

> In focusing on either empowering consumers to reduce their demand or designing more efficient supply systems and household technologies, demand managers reinforce this production–consumption divide and overlook the reasons why people use resources, how these 'needs' and 'wants' are constituted and how they are changing within the broader context of everyday life, where day-to-day practices, such as bathing, cooking, laundering and house cleaning, take place.
>
> (Strengers, 2011, 36)

Bringing practice thinking to bear in attempting to instigate change is therefore an opportunity to leave behind our tendency to think in binary ways – individual or society, behaviour or attitude, and so on. Production-consumption relations are revisited in Chapter 10.

Nicola Spurling and colleagues use the insights from practice approaches to frame the problem of change differently: instead of thinking merely about changing behaviour or changing infrastructure, practice approaches suggest we should focus on re-crafting, or substituting practices, or changing how they interlock (Spurling et al., 2013). Drawing on Shove and colleagues' (2012) concepts of materials, competences and meanings, they characterise these three forms of change:

- *Re-crafting practices*: this involves reducing the resource-intensity of practices by changing one or more of their elements (meanings, competences, or materials). An intervention in this context could include a university canteen committing to 'meatless Monday' (change in material), marketing this to students as an environmental intervention (meanings), and training its chefs to produce high-quality vegetarian food (competences).
- *Substituting practices*: this involves replacing less sustainable practices with more sustainable alternatives. This might include interventions that promote modal change in mobility practices: from driving to walking or cycling.
- *Changing how they interlock*: this involves harnessing the complex interactions between practices so that change ripples through a series of interconnected practices. For instance, an intervention could look at designing neighbourhoods for working, living and playing in, and thus reducing the need to travel further afield (Spurling et al., 2013).

Spurling and colleagues advocate a holistic understanding of how change can come about, which starts from a belief that practices consist of this relationship of meanings, competences and materials, and as a result it is impossible to change one element without the others being affected. This approach is holistic in the sense that it does not imagine that a complex world, and its resulting unsustainable effects, can be changed merely by changing the way people think, or by changing the incentive structures around specific actions (see Chapter 13 for more on systemic change). While this is instinctively attractive, it can also be rather unsettling, because it is likely to require more substantial commitment, something which is not always present in political responses to environmental issues. Having said that, in a further application of this thinking, Spurling and McMeekin (2015) note that recent policy on sustainable mobility focus on recrafting or substituting practices, less radical framings. For instance, they document that these two framings in operation in England do not question the need to reduce demand for mobility.

So Spurling and colleagues give us an idea about what kinds of change we could imagine through a practice lens. Melanie Jaeger-Erben and colleagues (2015) help us think about the processes through which these kinds of change might come about. These authors combine insights from transitions thinking (see Chapter 13) with practice theory to anticipate how change might come about. Jaeger-Erben and colleagues imagine that change will result from social innovations, which eventually become established as more widespread practices. The process of change would involve (in my words):

1   Identifying established practices for which conventional solutions no longer address everyday challenges and problems;
2   Finding alternative practices or practice elements, and experimenting with implementing these, and
3   Finding ways of stabilising alternative practices, and ensuring that they both persist and spread beyond their initial context.

This seems rather abstract, but you can imagine that each of these steps would require very different forms of support, and likely more consistent forms of support, than, for instance, the introduction of a tax or incentive. Policy makers might be required to provide experimental spaces in order to encourage innovative practices to emerge in place of those that have big environmental impacts. Once these alternatives have emerged, they might need support from the education system (skilling-up) or through subsidies on key materials. In order to ensure adoption more broadly, government could stimulate demand through public institutions. We begin to imagine a world in which change must consist of multiple coordinated interventions, flexible and responsive through time according to how innovations develop.

Coordination, holistic thinking, flexibility, innovation, continuous adjustment are all key words here, and these paint a very different picture of intervention for sustainability, than, for instance, the idea of 'nudge' we covered in Chapter 5. When we take such a holistic approach, we have to conceive of governance holistically, for instance:

•   To recognise that as interventions have an impact, conditions change and require different kinds of interventions (Shove and Walker, 2010);

- To conceive of interventions as continuous and reflexive as a result (Spurling and McMeekin, 2015), and
- To accept that interventions will rely on multiple actors, sometimes across sectors, engaging with a problem to produce workable solutions (Browne, 2015).

This community of thinkers conceives of change happening in incremental ways, with a gradual refinement of a number of interventions which gradually meet sustainability goals. Make no mistake, however, these are radical ideas in a context in which we often see one intervention – a subsidy, a behaviour change initiative, an insulation programme – touted as the solution to all ills. In my view, the practice community is trying to propose a mature and comprehensive response to this massive social issue, in the face of rather conservative governments. As we will see, some of the critiques of a practice approach come from this conservative place: a discomfort with the idea of radical social change, even when this is reached through incremental steps.

Critiques of a practice approach

Given that I started this chapter by calling practice work 'ground-breaking' and am using the adjective 'radical' to describe the policy intentions of these scholars, you will not be surprised to hear that this approach has come under some fire. This has not been helped by the rather combative approach of some members of this community, which is clearly seen in Shove's 'Beyond the ABC' paper, and the responses to this from various academic interest groups (Shove, 2010a,;Whitmarsh et al., 2011; Shove, 2011; Wilson and Chatterton, 2011). In this section, I outline a series of critiques of this body of work, with some discussion as to their validity.

The first critique is that this academic community has tended towards insularity, resisting other disciplines, and any concept of interdisciplinarity. In effect, the claim is that the practice community has established itself in opposition to other academic communities working on sustainable consumption. Those other communities, in turn, claim to be open to a more collaborative approach (Whitmarsh et al., 2011). The challenge here is that the 'practice' community sees its own truths (practices are habitual, and structured by skills, materials and competences) as excluding truths from other disciplines (behaviour is formed by attitudes). Such exclusivity is contested by writers in other disciplines. As psychologists Lorraine Whitmarsh and colleagues put it: 'individuals do have and should have some self-direction of their own behaviour. Asserting this does not require rejection of the evidence that "choices" are constrained and culturally shaped, and that behaviour is often not the outcome of conscious deliberation' (ibid., 259). Those who value interdisciplinarity argue that these different ways of thinking complement each other in asking and answering different questions about the topic of sustainable consumption (Wilson and Chatterton, 2011).

This first critique forces us to think about the value of interdisciplinarity. Shove (2011), for instance, argues that the various disciplines concerned with sustainable consumption operate within paradigms (or ways of thinking) that are incompatible. These paradigms structure the research agendas of a discipline, the methods it uses and the meaning of any results it produces. If paradigms are incompatible, calling for interdisciplinarity is problematic, as it fails to recognise these tensions between the disciplines. For instance, Shove finds that 'interdisciplinary' talks frequently turn out to be discussions within the psychological paradigm. As she puts it: 'On closer inspection, many calls for interdisciplinarity turn out to be calls for different sorts of experts to contribute to questions that are already defined and framed in a certain way' (ibid., 262).

Calls for interdisciplinarity assume that there is just one problem, and that the different disciplines can add to the understanding of that problem by creating a new layer of knowledge (ibid.). Shove would argue strongly against this: if we define the problem differently who is to say it is the same kind of problem?

A second (linked) criticism comes from a more pragmatic perspective, which suggests that work on practice provides rich depictions of daily life, in historical context, but that such work only has limited value in addressing present-day (and future) problems (Maller and Strengers, 2015). To some extent, this amounts to a reaction against the mainly qualitative and historical nature of the evidence mobilised by this community, which is not the kind of evidence that environmental policy-makers are used to engaging with (Shove, 2010a). One of the big challenges for this academic community is that a practice approach also requires engaging with a new way of seeing the world, and a new way of understanding change. In engaging with policy-makers through practice language and ideas, Strengers and colleagues recognised that practice thinking is transformational, and this provides a challenge to policy makers (Strengers et al., 2015). In many ways, this links to the first critique: policy-makers are used to the language of economics, and to some extent to that of psychology, but not to these sociological terms. Policy-makers are often wanting to construct standard, replicable programmes, which is the sort of 'solution' they are more likely to find in psychology or economics (Maller and Strengers, 2015). Further, the kind of holistic change often recommended by practice scholars sounds expensive, and institutionally challenging.

A third critique comes out of the intense focus on practice itself, which some argue is to the detriment of an understanding of the role that people play in leading their own lives (the role of agency). Given that this school of thought has avoided explanations based on choice or attitudes, it can seem that people, their interests and experiences, even their belonging in bigger categories of gender, age or ethnicity, are excluded from explanations of change in favour of more material explanations. Certainly the agency of human beings is rather underplayed here, which is problematic. As sociologist Andrew Sayer points out: we cannot ignore human agency:

Whatever the limitations of the more cognitivist approaches to behaviour change, such as the ABC model, they at least (a) acknowledge people as capable of reasoning and judgement, and (b) imply a respect for their right to decide how to respond as they see fit.

(Sayer, 2013, 170)

Sayer's second point here is also important, and also raised by Whitmarsh and colleagues who point out that it would be foolhardy to ignore individuals to the extent that they 'are excluded from societal decision making and participation in enacting change' (Whitmarsh et al., 2011, 259). If we see the world principally as a series of practices, which happen to be enacted by practice carriers, the latter become rather unimportant in thinking about interventions. There is a risk of practice theory being used to back up intrusive state intervention, which pays little heed to the specific individuals on the receiving end. In a worst-case scenario:

It can allow social scientists to present policy makers with instrumentally-useful knowledge for manipulating practices so as to achieve external policy goals, whatever they may be (green or otherwise) over the head of those involved in the practices.

(Sayer, 2013, 172)

There are echoes of the critique of nudge approaches here, profiled in Chapter 5. In effect, neglecting agency (in either nudge or practice) is a way of neglecting the power (or indeed powerlessness) of individuals. If we think mainly of practices and practice 'carriers', we are likely to miss the distinctions between practice carriers that might allow them to engage in a practice or not. Agency can also be exercised collectively, by governments or corporations, for instance, and this way of explaining change, through 'coevolution' of practices, is rather silent on the possibility of power being used or abused by vested interests (Welch and Warde, 2015). Welch and Warde argue that collective agency needs to be a focus in future work (ibid.).

Conclusion

The body of research on practice has been a radical and exciting development in the study of sustainable consumption, which has provided a thought-provoking alternative to the more established individualistic approaches. After the detailed work in the early days about practices in particular contexts and over time, a new interest in change has emerged as the academic community tried to find ways of engaging with the world of policy. For me, reading *Comfort, Cleanliness and Convenience* in 2004 was a transformative experience, and one which made it impossible to make the same (rather lazy) assumptions about consumption.

Consumption is not merely about individuals; it is often habitual, it also relies on infrastructure and materials being in existence and available, and as a result it is sometimes irrelevant to talk about attitudes and choices in the context of sustainability. The debate that practice scholars have stimulated about interdisciplinarity also has some important lessons. We should not assume that this is a 'good' thing, that adding a new discipline merely increases knowledge. Shove's combative stance on this topic, albeit rather too dismissive of other disciplines for my liking, is a healthy dose of rigour in a context which has a tendency to make interdisciplinarity look easy. If we are going to engage in mixing disciplines, we must understand the inherent contradictions between them. I will return to this theme in my conclusions in Chapter 14.

References

ANANTHARAMAN, M. 2016. Elite and ethical: The defensive distinctions of middle-class bicycling in Bangalore, India. *Journal of Consumer Culture*, 17, 864–886.

BARBOSA, L. & VELOSO, L. 2014. Consumption, domestic life and sustainability in Brazil. *Journal of Cleaner Production*, 63, 166–172.

BROWNE, A. L. 2015. Insights from the everyday: Implications of reframing the governance of water supply and demand from 'people' to 'practice'. *Wiley Interdisciplinary Reviews: Water*, 2, 415–424.

BROWNE, A., MEDD, W., ANDERSON, B. & PULLINGER, M. 2015. Method as intervention: intervening in practise through quantitative and mixed methodologies. In: STRENGERS, Y. & MALLER, C. (eds) *Social Practices, Intervention and Sustainability: Beyond Behaviour Change*. Abingdon, UK: Routledge.

EVANS, D., MCMEEKIN, A. & SOUTHERTON, D. 2012. Sustainable consumption, behaviour change policies and theories of practice. In: WARDE, A. & SOUTHERTON, D. (eds) *The Habits of Consumption*. COLLeGIUM: Studies across Disciplines in the Humanities and Social Sciences. Helsinki: Open Access Book Series of the Helsinki Collegium of Advanced Studies, 113–129.

GEELS, F. W., MCMEEKIN, A., MYLAN, J. & SOUTHERTON, D. 2015. A critical appraisal of Sustainable Consumption and Production research: The reformist, revolutionary and reconfiguration positions. *Global Environmental Change*, 34, 1–12.

JACK, T. 2013. Nobody was dirty: Intervening in inconspicuous consumption of laundry routines. *Journal of Consumer Culture*, 13, 406–421.

JAEGER-ERBEN, M., RÜCKERT-JOHN, J. & SCHÄFER, M. 2015. Sustainable consumption through social innovation: A typology of innovations for sustainable consumption practices. *Journal of Cleaner Production*, 108, 784–798.

KENNEDY, E. H., COHEN, M. J. & KROGMAN, N. 2015. Social practice theories and research into sustainable consumption. In: KENNEDY, E. H., COHEN, M. J. & KROGMAN, N. (eds) *Putting Sustainability into Practice: Applications and Advances in Research on Sustainable Consumption*. Cheltenham, UK: Edward Elgar.

KIRKLEES COUNCIL. 2010. *Kirklees Warm Zone – Case Study* [Online]. Available: www.carbondescent.org.uk/case-studies/kirklees-warm-zone-final-report [Accessed 29 March 2018].

LEVETT, R., CHRISTIE, I., JACOBS, M. & THERIVEL, R. 2003. *A Better Choice of Choice: Quality of Life, Consumption and Economic Growth*. London: Fabian Society.

MALLER, C. & STRENGERS, Y. 2015. Transforming practice interventions. In: STRENGERS, Y. & MALLER, C. (eds) *Social Practices, Intervention and Sustainability: Beyond Behaviour Change*. Abingdon, UK: Routledge.

SAYER, A. 2013. Power, sustainability and wellbeing. *In:* SHOVE, E. & SPURLING, N. (eds) *Sustainable Practices: Social Theory and Climate Change.* Abingdon, UK: Routledge.

SHOVE, E. 2003. *Comfort, Cleanliness and Convenience: The Social Organization of Normality.* Oxford, UK: Berg Publishers.

SHOVE, E. 2010a. Beyond the ABC: Climate change policy and theories of social change. *Environment and Planning A,* 42, 1273–1285.

SHOVE, E. 2010b. Social theory and climate change: Questions often, sometimes and not yet asked. *Theory, Culture and Society,* 27, 277–288.

SHOVE, E. 2011. On the difference between chalk and cheese? A response to Whitmarsh et al.'s comments on 'Beyond the ABC: climate change policy and theories of social change'. *Environment and Planning A,* 43, 262–264.

SHOVE, E. & WALKER, G. 2010. Governing transitions in the sustainability of everyday life. *Research Policy,* 39, 471–476.

SHOVE, E., PANTZAR, M. & WATSON, M. 2012. *The Dynamics of Social Practice: Everyday Life and How It Changes.* Thousand Oaks, CA: Sage Publications.

SOUTHERTON, D., VAN VLIET, B. & CHAPPELLS, H. 2004. Introduction: Consumption, infrastructures and environmental sustainability. *In:* SOUTHERTON, D., CHAPPELLS, H. & VAN VLIET, B. (eds) *Sustainable Consumption: The Implications of Changing Infrastructures of Provision.* Cheltenham, UK: Edward Elgar.

SPAARGAREN, G. 2000. Lifestyles, consumption and the environment: The ecological modernisation of domestic consumption. *In:* MOL, A. P. J. & SONNENFELD, D. A. (eds) *Ecological Modernisation Around the World: Perspectives and Critical Debates.* London: Frank Cass.

SPAARGAREN, G. 2003. Sustainable consumption: A theoretical and environmental policy perspective. *Society & Natural Resources,* 16, 687–701.

SPURLING, N. & MCMEEKIN, A. 2015. Interventions in practices: Sustainable mobility policies in England. *In:* STRENGERS, Y. & MALLER, C. (eds) *Social Practices, Interventions and Sustainability.* Abingdon, UK: Routledge.

SPURLING, N., MCMEEKIN, A., SHOVE, E., SOUTHERTON, D. & WELCH, D. 2013. *Interventions in Practice: Re-Framing Policy Approaches to Consumer Behaviour* [Online]. Sustainable Practices Research Group. Available: www.sprg.ac.uk/projects-fellowships/theoretical-development-and-integration/interventions-in-practice---sprg-report [Accessed 18 December 2017].

STRENGERS, Y. 2011. Beyond demand management: Co-managing energy and water practices with Australian households. *Policy Studies,* 32, 35–58.

STRENGERS, Y., MOLONEY, S., MALLER, C. & HORNE, R. 2015. Beyond behaviour change: Practical applications of social practice theory in behaviour change programmes. *In:* STRENGERS, Y. & MALLER, C. (eds) *Social Practices, Intervention and Sustainability: Beyond Behaviour Change.* Abingdon, UK: Routledge.

VLIET, B. V., CHAPPELLS, H. & SHOVE, E. 2005. *Infrastructures of Consumption: Environmental Innovation in the Utility Industries.* London: Earthscan.

WALLENBORN, G. & WILHITE, H. 2014. Rethinking embodied knowledge and household consumption. *Energy Research & Social Science,* 1, 56–64.

WARDE, A. 2005. Consumption and theories of practice. *Journal of Consumer Culture,* 5, 131–153.

WELCH, D. & WARDE, A. 2015. Theories of practice and sustainable consumption. *In:* REISCH, L. & THØGERSEN, J. (eds) *Handbook of Research on Sustainable Consumption.* Cheltenham, UK: Edward Elgar.

WHITMARSH, L., O'NEILL, S. & LORENZONI, I. 2011. Climate change or social change? Debate within, amongst, and beyond disciplines. *Environment and Planning A*, 43, 258–261.

WILSON, C. & CHATTERTON, T. 2011. Multiple models to inform climate change policy: A pragmatic response to the 'beyond the ABC' debate. *Environment and Planning A*, 43, 2781–2787.

9 'Consumption is meaningful!'

In the final chapter of this section, we tackle a story which environmentalists tend to ignore, or find difficult to incorporate in their thinking about sustainable consumption. This story understands consumption as valuable, significant and socially meaningful. Consumption is an important part of our daily lives, and is one of the key ways in which we create meaning and significance, particularly with regards to our relationships with other people. When we understand consumption as a meaningful, social act, the various ambitions of environmentalism (including reducing consumption and changing consumption) become highly challenging. How do we do 'less consumption' if each act has social and personal significance?

The key contributors here come from a culturalist perspective, rooted in the discipline of anthropology. These ideas are also widespread in society: this is not surprising given the ways in which this perspective is evidenced. Anthropology is itself an approach to understanding the world which aims for deep accounts of how and why people act as they do, understood through the daily lives of ordinary people. Much of the research we will talk about in this chapter is based on ethnographic methods, that is, where the researcher embeds him or herself with a group of people in order to understand what their lifeworld entails. Given this ethnographic approach, in particular the importance placed on understanding everyday life, we also find that much of this work is trying to understand 'why do people consume in the way they do?', rather than to look at how what people do might be changed through policy or other initiatives. This contrasts very strongly with some of the disciplines we have already seen (especially psychology and economics).

Intriguingly, alongside those that build their research on bottom-up, in-depth understandings of everyday life, some much more abstract thinkers also advocate this point of view. Social theoreticians based in sociology and anthropology have noticed a shift from an agrarian, to a producer and finally a consumer society, and commented on how this changes what consumption means in people's everyday lives (Cohen, 2016). It is important to note at this point that both culturalist research and social theory have a limited history of engagement with sustainable consumption questions. This means that this is a rather new area of enquiry in relation to sustainable consumption. Many writers in this field use the term 'ethical consumption' as opposed to 'sustainable consumption' – I will alternate between these as appropriate in the chapter.

As in the other chapters based around a story, the idea that 'consumption is meaningful' is a (deliberately) over-simplistic representation of this field, and, as we will see, many writers in this area are quick to go beyond this statement. It is also not indicative of the starting point of all anthropologists studying sustainable consumption, as we will see. Having said that, it is a powerful and influential idea, and one which writers on environment tend to feel uncomfortable with, hence my inclusion of it here. In the rest of the chapter, I will consider a range of inputs from empirical and theoretical work, which at least accounts for the meaningfulness of consumption. I will also address what we should do with these insights, to help you understand how the idea that 'consumption is meaningful' impacts on what we know about sustainable consumption, and what we can do about it.

A consumer society

The idea that consumption has meaning is connected to a bigger story about the kind of societies that people inhabit. Authors on this topic would argue that a late capitalist society is frequently one which revolves around consumption: a consumer society (Campbell, 1995; Bauman, 2007; Miller, 2012; Cohen, 2016). This is in contrast to societies which revolve around agriculture or industry. Daniel Miller defines a consumer society: 'By "consumer society", I mean one in which commodities are increasingly used to express the core values of that society but also become the principal form through which people come to see, recognise and understand those values' (Miller, 2012, 40).

Whereas in agrarian society your 'core values', as Miller puts it, might be your connection to the land, and in an industrial society to the things that you produce, in a consumer society the things you buy and own become more important to your identity, and to your relationships with other people. This also suggests that a host of other identifiers become less important:

> such basic definers as gender, race, nationality, ethnicity and religion . . . do no more than 'frame' the parameters of who we consider ourselves to be . . . the person we really consider ourselves to be, the 'real me' if you like, is to be found in our special mix or combination of tastes.
>
> (Campbell, 2004, 31)

In other words, in a consumer society, we are what we choose. Consumption, in this vision, is absolutely central to our identity.

Miller gives an example from his ethnographic fieldwork in the 1980s in Trinidad, which he categorised as a consumer society, due to its reliance only on oil as an export product. He found that asking what people 'do' in Trinidad, in other words asking what their work is, is considered offensive, because it suggests that their identity associated with work life is more important than their leisure identity (Miller, 2012). To put this in context, at the time of the study, Trinidad had recently transitioned to a consumer society, and as such, people were more sensitive to these kinds of identity issues. In other places, a consumer society is seen in an increasing emphasis on what we have, instead of what we do.

Box 9.1 Environment in a consumer society: the case of Singapore

Chris Hudson's work in Singapore is a particularly insightful example of how a consumer society might interpret environment (Hudson, 2014). She shows how Singapore has been using its environment as a means of differentiation, a selling point, in order to position itself as a tourism destination with a difference. After slum clearances in the 1960s, the then Prime Minister Lee Kwan Yew spearheaded tree planting all over the island, and the creation of a 'garden city' which has in more recent years extended to green corridors along roads, greenery around shopping malls and nature-based tourist attractions, such as Gardens by the Bay, albeit focused in the wealthier neighbourhoods (ibid.). Singapore is also a city with a strong consumer culture; indeed, it is a good example of a consumer society. Hudson sees the environment being used in two ways in this consumer society: first, as a means of expressing symbolic values (sustainability, eco-friendliness); though note that these are only symbolic, because much of the country's economy depends on consumption in abundance. Second, the environment is seen as an opportunity to consume nature, which offers 'aesthetic gratification . . . sheer delight, and sensual pleasure' (ibid., 88). Clearly the vision of sustainability or eco-friendliness here is a long way from one which might actually have an impact on the problem we defined in Chapter 2.

There is some resistance to the idea of a consumer society. You may have a negative reaction to this idea yourself. Am I really just the sum of my consumption choices? Is my identity merely a matter of taste? This is often unpalatable for environmentalists, who (in principle at least) would resist defining themselves in relation to their consumption choices. Environmentalists (and others) are quick to denigrate the ideas of consumption, consumerism and the consumer society. Critics are likely to talk about consumerism and the consumer society as frivolous, hedonistic and meaningless (Campbell, 2006; Humphery, 2010). Campbell (2006) calls this critique puritanical (after a form of Protestant Christianity), where it is acceptable to meet basic needs, but where luxury is unnecessary and wrong. Puritans would place more value on work than leisure, and see leisure as trivial, and likely connected to sins such as greed, pride and envy. I will come back to puritanism and the environmental movement below (Littler, 2009).

The idea that 'consumption is meaningful', and the very existence of a consumer society, have important implications for thinking about sustainable consumption. If consumption is so tied up with identity, then we need to tread carefully when thinking about changing things. This is only a starting point for the 'consumption is meaningful' perspective, however, and as we will see, in this story, the meaning and value placed on daily acts of consumption are also very important.

Making ourselves and our relationships

Some of the common assumptions we hold about what consumption is for, and why people consume, are taken to task by the story that 'consumption is meaningful'. As I have pointed out, this approach is critical of our tendency to paint acts of consumption, and acts of shopping, as frivolous, hedonistic and individualistic. The starting point here is that consumption has a highly social nature, that consuming 'stuff' is about communicating to other people, rather than about owning 'stuff' for a more practical reason: 'Material culture tends to be symbolic before it is functional . . . One of our links to that aura of authentic society is that we remain interested in totally useless stuff, because useless stuff generally has a social and symbolic role' (Miller, 2012, 18).

In other words, in a consumer society, we do not consume to survive in a functional sense; we consume because we need to maintain social relations, to negotiate our space within the social world. Note that the word 'symbolic' also implies communication: that we use consumption as a means of communicating our identity to our peers.

The symbolic and social roles of consumption are also clearly identified by Mary Douglas, a key voice in the anthropology of consumption. She describes the process and purpose of consumption as a means of presenting (symbolic) and sharing (social) goods:

> An individual's main objective in consumption is to help to create the social universe and find in it a creditable place. To achieve his main objective he needs to mobilize marking services from other consumers. Successful consumption requires a deployment of goods in consumption rituals that will mobilize the maximum marking services from other consumers.
>
> (Douglas, 2006, 243)

For clarity, in Douglas's vision, people consume to fit in with their peers, and consider themselves successful when others approve of how they consume. This does not necessarily mean that everyone must consume lots of expensive and flashy stuff to be considered successful, as in some social circles this would be considered bad taste or inappropriate. The bigger point here is that in this story, all consumption is relational, and its meaning is derived from how it helps to construct social relations.

A nice example of this in practice comes from Cindy Isenhour's study of Swedish ethical consumers, when one of her environmentally engaged respondents talks about the challenges of attempting to live a green lifestyle, in particular the challenges of consuming less, in Swedish society:

> Well it's very difficult to live as I would like . . . socially, that's a big problem . . . not having certain things like a mobile phone, it's not accepted. People think you are really weird, (they say) 'why are you doing this?' – they just simply can't understand and find it somehow offensive and a huge inconvenience. Even not having a driver's license . . . it's not a problem for me but it's questioned socially.
>
> (Isenhour, 2010, 465)

While in some social circles (for instance, among environmentalists), not having a mobile phone or a driver's licence might be socially acceptable, this Swedish respondent finds that he is failing to meet more conventional expectations. Isenhour argues that this is compounded by the strong culture of conformity in Sweden, which makes such 'deviant' behaviour even more challenging, and causes stress for those that are bucking the trend (ibid.). In Douglas's terms, this respondent is failing to attract the requisite level of marking services, and as such, is being understood socially as 'failing to consume correctly'.

While symbolic consumption is important, it is not the same as conspicuous consumption – that is, luxury consumption, or consumption of showy goods. Indeed, this strand of research also finds that most consumption is actually associated with fairly basic daily needs. The significance of shopping on a day-to-day basis is in providing food and clothing for the people that we have responsibility for, making sure that everyone has their basic needs met in an adequate and appropriate way (Miller, 2012). Note that Miller would still see such consumption as both symbolic (communicating relationships) and social (constituting relationships). Lodziak (2002) argues that this is a result of macro-economic changes: in the late modern era, most people have less money to spend on frivolous things, given increases in survival costs, and slower increases in incomes. The symbolic and the social in such basic provisioning can be seen, for instance, when the shopper chooses their family members' favourite foods, as a means of gifting to others at the same time as meeting basic needs.

These insights have hugely important implications for thinking about sustainable consumption, and we could build a rather radical argument based on this starting point. For instance, if we adopt the story that 'consumption is meaningful!', it is difficult to say that some consumption is necessary and some consumption is a 'luxury'. Logically if all consumption is relational and has meaning, none can be unnecessary. Indeed, by condemning specific forms of consumption as unnecessary, we might be condemning some forms of social relation that are dependent on that consumption act. Further, the idea of 'reducing consumption' seems nonsensical from this point of view, as it suggests that consumers might have to engage in 'reducing' social relations.

In practice, writers in this field are more measured in their assessment of the possibility for change. Authors also point out how the meaning of consumption is shaped by corporations and governments: in effect, that the social relations inherent in these institutions also impact on the meaning and value of consumption (Isenhour, 2017). Much of the work done by anthropologists on sustainable consumption takes into account the idea that 'consumption is meaningful', but is not entirely driven by it, and is still trying to find room for change. In the following two sections, I take some examples from empirical work which look at understandings of ethical consumption by both 'outsiders' and 'insiders', informed by the idea that consumption is meaningful. In doing so, I also profile how the idea that 'consumption is meaningful' plays out in empirical work.

Outsider meanings of ethical consumption

As I have pointed out, ethnographic methods build a deep understanding of people's everyday lives. Such studies have attempted to understand what being 'ethical' means in the context of shopping for daily life. This has included ethnographic research on the daily lives of those who define themselves as ethical consumers, and those who do not. Here we start by looking at original research and commentary on people who do not identify with the label of 'ethical consumer'. Intriguingly, we find that these people do take ethical considerations when shopping, although these are bound up in complex and broad moral considerations about their daily lives.

There is plenty of evidence to show that people are aware of ethical considerations as we tend to define them (concern for the environment and for distant others) in their shopping practices, but the more useful insight here is to do with the relationship of such ethical considerations to people's broader concerns. Sarah Marie Hall (2011, 2015) argues that all consumption has a moral 'reading', and proposes that we look for ethics in *all* acts of consumption, rather than confining our research to the consumption of a limited number of products or to a set of practices. Miller (2012) makes a distinction between being ethical (thinking of distant others) and being moral (thinking about one's immediate family) when shopping, and finds that the morality of home often wins out. In his ethnographic study of residents of a London street, he shows that people care about the impact of their shopping on distant others and on the environment, although they tend to prioritise moral concerns about their families, including the need to get the most out of their budget (ethical choices are widely seen to be more expensive). Miller uses his finding that morality permeates shopping practice to claim that shopping is about expressing one's love to one's significant others. Hall (2011) is less romantic about people's intentions, but points out that care for either distant or significant others is part of a wider set of drivers including health priorities, affordability and personal preferences.

Around the time of the global financial recession in 2008, there was a commonplace discussion amongst environmentalists that hard times might 'make' environmentalists out of us all, as a result of a need to reduce consumption of goods to make tight budgets go further. The possibility that the recession would result in less (relatively expensive) 'ethical consumption' was also raised (Hall, 2015).

The real picture has been mixed, with some product sales increasing (e.g. Fairtrade food) and others decreasing (e.g. green energy) (ibid.). Of course, different demographics, and indeed people from nations with more or less of a social security net, will be affected differently by a financial crisis. Thinking about recession, and researching the impacts of this on everyday lives, has led to some useful insights on the differences between reducing consumption as a result of poverty, and choosing to consume less because of environmentalist values. At the least, the contribution here is to remind environmental thinkers that the calls for 'voluntary simplicity' (see Chapter 12 for more on this) are problematic in a context where households are struggling to meet their basic needs.

In reflections on work with consumers with environmental concerns, David Evans (2011) points out that there is a critical distinction between frugality and thrift, the former linked to the environmental ethic of 'giving stuff up' and the latter more akin to Miller's 'moral consumption'. In a time of economic hardship, this is particularly important to take account of, in order to understand the meaning of consumption acts. Frugality is a choice, not a result of economic scarcity, and has a deliberate and ethical starting point: 'a moral restraint that is grounded in ascetic critique of consumption, excess and waste' (ibid., 554). Thrift, on the other hand, 'is the art of doing more (consumption) with less (money) and so thrifty practices are practices of savvy consumption' (ibid., 551). These practices are driven by very different meanings, and we must maintain a distinction between poverty-induced and voluntary simplicity practices (Hall, 2015). You can probably see that people who practice thrift and people who practice frugality would have a different response to a policy aimed at reducing consumption, for instance.

These differences between 'ordinary' people and self-defined ethical consumers, are not only about what structures specific acts of consumption, but also what each of these types of people think of each other. Researchers in this area note how 'ordinary' people commonly stereotype environmental life choices as anachronistic, and Jo Littler (2009) notes that rather than being concerned with morality (a 'galvanising moral vision'), environmentalists are widely understood to be moralistic ('reproachful' and 'moralizing'). There is certainly a strong sense that environmentalists are somehow 'other', or different to 'us', in the experiences of people outside of the movement (Miller, 2012). Littler argues that when people dismiss ethical consumption as 'worthy', they are associating it with a religion-like puritanism, and in doing so make it look both ridiculous, and distant from the ideas of pleasure and desire that are dominant in other walks of life. Note that this antipathy can work both ways: for instance, ethical consumers sometimes look down on the thrifty practices of the working classes, associated with purchase of cheap but new goods, as opposed to buying quality goods to make sure they last (Isenhour, 2012).

There are plentiful connections to concepts of identity, distinction, stigma and class in Chapter 3, not least in the idea that goods are a means of signalling one's status to one's peers. Certainly in the discussion of environmentalism, it becomes clear that frugality is a form of middle-class distinction, as opposed to the more working-class thrift. Part of the challenge that is revealed through the 'consumption is meaningful' perspective is that only a relatively small group of people are likely to be happy to subscribe to the common understanding of an environmentalist identity. In doing so, they deliberately position themselves, through their consumption choices, as different (to the mainstream middle classes, and to the working classes) (Horton, 2003). This distinction makes it more difficult for outsiders to be involved in environmentalism. In the next section, we see what researchers looking at meaning have to say about such insider (or ethical consumer) perspectives on ethical consumption.

Insider meanings of ethical consumption

One of Cindy Isenhour's (2012) starting points in her study of ethical consumers in Sweden, is to tackle the question of how ethical consumers maintain their symbolic and social capital while also consuming less (or at least consuming differently). This is an intriguing question – if we think of consumption as intrinsically linked to both material use, and to the creation of the social world, it is hard to understand how meaning continues to be created in an ethical lifestyle, when using less stuff. Isenhour finds that her ethical consumers have different strategies to get round this problem (ibid.). For instance, in the 'retro chic' strategy that she identifies, consumers signal taste and ethics by buying and displaying second-hand, stylish furniture. This allows people both to maintain their status as 'ethical' and to identity as tasteful and stylish people. Alternatively, if consumers adopt a 'beyond the mainstream' strategy, they might have to change their social circle in order to make this work. For instance, if you adopt veganism, it becomes easier to spend your free time with other vegans, who understand what you eat. A full description of the strategies that Isenhour identifies is shown in Box 9.2.

This range of strategies adopted by ethical consumers supports an overarching thesis that ethical consumption has shifted in recent years. The consensus is that ethical consumption has been normalised, that it is no longer a radical or marginal set of practices, but one of a range of lifestyle choices in late capitalism (Lewis and Potter, 2011; Barendregt and Jaffe, 2014). Barendregt and Jaffe's characterisation of this sphere as 'eco-chic' is helpful here, which they summarise as 'a combination of lifestyle politics, environmentalism, spirituality, beauty, and health, combined with a call to return to simple living' (2014, 1). As I hint in my description of Isenhour's Swedish ethical consumer strategies above, this is not simply a case of people becoming more virtuous, but rather a series of social drivers leading people to choose ethically. Barendregt and Jaffe, for instance, connect this trend to a perceived need to slow down, and see ethical consumers as leading socially committed lifestyles, but (in contrast to our insights in Chapter 7) somewhat apolitical ones. The increasing popularity of ethical living among hipsters is a nice example here. Further, ethical consumerism is tightly bound up with class identity:

These practices also represent forms of cultural and moral capital that are central to the creation and maintenance of class distinction. Eco-chic is increasingly a part of the identity kit of the upper classes, offering an attractive way to combine taste and style with care for personal wellness and the environment.

(Barendregt and Jaffe, 2014, 1)

Jo Littler points out the importance of distinguishing between forms of ethical consumption, some of which are much more lifestyle oriented, others more political (as discussed in Chapter 7). Anti-consumerism consists of a political stance against capitalist consumer culture, whereas anti-consumption marks a radical lifestyle orientation: buying and using less stuff (Littler, 2011). A third category, reminiscent of 'weak' sustainable consumption (Lorek and Fuchs, 2013), would merely focus on buying more ethical products (Littler, 2011).

Box 9.2 Four Swedish strategies for ethical consumption

The four strategies for ethical consumption that Isenhour (2012) identifies in her study of Swedish consumers, are interesting because they show the range of practices that people can engage in under a similar banner:

1 **Conspicuous green consumption**: where green products (a hybrid car, solar panels, a hemp-covered sofa, labelled dish soap, kitchen composter) are displayed prominently in the home.
2 **Retro chic**: where consumers look to the past to provide meaning, by refraining from flying, biking where possible, buying stylish second-hand goods.
3 **Prestige posh**: buying high-quality products in the expectation that these will last longer.
4 **Beyond the mainstream**: where consumers consume less. They do not feel the need to display rare or valuable products, although they are likely to own lots of books.

I recognise these strategies from the UK context, and suspect that they have some relevance elsewhere too. Can you see these strategies being used in your local context?

This body of work, then, shows us that ethical consumers make up a broad, and growing, cross-section of people, with varying values, strongly contrasting practices and different ideas about what kind of change is and is not acceptable in their daily lives. This presents further challenges for thinking about sustainable consumption policy. Not only does consumption have meaning, most people do not identify with the identity of an ethical consumer, and those that do have a broad range of backgrounds. Perhaps as a result of this, there has been relatively little focus on what we can do about environmental and social problems associated with unsustainable consumption in this field. The picture sometimes seems so complex, it is difficult to see what the solutions might be.

What do we do with these insights?

Much of the work in this field, then, is concerned with describing how people live, and in doing so revealing the challenges and opportunities of engaging in ethical consumption. Suggestions as to how this knowledge could be used to think about change has not been a focus to date. Perhaps this is partly because thinking about change is difficult in the light of this knowledge of consumption's cultural importance. When we understand that consumption has meaning, that the material world is one of the ways in which relationships are constructed, and that ethical consumption depends on people identifying with a complex range of ideas, this makes it challenging to conceive of how change might happen. For me, this perspective consists of a very broad approach to understanding the problem, based in everyday life (through ethnographic techniques). As a result, it provides a strong contrast to many of the other disciplinary perspectives, which tend to narrow their focus to people's preferences or values, and to move on to thinking about solutions to these narrow problem definitions.

In my opinion, one of the things we must do with this way of thinking is to treat it as a critical friend: to use these insights to see how the solutions proposed by other disciplines are problematic. Insights from daily life force us to be more critical about sustainable consumption. This is nicely captured in an example from Miller on how consumer choice is positioned as a solution to environmental problems: 'housewives, who are generally also in employment, as well as responsible for their families, are already landed with enough responsibilities without being expected to save the planet somewhere between childcare and washing up' (2012, 157).

Note that because Miller begins from the lived experience, he notices both who is affected by calls for consumer choice (women, housewives, and mothers – see also Chapter 3) and how this is likely to be experienced (as an additional responsibility). At the very least then, this perspective mitigates for a more socially coordinated approach to sustainable consumption, rather than an individualised one.

In producing rich and deep understandings of daily life, a 'consumption is meaningful' perspective allows us to argue for policy that does not focus on the individual – policy that is systemic or that addresses multiple levers simultaneously within the production/consumption system (see Chapters 10 and 13). It also would suggest that collective solutions (see Chapter 11) are an appropriate response to the sustainable consumption problem, given the emphasis on consumption as an outcome of social relations. Indeed, an appreciation of the cultural importance of consumption presents a powerful challenge to the individualist perspectives of economics and psychology that I covered in Chapters 5 and 6. This 'consumption is meaningful' perspective teaches us that consumption choices are socially constructed and guided by culturally embedded expectations, and that they are unlikely to be adequately captured by focusing on rational drivers (preferences or values). It also challenges the stronger interpretations of practice approaches seen in Chapter 8, which characterise people as 'practice carriers'. In this cultural perspective, meaning is created through people's relationships with each other and with other social institutions. This makes groups of people both carriers of practices and generators of meaning.

The work of the philosopher Kate Soper on alternative hedonism, which also relates to work on happiness and well-being in Chapter 12, offers one way into thinking about how the idea that 'consumption is meaningful' might translate into action. Soper starts with the perspective that any value produced in the current consumption paradigm must be replaced with an alternative vision (or an alternative meaning):

> the chances of developing or reverting to a more ecologically sustainable use of resources, and hence of removing some of the key sources of social and environmental exploitation, are dependent on the emergence and embrace of new modes of thinking about human pleasure and self-realization, especially, in the first instance, on the part of the affluent global elites.
>
> (Soper, 2008, 571)

There are two key claims here: first, that in order to counter consumerism, we must be able to point to an alternative kind of 'good life' than that which involves owning and buying stuff. Second, Soper believes there are already signs of alternative hedonism emerging. Effectively, Soper is arguing that meaning (particularly meaning that affects human pleasure and self-realisation) can be made in different ways, and if the wealthiest people on the planet take action in helping to craft an alternative vision, this may pave the way for others to engage. Note that there is an assumption here that an alternative hedonistic culture will 'trickle down' to the rest of society.

As a philosopher, Soper is mainly concerned with possibilities for change in a philosophical sense, not the practical means by which this might be achieved. Her idea of alternative hedonism is relevant here because it sees 'consumption as meaningful' as a starting point, from which to think about how meaning might be constructed differently. Soper points to the way in which voluntary simplists look for new meaning in simple living, whether by downshifting their lifestyles, or by simplifying more dramatically, as a sign of alternative hedonism in action. She points out that voluntary simplicity combines self-interested and altruistic motives, which bring together a belief in simplicity being better for one's health, and for one's impact on others and the planet. Soper sees a specific role for the 'disillusioned seduced' here – people who are relatively wealthy, and have already fulfilled their own needs, who are therefore able to rescue the 'repressed' through their action.

In simple terms, alternative hedonism is a hope that if the very rich change what is considered desirable (in effect, change the meaning of consumption) – that is, finding pleasure in less, rather than more, stuff – others will follow. Soper is (perhaps rather optimistically) thinking through how the meaning associated with stuff can be changed, and as a result how different kinds of stuff (by implication, less ethically problematic stuff) might be consumed. This is also the implication of Isenhour's work on the ways in which ethical consumers create meaning (Isenhour, 2012) One of the most hopeful insights from this work is that ethical consumers can find different ways of communicating their identity through stuff. The hope here is that it might be possible for ethical consumers to consume less stuff but still live a socially fulfilling life.

As we have seen in Chapter 3, and in the section on 'insider meanings' above, ethical consumer lifestyles tends to be the domain of cultural elites, who use ethical consumption as a form of distinction. One of the contributions of a 'consumption is meaningful' approach in the future, might be to ask the question: how can ethical consumption become more than a pursuit for cultural elites? In the spirit of Kate Soper's work on re-imagining the good life, scholars with an appreciation of the meaning of consumption are ideally placed to think about alternative green identities, which work for a range of people. Hall and Miller's understandings of daily shopping practices among 'ordinary people', where they find that ethics or morality are already present in many consumption decisions, are a promising start here (Hall, 2011; Miller, 2012; Hall, 2015). Certainly the insights from this field mean that we need to think creatively about how more people can be engaged in this agenda.

Conclusions

This perspective offers a series of important contributions to understanding sustainable consumption based on the starting point that 'consumption is meaningful', and the methods it draws on to understand the world (researching everyday life). Substantively, then, we learn from this perspective that shopping and consumption are meaningful activities, embedded in day-to-day social life, which have both symbolic and social value. People have complex lives with multiple allegiances, but ethnographers find that morality and/or ethics do have a bearing on how people talk about their consumption activities in daily life. This perspective also teaches us that ethical consumers are different to other people, because they make meaning out of the stuff in their lives in different ways. Hope for change here lies in the possibility of the meanings associated with stuff being shifted in ways that reduce the total material use by humankind. This way of thinking also offers the opportunity to think about alternative meanings and identities that could widen the scope of environmentalism.

References

BARENDREGT, B. & JAFFE, R. 2014. The paradoxes of eco-chic. *In:* BARENDREGT, B. & JAFFE, R. (eds) *Green Consumption: The Global Rise of Eco-Chic.* London: Bloomsbury.
BAUMAN, Z. 2007. *Consuming Life.* Cambridge, UK: Polity.

CAMPBELL, C. 1995. The sociology of consumption. *In*: MILLER, D. (ed.) *Acknowledging Consumption: A Review of New Studies*. London: Routledge.

CAMPBELL, C. 2004. I shop therefore I know that I am: The metaphysical basis of modern consumerism. *In*: EKSTRÖM, K. M. & BREMBECK, H. (eds) *Elusive Consumption*. Oxford: Berg.

CAMPBELL, C. 2006. Consuming goods and the goods of consuming. *In*: JACKSON, T. (ed.) *The Earthscan Reader in Sustainable Consumption*. London: Earthscan.

COHEN, M. J. 2016. *The Future of Consumer Society*. Oxford, UK: Oxford University Press.

DOUGLAS, M. 2006. Relative poverty – Relative communication. *In*: JACKSON, T. (ed.) *The Earthscan Reader in Sustainable Consumption*. London: Earthscan.

EVANS, D. 2011. Thrifty, green or frugal: Reflections on sustainable consumption in a changing economic climate. *Geoforum*, 42, 550–557.

HALL, S. M. 2011. Exploring the 'ethical everyday': An ethnography of the ethics of family consumption. *Geoforum*, 42, 627–637.

HALL, S. M. 2015. Everyday ethics of consumption in the austere city. *Geography Compass*, 9, 140–151.

HORTON, D. 2003. Green distinctions: The performance of identity among environmental activists. *The Sociological Review*, 51, 63–77.

HUDSON, C. 2014. Green is the new green: Eco-aesthetics in Singapore. *In*: BARENDREGT, B. & JAFFE, R. (eds) *Green Consumption: The Global Rise of Eco-Chic*. London: Bloomsbury.

HUMPHERY, K. 2010. *Excess: Anti-Consumerism in the West*. Cambridge, UK: Polity.

ISENHOUR, C. 2010. On conflicted Swedish consumers, the effort to stop shopping and neoliberal environmental governance. *Journal of Consumer Behaviour*, 9, 454–469.

ISENHOUR, C. 2012. On the challenges of signaling ethics without the stuff: Tales of conspicuous green anti-consumption. *In*: CARRIER, J. G. & LUETCHFORD, P. G. (eds) *Ethical Consumption: Social Value and Economic Practice*. Oxford, UK: Berghahn Books.

ISENHOUR, C. 2017. When 'gestures of change' demand policy support: Social change and the structural underpinnings of consumer culture in the United States. *In*: COHEN, M., SZEJNWALD BROWN, H. & VERGRAGT, P. (eds) *Social Change and the Coming of Post-Consumer Society*. Oxford, UK: Routledge.

LEWIS, T. & POTTER, E. 2011. Introducing ethical Consumption. *In*: LEWIS, T. & POTTER, E. (eds) *Ethical Consumption: A Critical Introduction*. Abingdon, UK: Routledge.

LITTLER, J. 2009. *Radical Consumption*. Maidenhead, UK: Open University Press.

LITTLER, J. 2011. What's wrong with ethical consumption? *In*: LEWIS, T. & POTTER, E. (eds) *Ethical Consumption: A Critical Introduction*. Abingdon, UK: Routledge.

LODZIAK, C. 2002. *The Myth of Consumerism*. London: Pluto Press.

LOREK, S. & FUCHS, D. 2013. Strong sustainable consumption governance – Precondition for a degrowth path? *Journal of Cleaner Production*, 38, 36–43.

MILLER, D. 2012. *Consumption and Its Consequences*. Cambridge, UK: Polity.

SOPER, K. 2008. Alternative hedonism, cultural theory and the role of aesthetic revisioning. *Cultural Studies*, 22, 567–587.

Part 3

Visions of the future in sustainable consumption

10 Production-consumption relationships

So far we have been talking about sustainable consumption principally from the consumer's point of view, including what the consumer understands (Chapter 4), how the consumer chooses (Chapters 5 and 6), and what is the political, social and cultural context of consumer actions (Chapters 7, 8 and 9). These last three chapters begin to reveal the fact that consumption does not exist within a vacuum, that any consideration of consumption must take into account the many structural elements (politics, society, culture) that help to shape what the consumer does. Here we look at a particular aspect of that structure: the relationship between the consumer and the producer. This is the first chapter in a section that looks towards solutions to sustainable consumption, and how these are characterised.

Many forms of consumption (particularly consumption of products and services) require producers to make or grow something before it can be bought, consumed and disposed of. This might be a business selling a product, a farmer growing food, or an owner providing a service. There are frequently long supply chains between producer and consumer, amounting to a chain of producers and consumers (Lebel and Lorek, 2008). As a product makes its way towards the final consumer, it is produced, transformed, transported and branded, accruing value along the way. Producer-consumer relationships are important: given that the supply chain, or indeed the network of production and consumption, is constituted of these relationships. By focusing on the relationships between producer and consumer: 'we can ask questions from both a production perspective (How could this industrial process be made more resource efficient?) and a consumption perspective (What are the underlying drivers of downstream demands in the network or value chain?)' (Lebel and Lorek, 2008, 266).

In treating consumption and production as two sides of the same problem, we are also likely to find ways of understanding both sustainability problems and solutions in a more systemic way.

The nature of the sustainable consumption problem, as described in Chapter 2, is that in a globalised world it has a tendency to spread geographically, with production-consumption chains often circling the whole globe. These geographical networks also have a tendency to reproduce inequality, to burden the poorest with environmental damage, and to allow the richest the most access to consumption opportunities. As a result, if we attempt to understand these problems as if they were either production or consumption issues, we are likely to miss the bigger picture. So, for instance, we might see deforestation as a by-product of global South production processes (Lehtoranta et al., 2011). However, much deforestation in the global South is caused by a demand for wood (or other) products in the global North, so this is also a consumption problem (ibid.).

This is not to say that consumption on its own is not a valid area of research – of course it is very important to understand how and why people consume. In this chapter, however, I look at the intersection of production and consumption research, profiling weak and strong sustainability approaches to thinking about change in the context of this relationship. You may also wish to read this chapter in conjunction with Chapter 13 ('Revolution or evolution') in which I look at more political approaches to systemic change.

What role for production in sustainable consumption?

As a starting point, we will take Lorek's (2016) list of mechanisms which might enable a more sustainable production-consumption system (see Table 10.1). This list should give you a flavour of the sort of initiatives that producers (and sometimes consumers) can engage in order to reduce the negative environmental and human impacts of consumption. These range from efficiency measures ('produce with less'), to information-provision or value-stimulating measures ('certify and label', 'produce/buy responsibly'), to more systemic transformation measures ('service rather than sell' or 'green supply chains'). They also include measures that affect different people differently ('increase wisely'; see also Chapter 3). Note that this list may not be complete, it is certainly more environmentally rather than socially oriented at first glance. In addition, it is interesting to note that these mechanisms may work together: they are not mutually exclusive.

In this list, there are measures which correspond with weak or strong visions of the role that production plays in sustainable consumption (Lorek and Fuchs, 2013; Akenji, 2014). The weaker vision, characterised as 'green consumerism', would typically put forward information-based measures ('certify and label' or 'buy responsibly'), promoting ethical options without challenging the larger structural determinants of unsustainable consumption (Akenji, 2014). In the weaker vision, efficiency of production is key ('produce with less'), and the potential of the market to resolve this problem is not doubted – hence a focus on information measures to ensure that the market runs most efficiently (Noblet and Teisl, 2015).

The stronger vision, the 'strong sustainable consumption' perspective, would typically emphasise the complex and systemic nature of production-consumption relationships, and argue for the need to go beyond efficiency and 'decoupling' of environmental harm from consumption (Lorek and Fuchs, 2013). Strong sustainable consumption visions are likely to see the need for transformation in the whole system from cradle to grave. The weak (green or ethical consumerism) and strong (systemic approaches) visions will be profiled in the sections below.

Table 10.1 Mechanisms which could enable a more sustainable production-consumption system (from Lorek, 2016; reprinted with permission from Springer)

Enabling mechanism	Short description
Produce with less	Innovations in production process reduce the environmental impact per unit made.
Green supply chains	Firms with leverage in a chain impose standards on their suppliers to improve environmental performance.
Co-design	Consumers are involved in design of products to meet functions with less environmental impact.
Produce responsibly	Producers are made responsible for waste from the disposal of products at the end of their life.
Service rather than sell	Producers provide service rather than sell products; this reduces the number of products made, while still providing to consumers the functions they need.
Certify and label	Consumers buy labelled products. As labels are based on independent certification, producers with good practices increase their market share.
Trade fairly	Agreements are made with producers that may include minimum price and other investments or benefits. Consumers buy products labelled as or sold through fair trade channels while producers get a better deal.
Market ethically	Reducing unethical practices in marketing and advertising would reduce wasteful and over-consumption practices.
Buy responsibly	Campaigns that educate consumers about impacts of individual products, classes of products and consumption patterns change behaviour overall.
Use less	Consumption may be reduced for a variety of reasons, for example, as a consequence of working less. There are many potential environmental gains from less overall consumption.
Increase wisely	Increasing consumption of under-consumers can be done in ways that minimize environmental impacts as economic activity expands.

Green consumerism

The possibility for producers to encourage sustainable consumption among consumers can be understood in relatively uncontroversial ways, which do not challenge the status quo for producers. This is sometimes characterised as 'green consumerism', or using the more ambiguous term 'ethical consumerism', which I avoid in this discussion as it is used to mean very different things. Green consumerism essentially means that businesses can continue to operate according to a similar logic, with some attention to ethical or environmental issues. This way of understanding the producer-consumer relationship, might for instance, characterise a rising interest in ethical issues as the emergence of a new market: 'there is an increasing body of evidence to suggest that shoppers take their morals, in addition to their wallets, when they visit the high street' (Freestone and McGoldrick, 2008, 445).

Here the increase in ethical motivation is seen as a market opportunity, rather than a transformation of the market and of production itself (in contrast to 'systemic approaches' below). This body of work tends to be based in psychology, and has an emphasis on understanding how values impact on how people consume (as in Chapter 6).

There is some cynicism in the sustainable consumption literature about green consumerism, which tends to be seen as a form of greenwash, or running the risk of creating a rebound effect (where savings in one area are spent on other environmentally detrimental products or services). This is certainly a risk. For instance, Lewis Akenji (2014) gives the example of the Japanese government rewarding people buying energy-efficient appliances (fridges, air-conditioning units, etc.) with 'eco-points', which can be used to buy other products. This had a substantial impact on sales of these products, but some of this increase is likely to have resulted in increased energy consumption overall (ibid.).

In the following section, I will detail a 'green consumerism'-type intervention: the drive towards setting corporate performance standards and transparency, and the resulting certification and labelling of products.

Standards and transparency, certification and labelling

The increase in environmental and ethical labelling is one of the reactions to rising consumer activism against environmental and human rights abuses (Egels-Zandén and Hansson, 2016). Standards, certification and labelling are connected in this context; companies are increasingly drawn to committing to standards in relation to their performance on environmental and ethical issues, and these standards are controlled through certification schemes, which then frequently result in the licence to display a label on a product. A plethora of labels exist: organic, fair trade, marine or forest stewardship council, and energy-efficiency labels. Some of these labels are legislated by government (e.g. energy-efficiency labels), many of them are voluntary schemes which corporations engage in to increase their legitimacy (Rasche, 2015). Note that from a consumer perspective, these initiatives tend to assume that the problem of unsustainable consumption is a lack of information, and the solution is to provide people with means to take more informed decisions (see Chapter 4). The assumed subject of these kinds of initiatives is someone who wants to make changes, and who just needs access to the right kind of information (Thøgersen et al., 2010; Noblet and Teisl, 2015). However, on the production side, standards associated with these labels require companies to change their business practices: to meet higher (albeit voluntary) standards set by the certification scheme.

Given that labelling has arisen in response to consumer activism on environmental damage and human rights abuse (see also Chapter 7 on political consumerism), there is a need for robust standards, and certification schemes. The suspicion that companies are greenwashing is indeed part of the motivation for them to engage in voluntary certification schemes (Noblet and Teisl, 2015). These schemes can both enable and inhibit sustainable consumption goals (Rasche, 2015). For instance, labelling helps to inform people about the conditions in which products are made, when companies adhere to standards they are often required to report more generally on progress towards sustainability goals, and these tools often help further entrench sustainability in companies (ibid.). On the other hand, the existence of competing standards and labels is confusing, and activist consumers frequently question the credibility of labels and standards (ibid.) as do suppliers (Giovannucci and Ponte, 2005). As a result, the effectiveness of labelling relates to people's (and companies') familiarity with the label, their trust in the process of labelling and the level of standardisation adhered to in the label (if information is communicated consistently and in a similar format, people are more able to judge its worth) (Noblet and Teisl, 2015).

The way labels work from a producer perspective is very important; inevitably, the presence of standards and certification has an impact on the business practices of those organisations that use them (ibid.). This can lead to positive outcomes, but there is also a risk that expectations of the certification scheme result in the exclusion of smaller players, or a change in governance structure. For instance, in Costa Rica, the poorest farmers are known to be excluded from fair trade certification as a result of the high-quality requirements of the scheme (Bryant and Goodman, 2013). Standards can also be implemented in more or less enthusiastic ways by suppliers, as shown by Sally Smith's study of the UK supermarket sector and Fairtrade (Smith, 2010). As Fairtrade, for instance, has become more mainstream, there are also risks of its credibility being diluted (Doherty et al., 2013). It is important to recognise that these labels and certification schemes are not benign; while on the surface they may seem like they are trying to do 'good', they still need to be open to criticism (Dolan, 2008).

A natural extension from certification is to attempt to increase transparency in the supply chain, particularly in a globalised marketplace where retailers buy from suppliers who in turn buy from further suppliers. The idea behind this is that providing information about the supply chain allows consumers to exert influence on corporations, and hold them accountable (Egels-Zandén and Hansson, 2016). This also offers opportunities to companies to improve their legitimacy (ibid.). In a study of the Swedish jeans company Nudie Jeans, which prides itself on supply-chain transparency, authors attempt to understand what impact transparency has on the consumer. They find that in this case, consumers 'do not seem to leverage increased transparency to pressure firms but, instead, when exposed to increased transparency, are almost twice as willing to purchase products' (ibid., 379).

In other words, the impact of increased information in this context is increased trust, without the added pressures on this company to justify its actions. Clearly, this is a study of only one company engaged in this kind of action, but we need to remain careful nevertheless of assuming that such action always results in 'better' corporate behaviour. Increased transparency can also risk pushing risky practices down the supply chain, so that they are not associated with the brand under which a product is sold.

Critiques of green consumerism

As you might expect, green consumerism strategies come in for substantial criticism in the sustainable consumption literature, not least because the systemic approach I will profile next is the response of 'strong sustainable consumption' authors to this field. The fear here is that green consumerism is merely a form of 'greenwash' or 'bluewash', a way of making it seem that corporations are engaged in environmental (green) or ethical (blue) work, when actually they are merely conducting their business as usual: 'From a critical perspective, ethical consumer strategies seem more like niche marketing opportunities allowing corporations to target privileged, conscientious consumers, than a substantive program for health, sustainability, and social justice at a global scale' (Johnson, 2008, 240).

One of the reasons green consumerism initiatives seem rather problematic is their voluntary nature; they tend to be reliant on the goodwill of companies or non-governmental organisations to implement and enforce change. It is difficult then both for outsiders to have faith that such initiatives are delivering genuine change, and for insiders to make meaningful changes when this depends on an abstract commitment, rather than a legal or financial duty. Green consumerism initiatives are often hailed as part of a 'post-political' era – a term used to describe a politics which avoids direct regulation, and instead relies on consensus and partnership working between government and other stakeholders (Foster, 2014). Post-political governance is also accused of being greenwash (ibid.).

In a sense, the challenge here is that green consumerism looks a lot like business as usual, mainly because many of the ideas behind these two strategies are very similar. As Johnston notes (2008):

- Both are wedded to the idea of consumer choice; in the case of green consumerism, this is about choice which reduces the impact of corporate activities on the environment and other people. Note that this is reminiscent of the economic understanding I profile in Chapter 5, and tends to ignore the possibility for more substantive political change (e.g. the introduction of trade unions, choice editing etc.);
- Both tend to see business as good for democracy; in the case of green consumerism, for instance, implying that buying ethical amounts to 'voting with your dollar' (Dickinson and Carsky, 2005). These kinds of initiatives, as we saw in Chapter 7, risk shrinking the space associated with politics, while also expanding that associated with consumption.

Note that green consumerist initiatives rather dodge the question of self-interest that I tackled in Chapter 5. For instance, if people, and indeed corporations, are self-interested, why would they engage in ethically 'correct' choices, and in 'voting' through their spending? Further, is there not a risk of self-interest prevailing, rather than people sticking to their values (as in Chapter 6) and doing the 'right' thing?

Robert Foster (2014) gives the example of a partnership between Conservation International (a large NGO) and Fiji Water (a corporation), to sell carbon-negative bottled water. This is typical of the partnership working I refer to above which is characterised as post-political. The idea of a conservation NGO selling water in plastic bottles inevitably attracts criticism, given the potential for harm from plastic waste on natural ecosystems, and the environmental costs of bottling and shipping water from Fiji around the world. Foster quotes the chairperson of Conservation International in response to criticism:

> Maybe it would be morally preferable to carry a bottle I filled at the tap, but bottled water is a consumer reality. So rather than operate in a moralistic framework, we'll use the economy as it exists to make a difference.
>
> (Ibid., 35)

This is a particularly strong example because the chairperson is evoking a sense of inevitability in relation to the strategic decision that this NGO has taken. We are left with the impression that it is not worth trying to challenge the status quo, that the maximum we can do is to reduce harm (by producing carbon-negative bottled water), rather than changing the practice of bottled water consumption in the first place.

In the study of sustainable consumption, strong approaches argue for the need for a systemic explanation of the relationship between producer and consumers. Green consumerism, from this perspective, is highly contradictory, as 'Individual consumers are urged to cycle and walk to work to help save their local and global environment – and then encouraged to fly halfway around the world for their holidays' (Lebel and Lorek, 2008, 242).

In the following section, I profile a series of more systemic perspectives on this relationship.

Systemic approaches

When writing about production-consumption relationships from a systemic perspective, it is necessary to understand the causal webs of relationships in production-consumption systems, in order to understand how they might successfully result in a transition to a more sustainable state. For example, food systems are often made up of complex supply chains of producers and consumers, processing and selling products until they get to their final market (Reisch et al., 2013). Contemporary food systems have particular characteristics which make them complex, high impact (on environment and on other people), and difficult to manage. For instance, global North food systems are typified by intensive agriculture, retailer market monopoly and globalised supply chains, and are subject to a range of national and international regulation (ibid.). The complexity of food systems has led to limited success of policy interventions in this space, because of:

> the tendency to view single aspects of sustainability as unrelated – to dissociate food production from nutritional behavior, economic aspects from social aspects, health aspects from environmental aspects, and everyday meal planning from other life areas like employment, housework, and leisure.
>
> (Ibid., 21)

In other words, because we do not treat the food system as a system, we do not address it appropriately through policy.

Further, as Oksana Mont explains in her work on measures that avoid ownership (car sharing, power-tool rental, washing services): 'institutionalisation of alternative consumption practices depends on institutional settings, on how the alternative systems are developed and on socio-cultural context' (Mont, 2004, 137).

Mont claims here that alternative consumption practices do not just 'happen', as they exist within a larger system, and as a result will fail or thrive in the context of that system. This evokes some of the issues that arose in Chapter 3 about how social context impacts on the effectiveness of different types of intervention. A systemic approach, therefore, would emphasise the need to consider the actions of multiple actors in tackling this kind of problem; even when alternative forms of consumption based on services exist, this does not necessarily mean that they will thrive unless social conditions are favourable (Mont, 2004).

A number of different concepts have emerged to talk about production-consumption relationships in a systemic way. I will profile 'industrial ecology', 'circular economy' and 'product-service systems' in the following three sections. Given the diversity of these examples, I also deal with critiques of these in turn, rather than offering an overall critique at the end of the section.

Industrial ecology

Industrial ecology emerged as an area of study in the 1990s, and focused particularly on transforming linear industrial systems (where raw materials are the input, and the outputs are the products and waste products) into circular systems (where waste products are reused as the input to further production processes) (Mont and Heiskanen, 2015). This amounts to an improvement of industrial efficiency: turning waste into value, and preventing 'leaks' of pollutants into ecological systems (Lehtoranta et al., 2011). The philosophy behind industrial ecology was to learn from ecosystem functioning, and apply this learning in an industrial context. This led to the concepts of industrial symbioses (finding ways that one industry's waste stream can be another's input) and eco-industrial parks (locating symbiotic industries in one place) (ibid.). As you can probably imagine, these ideas can have substantial economic benefits, allowing industries to avoid the costs of waste disposal and buying raw materials; however, this is not necessarily enough to stimulate such action. There is often also a need for governments to introduce policy to stimulate such activities (ibid.).

The ideas of industrial ecology have not frequently been applied in consumption research, although concepts of household or urban metabolism have been developed from this starting point (Moll et al., 2005). We can also find connections to industrial ecology through the concept of 'planned obsolescence':

the design of products which deliberately fail, so that people will throw them away and then go out and buy more of the same. Harald Wieser has documented how, particularly in the context of consumer electronics, product lifespans are decreasing (2016). As we will see, however, the consumer is also entering into the conversation about the circular economy, a new iteration of industrial ecology thinking.

The circular economy

The concept of the 'circular economy' is one that has emerged from practitioners working on environmental issues from a business perspective. It has been enthusiastically adopted in China, including being written into government policy (Murray et al., 2017). In Europe, the Ellen MacArthur Foundation has been central to this initiative; the foundation is a non-profit organisation which promotes the concept, and acts as a hub to bring together academics, businesses and policy-makers (Geissdoerfer et al., 2017). The concept is also being taken up by governments and NGOs in the UK, France, and the Netherlands, as well as the European Union.

The main thrust of the circular economy arguments are: first, that we need to aim to operate as a 'closed-loop economy', which is an economy that reduces waste and pollution at every step of manufacture, use and disposal of a product (ibid.); and second, that such an economy should incorporate 'design to re-design' thinking (Hobson, 2016). The latter means designing with the opposite goals to planned obsolescence (as explained above), that is, creating products which last, and which can be redesigned to work as something else at the end of their working life. Geissdoerfer and colleagues' definition of a circular economy is useful here: 'a regenerative system in which resource input and waste, emission, and energy leakage are minimised by slowing, closing, and narrowing material and energy loops. This can be achieved through long-lasting design, maintenance, repair, reuse, remanufacturing, refurbishing, and recycling' (Geissdoerfer et al., 2017, 759).

Note the word 'regenerative', which is often used in relation to a circular economy, meaning that the economy can regenerate using much the same materials. There is a substantial overlap with the idea of industrial ecology described above – the circular economy is an extension of this. Kersty Hobson believes that the new concept has emerged because the practice of reusing and repurposing materials is becoming more feasible (2016). Both industrial ecology and the circular economy tend to focus on a single business, a cluster of businesses, or a city as a working unit (Murray et al., 2017). There is a strong business orientation here; this concept is seen as an opportunity for businesses to engage meaningfully with an environmental agenda.

So how does this relate to sustainable consumption? Oksana Mont and Eva Heiskanen (2015) identify three ways of introducing closed loops in the consumption phase:

1   Reusing the product: by repairing it or upcycling it (could be for a different purpose);
2   Dismantling the product: using the parts for something new, and
3   Recycling the product: reducing the use of raw materials.

These consumption closed loops are somewhat dependent on the presence of appropriate production strategies. For instance, it is difficult to dismantle a product and reuse the parts if it was produced in a way to prevent this happening. This could relate to design (designing for redesign, incorporating old products in new designs), and retail (rental rather than ownership) of products (ibid., 2015). Having said this, the consumer is also expected to move towards a more dynamic, co-productive role in the circular economy (ibid.). This might mean:

- the consumer playing a role in producing or redesigning products,
- the consumer engaging in collaborative consumption: sharing products, or helping to turn products into services,
- the consumer engaging with a 'service rather than sell' business model (as described in more detail in the next section).

As well as producers and consumers having a role in this new kind of economy, governments would also need to support these new roles for consumers and approaches to business. We can imagine, for instance, governments instigating policies to support markets for recyclable and recycled materials. An example of this is the Swedish government reducing tax on repair businesses in 2016, to make them more competitive.

As well as bearing similarities to industrial ecology, the circular economy also has parallels to the broader concept of sustainability. The key difference here is that while sustainability sets economic, environmental and social goals, the circular economy has a strong focus on economic and environmental aspects, with limited attention to social issues (Murray et al., 2017): 'The Circular Economy clearly seems to prioritise the economic systems with primary benefits for the environment, and only implicit gains for social aspects' (Geissdoerfer et al., 2017, 764).

There are consequences to this way of thinking, which relate to the way that people are conceived of in this model. Given its roots in economics, work on the circular economy tends to replace the 'rational actor' as product consumer, with the rational actor as service user (Hobson, 2016). These subjects act in a very similar way: choosing rationally between options, using environmental values to make decisions about consumption (see Chapters 5 and 6). Kersty Hobson argues that there is much more room for radicalism here, and that circular economy thinking is missing the opportunity to rethink the consumer's role in consumption and production (2016). For instance, there is potential through the circular economy to reframe the consumer as a co-producer, a collaborative consumer and even an everyday activist. Being more radical in our reframing of the role of the consumer is important, because, as Mont and Heiskanen put it, a 'rational choice' vision of the consumer falls well short of the envisaged role of the consumer in a circular economy: 'this process is likely to require a stronger cultural narrative than the depoliticized notion of 'green consumerism' to support the transformative role of new consumer practices of non-market production' (Mont and Heiskanen, 2015, 43).

The lack of interest in social issues also impacts on the way that the problem of unsustainable consumption is characterised. The focus on economics first, and the environment as a beneficiary of reformed economics, results in social issues taking a back seat. For instance, Hobson shows how the consumption of rare earth metals, some of which are mined in conflict zones and therefore difficult to recover, becomes framed as a problem of access, rather than as a human rights issue: 'given the projections that numerous crucial minerals will become inaccessible, whether their sourcing takes place unjustly or not, it is their substitutability and recoverability that has become a focus for industry, research and government' (Hobson, 2016, 92).

In characterising rare earth metals using a circular economy lens, we have no sense of the social impacts and political implications of either mining, or not mining these materials.

From product to service

The 'service rather than sell' mechanism, as Lebel and Lorek put it (2008), represents an attempt to reduce the amount of material being used by consumers and producers, by moving away from business models and cultural expectations of product ownership, and towards an economy that relies on sharing or rental of services. There are links here with the idea of a sharing economy which is profiled in Chapter 11. The kinds of service that could be included here are exemplified by the product-to-service businesses that Monique Retamal (2017) found in her study of Hanoi, Bangkok and Manila; these included bike shares, ride and taxi shares, tool rental, laundry services, fashion and designer bag rental, and toy and baby equipment rental. Arnold Tukker (2004) characterises product service systems as existing on a spectrum between those that are principally product oriented (with some additional services) to those which are result oriented (the consumer and producer agree on a result without a preconceived idea of what kind of product is needed). The latter category points towards the more radical potential of this kind of business model (ibid.).

Retamal offers a set of criteria that these kinds of businesses must fulfil in order to offer a genuinely less environmentally impactful choice:

> 1) using durable, quality goods; 2) intensifying use of goods; 3) enabling repair, take back and recycling of goods; 4) ensuring rental replaces purchase; 5) minimising transport and disposable packaging of goods; and for transport – 6) reducing private vehicle kilometres travelled.
>
> (Retamal, 2017, 894)

Note that while we can see these kinds of initiatives as producer-led, for many of the criteria above, more than one stakeholder must be involved in implementation. For instance, government legislation would help to achieve criteria 5 above, and criteria 3 and 4 require at least consumer participation in order to succeed (ibid.). Intriguingly, Retamal notes that the opportunities for product-service systems are different in the global South. In her study, she found that people were more likely to use these initiatives to gain access to products for the first time, rather than shifting from ownership to rental of these kinds of products (ibid.).

The idea of turning products into services fits well with a practice approach (see Chapter 8). Josephine Mylan (2015) shows how practice approaches reveal the challenges of shifting from one system to another; in their terms, how meanings, competences and materials might change as a product/ownership based system shifts to a service/rental one. She calls these changes part of a 'transformation' of consumer demand, rather than just 'meeting' consumer needs (ibid.). Even when a consumer might have a very similar outcome (e.g. driving to work) when they achieve this through a service (e.g. car share) rather than through a product (e.g. car ownership), this amounts to a very different consumption experience. Further, she notes that where meanings would have to change in order to accommodate a service rather than a product (as in our car example) this is particularly challenging to effect.

This may help to explain why, in an extensive review paper, Arnold Tukker (2015) finds that so-called 'product service systems' are still not regularly implemented in business-to-consumer relationships. As he summarises, customers have less control over a service than they would a product, services are often less accessible than products, and there is less intangible value in a service than a product. Further, customers sometimes have the impression that a service will control their behaviour, which is not a desirable attribute. In a study of young people's attitudes to alternative business models (including buying second hand, product-to-service, and collaborative consumption), it was also found that that lack of ownership is particularly challenging (Gullstrand Edbring et al., 2016). The idea of owning second hand, is a lot more attractive here than the other two business models, and the value of product-to-service models is even more compromised by the fact that there is not always an economic incentive to hire rather than own (ibid.). All three of these models are affected by people's perceptions of hygiene – the more intimate the product (e.g. a bed) the less convinced people are that they could rent or borrow it (ibid.).

Conclusion

In this chapter, I profiled two bodies of work on the relationship between production and consumption: green consumerism and more systemic approaches. Green consumerism amounts to a rather weak interpretation of sustainable consumption (Akenji, 2014), which promotes relatively minor modifications to business as usual, adding environmental/ethical conscience to existing business practices. More systemic approaches align themselves with ideas around strong sustainable consumption, and tend to promote holistic thinking across the producer–consumer divide.

While green consumerism offers a relatively easy target, it is important that we also take a critical eye to the more systemic approaches. As we saw above, these are no means proven from a sustainability perspective (O'Rourke and Lollo, 2015). Product-service systems seem to be difficult to implement (Tukker, 2015). We have seen that the concept of the circular economy leaves out the social from sustainability, a rather dangerous development (see Chapter 3). In addition, the ideas of the circular economy that are popular with policy-makers tend to align better with weak sustainable consumption (Hobson, 2016). Indeed, there are almost always stronger and weaker versions of most of the popular ideas in circulation for solving the problem of unsustainable consumption. This is something we need to remain alert to.

References

AKENJI, L. 2014. Consumer scapegoatism and limits to green consumerism. *Journal of Cleaner Production*, 63, 13–23.

BRYANT, R. & GOODMAN, M. 2013. Peopling the practices of sustainable consumption: Eco-chic and the limits to the spaces of intention. *In:* BARENDREGT, B. & JAFFE, R. (eds) *Green Consumption: The Global Rise of Eco-Chic.* London: Bloomsbury.

DICKINSON, R. A. & CARSKY, M. L. 2005. The consumer as economic voter. *In:* HARRISON, R., NEWHOLM, T. & SHAW, D. (eds) *The Ethical Consumer.* London: Sage Publications.

DOHERTY, B., DAVIES, I. A. & TRANCHELL, S. 2013. Where now for fair trade? *Business History*, 55, 161–189.

DOLAN, C. 2008. Arbitrating risk through moral values: The case of Kenyan fairtrade. *Research in Economic Anthropology*, 28, 271–296.

EGELS-ZANDÉN, N. & HANSSON, N. 2016. Supply chain transparency as a consumer or corporate tool: The case of Nudie Jeans Co. *Journal of Consumer Policy*, 39, 377–395.

FOSTER, R. J. 2014. Adversaries into partners? Brand Coca-Cola and the politics of consumer-citizenship, *In:* BARENDREGT, B. & JAFFE, R. (eds) *Green Consumption: The Global Rise of Eco-Chic.* London: Bloomsbury.

FREESTONE, O. M. & MCGOLDRICK, P. J. 2008. Motivations of the ethical consumer. *Journal of Business Ethics*, 79, 445–467.

GEISSDOERFER, M., SAVAGET, P., BOCKEN, N. M. & HULTINK, E. J. 2017. The Circular Economy – A new sustainability paradigm? *Journal of Cleaner Production*, 143, 757–768.

GIOVANNUCCI, D. & PONTE, S. 2005. Standards as a new form of social contract? Sustainability initiatives in the coffee industry. *Food policy*, 30, 284–301.

GULLSTRAND EDBRING, E., LEHNER, M. & MONT, O. 2016. Exploring consumer attitudes to alternative models of consumption: motivations and barriers. *Journal of Cleaner Production*, 123, 5–15.

HOBSON, K. 2016. Closing the loop or squaring the circle? Locating generative spaces for the circular economy. *Progress in Human Geography*, 40, 88–104.

JOHNSTON, J. 2008. The citizen-consumer hybrid: Ideological tensions and the case of Whole Foods Market. *Theory and Society*, 37, 229–270.

LEBEL, L. & LOREK, S. 2008. Enabling sustainable production-consumption systems. *Annual Review of Environment and Resources*, 33, 241–275.

LEHTORANTA, S., NISSINEN, A., MATTILA, T. & MELANEN, M. 2011. Industrial symbiosis and the policy instruments of sustainable consumption and production. *Journal of Cleaner Production*, 19, 1865–1875.

LOREK, S. 2016. Sustainable consumption. *In*: BRAUCH, H. G., SPRING, Ú. O., GRIN, J. & SCHEFFRAN, J. (eds) *Handbook on Sustainability Transition and Sustainable Peace*. New York: Springer.

LOREK, S. & FUCHS, D. 2013. Strong sustainable consumption governance – Precondition for a degrowth path? *Journal of Cleaner Production*, 38, 36–43.

MOLL, H. C., NOORMAN, K. J., KOK, R., ENGSTRÖM, R., THRONE-HOLST, H. & CLARK, C. 2005. Pursuing more sustainable consumption by analyzing household metabolism in European countries and cities. *Journal of Industrial Ecology*, 9, 259–275.

MONT, O. 2004. Institutionalisation of sustainable consumption patterns based on shared use. *Ecological Economics*, 50, 135–153.

MONT, O. & HEISKANEN, E. 2015. Breaking the stalemate of sustainable consumption with industrial ecology and a circular economy. *In*: REISCH, L. & THØGERSEN, J. (eds) *Handbook of Research on Sustainable Consumption*. Cheltenham, UK: Edward Elgar.

MURRAY, A., SKENE, K. & HAYNES, K. 2017. The circular economy: An interdisciplinary exploration of the concept and application in a global context. *Journal of Business Ethics*, 140, 369–380.

MYLAN, J. 2015. Understanding the diffusion of Sustainable Product-Service Systems: Insights from the sociology of consumption and practice theory. *Journal of Cleaner Production*, 97, 13–20.

NOBLET, C. L. & TEISL, M. F. 2015. Eco-labelling as sustainable consumption policy. *In*: REISCH, L. & THØGERSEN, J. (eds) *Handbook of Research on Sustainable Consumption*. Cheltenham, UK: Edward Elgar.

O'ROURKE, D. & LOLLO, N. 2015. Transforming consumption: From decoupling, to behavior change, to system changes for sustainable consumption. *Annual Review of Environment and Resources*, 40, 233–259.

RASCHE, A. 2015. Voluntary standards as enablers and impediments to sustainable consumption. *In*: REISCH, L. & THØGERSEN, J. (eds) *Handbook of Research on Sustainable Consumption*. Cheltenham, UK: Edward Elgar.

REISCH, L., EBERLE, U. & LOREK, S. 2013. Sustainable food consumption: An overview of contemporary issues and policies. *Sustainability: Science, Practice, & Policy*, 9, 7–25.

RETAMAL, M. 2017. Product-service systems in Southeast Asia: Business practices and factors influencing environmental sustainability. *Journal of Cleaner Production*, 143, 894–903.

SMITH, S. 2010. For love or money? Fairtrade business models in the UK supermarket sector. *Journal of Business Ethics*, 92, 257–266.

THØGERSEN, J., HAUGAARD, P. & OLESEN, A. 2010. Consumer responses to eco-labels. *European Journal of Marketing*, 44, 1787–1810.

TUKKER, A. 2004. Eight types of product–service system: Eight ways to sustainability? Experiences from SusProNet. *Business Strategy and the Environment*, 13, 246–260.

TUKKER, A. 2015. Product services for a resource-efficient and circular economy – a review. *Journal of Cleaner Production*, 97, 76–91.

WIESER, H. 2016. Beyond planned obsolescence: Product lifespans and the challenges to a circular economy. *GAIA – Ecological Perspectives for Science and Society*, 25, 156–160.

11 The solution is collective

One of the long-standing starting points for many scholars and practitioners working on environmental issues is a belief that whatever we do, we must do it together. In the first instance, calls to arms mainly referred to the need for collective decision-making on contentious environmental issues, effectively calling for increased democracy when addressing problems that will have substantial effects on people's lives. The assumption here is that people will help to make solutions happen if they are invited to participate in crafting those solutions (de Geus, 2004). There is also an assumption that people will do the 'right' (or 'green') thing if they are included (Machin, 2013). These ideas have also inspired a belief in collective action on consumption, starting with the kinds of political consumerism we saw in Chapter 9, moving through an interest in community-based change, and an enthusiastic response to the sharing economy and its potential for stimulating change.

In this chapter, I consider these various initiatives through the academic literature on different forms of collective action. This literature varies quite substantially in terms of its disciplinary basis (writers are economists, geographers, sociologists, and political scientists) and in terms of its intent. Some authors embrace the idea of collective action with enthusiasm, others take a rather more critical view. There is also a diverse range of collective action under consideration here, from action by intentional communities, to coordination within the voluntary sector, to an act of sharing between two people, to action with others in the home. All the research and practice profiled in this chapter has in common a fascination with how people interacting together might impact either positively or negatively on the possibility for a more environmentally and socially sustainable world.

Note that one of the interests in looking at collective action in response to environmental problems is a reaction to the idea of sustainable consumption itself. In a narrow interpretation of sustainable consumption, perhaps one most clearly linked to the economic and psychological theories of 'behaviour change', we might understand this as relying on individuals to change behaviour, and in doing so to reduce their impacts on the environment. Anneleen Kenis, in her study of two collective action initiatives (Transition Towns and Climate Justice Action), is critical of an individualising perspective, and notes that her interviewees are also very much aware of the problems with a focus on behaviour change (Kenis, 2016). As one of her respondents summarises:

> It's not that individual behaviour change is not important, but I still have some second thoughts about it. Because the solutions are not individual. They can only be collective. And I think this stress on individual responsibility, that this is sometimes very blaming.
>
> (Jean-François, climate justice activist, in
> Kenis, 2016, 956)

While Kenis's participants understand that individual action has some value, they are resistant to this being portrayed as the answer to the whole problem. This respondent sees an emphasis on individual action as depoliticising, as detracting from collective responsibility. The interest in collective action on sustainability is first, a reaction to the unhelpful (and apolitical) emphasis on individual behaviour, and second, (in some cases) an opportunity to re-politicise these issues.

I begin here by discussing the history of interest in sustainability and collective action. I proceed by looking at three different forms of collective action on sustainable consumption: at the community, economy and household levels. I will then offer a critique of these initiatives, in order to show how careful we must be about making assumptions. Generally speaking, we have a tendency to think 'collective/community/family = good', perhaps also 'individualistic = bad'. I will argue here that, the whole picture is not so clear-cut.

Sustainability and collective action

Writings on sustainable development very often include a 'call to arms', highlighting a need to engage people in both decision-making and action in order to secure common goals. The *Brundtland Report*, a key document in the environmental movement, for instance, claims that 'effective participation in decision-making processes by local communities can help them articulate and effectively enforce their common interest' (World Commission on Environment and Development, 1987, 47). This tendency to call for collective action stems partly from the nature of the environmental movement as a radical one, which sees deliberative democracy as fundamental both to making good decisions, and to persuading people to engage in change. It also originates from a concern that many environmental problems come about as a result of small actions taken by large numbers of people, a challenge that can feel insurmountable at times.

The sub-discipline of ecological economics has also had a focus on participation. In his article 'The tragedy of the commons', the ecologist Garrett Hardin (1968) challenged a key tenet of economics: the belief that a rational actor can act both in their own interests, and in the interests of society at large. Hardin described the effects of allowing a group of herdsmen to graze their animals on common land, which results in overgrazing and ecological collapse as each herdsman tries to maximise his own interests by grazing more animals than he should.

This is a challenge to economic theory (Chapter 5), as it suggests that rational acts by individuals do not necessarily achieve socially rational results. The Nobel Prize-winning ecological economist Elinor Ostrom dedicated her life's work to understanding how common pool resources could be better managed (Ostrom, 1990). The idea of participation is central here; in particular, Ostrom believed that people will behave in the common interest if they are able to participate in institutions that are established to manage the resource in question.

Writers on sustainable consumption do not consistently use the terms 'participation' or 'collective action', but often assume that people need to make changes in their daily lives for the sake of the common good. In the next three sections, we will explore how ideas of collective action and consumption have been brought together in this field. This includes collective action at three different scales – the community, the economy and the household. It also ties in with developments in policy and practice, where there is increasing interest in bottom-up collective approaches to change. In particular, these writers speak to the surge of interest in community-based change (community energy, transition towns, etc.), the social, solidarity and sharing economies, and consumption within the home.

Community-based sustainable consumption initiatives

Since the early 2000s, a series of initiatives have emerged in the global North that explicitly link the idea of community and that of consumption. Some examples of these include Transition Towns, Incredible Edible, community gardens and Carbon Rationing Action Groups (CRAGs). These movements have also sparked enthusiasm among academics and practitioners for investigating the role of community, or some form of collective action, in making consumption more sustainable (Middlemiss, 2011a, 2011b; Seyfang, 2009). Note that this interest is quite culturally specific. It is no coincidence that many of these initiatives have emerged initially in Anglo-Saxon countries such as the UK, the US and Australia, where there are strong traditions of local activism and volunteering. The distinctiveness of this movement since the early 2000s is that initiatives emerged from the grass roots, from groups of enthusiastic volunteers rather than from local government.

Community-based sustainable consumption initiatives consist mostly of volunteer-led projects to promote pro-environmental change in a community of place, interest, or practice. These projects often have global environmental concerns at their heart, and express both an urgency for action (especially on climate change) and a belief that the local or small-scale offers the potential for this action to have a more substantial impact (Taylor Aiken, 2014b). Among governments, there is a sense that community-based initiatives might be 'trusted intermediaries' which can convincingly communicate messages to their peers (DEFRA, 2005). Among the initiatives themselves, there is a widespread belief that the challenges of attempting to reduce one's impact as an individual are reduced by collective action. Equally, many of the participants in these initiatives are disappointed by government's lack of action on climate change. As the

Transition movement commonly frames it: 'if we leave it to the governments, it will be too little, too late' (Transition Network, 2016).

Box 11.1 Case study: Transition Towns

Transition Towns projects are volunteer-led attempts to reduce the collective impacts of the community on the environment, with a particular focus on climate change. After setting up a Transition Town project in Totnes, Devon, UK in 2004, which attempted to engage the local community in positive change (to some success), the founders developed the Transition Network, which used the group's experiences in Totnes to promote the establishment of other Transition Town projects around the UK and further afield. The Transition Network provides various tools to help communities to think about how they can create change, including books, films and a process which a community can use to plan and manage their reduction in impact. Transition Town projects now exist in many parts of the developed world, including Australia, Canada, England, Germany, Ireland, Italy, the Netherlands, New Zealand, Scotland, South Africa, Spain, Sweden, the US, and Wales, and those recognised by the network amount to 480 projects (Transition Network, 2016).

While the process is not prescriptive, transition projects tend to engage with similar types of action, probably as a result of these shared tools, resources and processes. These include 'reskilling' – learning lost skills which result in more environmentally benign action, often triggered by the 'honouring the elders' part of the process. Arguably, these initiatives also tend to happen in similar types of communities, with rural, relatively wealthy communities well represented (Grossmann and Creamer, 2016; Kenis and Mathijs, 2014). Certainly the Transition Town initiative has grown into a mainstay of the environmental movement since its foundation, and has also put local community action on sustainable consumption-related issues on the map (see also Aiken, 2012; Chatterton and Cutler, 2008; Connors and McDonald, 2011; Kenis, 2016).

Community action on sustainability has been studied by scholars from many different disciplinary and theoretical starting points. As a result, there is a plethora of terminology used to refer to these initiatives: grass-roots innovations, community energy, sustainable communities, grass-roots associations and more. Over time, there has been a gradual shift in the kinds of questions asked about these initiatives, which perhaps indicates that an initial enthusiasm for collective change has given way to a more critical assessment of the potential for these initiatives to have an impact on major social and environmental problems. Initially, for instance, some were concerned with establishing whether these initiatives could make a difference to people's lifestyles (Hargreaves, 2011; Middlemiss, 2011a; Taylor Aiken, 2014b). A further question has involved thinking about the potential for such small-scale action to 'scale-up' and have a greater impacts on these substantial societal challenges (Seyfang and Smith, 2007; Global Environmental Change, 2013). More recently, critical questions have emerged about these initiatives, including questions about what community is being used for and by whom, and how it is mobilised for a range of different objectives (Creamer, 2014; Kenis, 2016; Taylor Aiken, 2016a).

So what is the balance of opinion here, on the value of community-based action on sustainability? While we cannot quantify such value, or indeed generalise about projects in all contexts, we can outline the successes of these initiatives to date, and the challenges that they face. Community action on sustainability has become highly prominent in recent years in the UK at least (Seyfang and Smith, 2007; Seyfang et al., 2013). It is clearly an area that strikes a chord in developed countries, given the enthusiasm with which some of the models have been replicated around the world. The Transition Town movement is probably the best known of these, but others (Incredible Edible, Community Energy, Carbon Conversations, and more) are also testament to the popularity of community action. These projects need certain resources to take off, principally the time and enthusiasm of a group of committed volunteers who have the energy to invest in their local communities (Middlemiss, 2010). Volunteers are also likely to need skills in inspiring, persuading and organising people, as well as the ability to find funding or other physical resources for their operations. Volunteers have a specific demographic profile: more female, better educated and more middle-aged than the general population (more middle-class) (Kendall, 2003), and as such these are not resources that are available to all communities.

The challenges that these initiatives face relate mostly to the contrast between the resources that each project holds, and the magnitude of the problem it is trying to address. Community projects here, that are reliant on volunteers and that hold limited funding, are attempting to resolve social problems where to date governments have failed (e.g. climate change, unsustainable food systems, localised energy provision). Community initiatives are also attempting to operate in a world which is set up for another vision of progress (economic growth, consumerism – see Chapter 13), and this makes creating change somewhat challenging. Researchers have found that even when funding is available, it can be highly problematic for these groups, which find themselves having to change their agenda in order to fulfil funders' requirements, sometimes to the detriment of their original goals (Creamer, 2014). Community volunteers are often subject to burnout, when years of volunteering alongside paid and family work take their toll. While these projects attract a fair amount of enthusiasm, it is essential to be realistic about these initiatives and about the sorts of changes they can achieve, so as not to place too much expectation on the army of volunteers involved in these initiatives.

In a review of 'social innovations' for sustainable consumption, Melanie Jaeger-Erben and colleagues point out that 'community empowering consumption' is

the 'most demanding type of social innovation, as it requires a network of personally engaged actors and high investment of personal resources' (Jaeger-Erben
et al., 2015, 792). It is particularly tricky to support these kinds of initiatives
because they tend to thrive when left to their own devices, and this is often difficult for government to do (given that funding awarded must be justified to the
taxpayer) (Creamer, 2014; Taylor Aiken, 2016b). Jaeger-Erben and colleagues'
characterisation of the *unconditional* support that these initiatives need, including spaces and resources for experimentation, financial and material resources,
indirect support for change agents and initiators, is rarely available, although it is
encouraging that their research was funded by German government actors who
are looking to make a difference in this sphere (ibid.).

Social, solidarity and sharing economies

The conviction that solutions to sustainability problems must be collective
has also resulted in discussions of alternative economies, including the ideas
of degrowth that I discuss in greater detail in Chapter 13. The term 'economy'
is used in its broadest sense here, including market, household, government
and the 'third sector', or civil society. Tim Jackson sees great potential in this
latter economy:

> the seeds for such an economy may already exist in local or community-based
> social enterprises: community energy projects, local farmers' markets, slow
> food cooperatives, sports clubs, libraries, community health and fitness cen-
> tres, local repair and maintenance services, craft workshops, writing centres,
> water sports, community music and drama, local training and skills.
>
> (Jackson, 2009, 139)

We are familiar by now with these kinds of organisations, and Jackson's description of these phenomena as a 'new economy' has strong connections to the 'social
and solidarity economy' concept which is well known in Europe, especially in
French-speaking countries, and Spain and Portugal (*économie sociale et solid-
aire*) (Sahakian and Dunand, 2014). Here, the social and solidarity economy is
one that aims towards 'systemic transformation of the economy or [is] part of a
"counter-hegemonic political economy"' (ibid., 2). This economy's function is to
engage people in collective, interdependent action towards producing social benefits for the community or region; critically, there is a sense of a need to organise
these efforts collectively and in a mutually supportive way. Sahakian and Dunand
estimate that in Geneva (Switzerland) about 10 per cent of the workforce
is employed in the social and solidarity economy, which is highly networked
(ibid.). Since the World Social Forum in 2002, the network Après Genève was
founded to ensure that organisations in this economy abide by agreed principles
and support each other in their aims.

Another way of ensuring that value is held in the local economy is through the
means of a community or alternative currency. These consist of alternative trading

systems designed to create new systems of provision, with a goal of creating more sustainable consumption patterns (Seyfang, 2009). Examples include Local Exchange Trading Schemes (LETS), time banks (where people exchange time with each other), barter markets and city-based currencies (such as Hours currency in Ithaca, New York). These institutions operate in many different countries, and constitute a 'mature, flourishing set of community-based initiatives for sustainability' (Seyfang and Longhurst, 2013; see also Sahakian, 2014). Specifically environment-focused community currencies are rare – most have social and economic goals (Seyfang and Longhurst, 2013). The impacts of these activities are summarised by a meta-analysis of the literature in this area (Michel and Hudon, 2015). These authors find that there are multiple economic and social outcomes, particularly for marginalised members of the population (e.g. unemployed, older people), although these impacts are not substantial enough to have a 'meaningful impact' on the local economy in general. Community currencies tend to operate on a relatively small scale, reducing their potential for impact. Evidence of environmental impact is limited, but there are some suggestions of changing consumption practices (ibid.).

A more recent use of the word 'economy' to invoke some sense of the collective is in the term 'sharing economy' (or 'collaborative economy'), which has come to prominence in the 2010s with the advent of a series of highly successful ventures that use the idea of sharing resources as a business model. Perhaps the best known of these are the commercial ventures Uber and Airbnb. Strictly speaking, these are not so much about 'sharing' as they are about making money from one's resources (Belk, 2014), and there is more interest for sustainable consumption in this phenomenon when it seems to originate from communitarian or altruistic values (Gruszka, 2016). Schor and Fitzmaurice (2015) define the sharing economy as involving sharing between strangers, a reliance on digital platforms, and typically engaging high 'cultural capital' consumers who choose to share as a mark of their taste, as opposed to needing to share. This trend has been greeted with enthusiasm by some academics, who argue that the sharing economy is an opportunity for efficient use of materials (e.g. cars, living space), as well as likely to build social capital as people make more meaningful connections (Botsman and Rogers, 2010; Heinrichs, 2013; Schor and Fitzmaurice, 2015; Gruszka, 2016).

The initial evidence on the sharing economy suggests that we should not be over-optimistic. In a discourse analysis of six organisations engaged in the sharing economy, Martin (2016) finds that these are more likely to privilege a framing of their work as an 'economic opportunity' as opposed to being a 'sustainable consumption' initiative. In a study of why people engage in the sharing economy, Hamari and colleagues find that an interest in sustainability does not strongly correlate to increased participation (Hamari et al., 2015), although Böcker and Meelen (2017) do find that car sharing is more often motivated by environmental values, and other forms of sharing (rides and meals for instance) are socially motivated. There are limited 'success stories' of sustainable consumption initiatives in this area, which are drowned out somewhat by the stories of business success (Martin, 2016), and business-driven cases seem to have grown much more quickly than sustainability-driven cases (Böcker and Meelen, 2017). Martin's case study of Freegle, a website in the UK that allows people to give away used goods for free to others that want them, also shows that this organisation has become increasingly commercial, as it experiences external pressures connected to the expectations that the sharing economy facilitates money making (Martin et al., 2015). While it is possible that business-oriented sharing economy ventures will have positive environmental and social effects, this is by no means certain (witness Martin and Shaheen's 2011 study of carsharing in the US, which found little change in emissions). Commercially driven organisations will prioritise economic gain over environmental and social considerations.

In their analysis of social innovations for sustainable consumption, Jaeger-Erben and colleagues characterise sharing economy initiatives as 'commonly organized consumption instead of community-creating consumption' (Jaeger-Erben et al., 2015, 789). As implied by Jaeger-Erben and colleagues here, the relationships that the sharing economy fosters will in many cases be of a different order to those created in, for instance, a community garden. An online interaction with someone, followed by a brief meeting in person, is not the same as sharing time and energy on a regular basis to cultivate a piece of land. The social intensity of the other initiatives covered in this section will vary also. The level of collective action here is important; one of the major benefits of these types of initiative is the possibility for community building – clearly that possibility is different for each type of initiative.

Household dynamics

Perhaps the most basic sense in which we act collectively is in our living arrangements, and the household or family provides another scale at which we can think about collective action. The household unit is an important one, at the least because it is an easily understood, and influential, form of collective action which most people are engaged in. Who we live with has a substantial impact on how we consume. Even when we live alone, our household's relationship with other households, and with other social structures (governments, markets) can affect our consumption impacts. Note that I have called this section household 'dynamics', by which I mean the properties which stimulate change in this context. I will discuss a series of studies here which take the household as a unit of analysis, and think about how the household affects the consumption of its occupants.

In my own qualitative work on fuel poverty (with Ross Gillard), I have found the relationships between people in the home to have an impact on people's energy consumption (Middlemiss and Gillard, 2015). The people we talked to here are members of households in the UK who cannot afford to keep their homes warm enough in the winter. We noticed how relationships between household members could result in more energy being used for some things (particularly by parents wanting to keep children warm and make sure they had a hot meal), and less for others (when the bill payer tolerated the cold when 'only' they were at home) (ibid.). People we met sometimes shared energy services with their friends and extended family in other households, by gathering in one place to keep warm, or by doing someone's washing for them. This allowed households to spend more on energy at other times. Relationships in the home also caused tension between household members, with, for instance, teenagers' use of electricity-hungry devices increasing the bill-payers' stress, and sometimes causing arguments. Our research begins to reveal how people's interactions in the home can have a complex relationship with energy consumption.

Isaksson and Ellegård (2015) look at how household food-provisioning tasks are distributed among members. They find that this has a big impact on the potential for change. For instance, if one person does all the work of food provisioning (including shopping, storing, cooking, and clearing up), they are less likely to have the time to engage in more environmentally friendly versions of these practices. Further, if more than one person is engaged in these processes, as they put it, 'one individual household member's replacing energy-intensive activities with less energy intensive ones does not necessarily mean reduced energy consumption at household level' (ibid., 182). These authors argue that this is why it is important to think about households as a focus for change, instead of individuals, given that the dynamics of how people use energy are both complex and impacted by social relations.

Other research has shown how practices are inflexible around particular times of day, and how some practices are less flexible than others (Powells et al., 2014; Nicholls and Strengers, 2015). For instance, Nicholls and Strengers show how the peak in energy consumption in Australia is the time when families cook dinner, bath and entertain their children, and get them to bed, all high-energy practices which are both intertwined (for instance, kids watching TV while parents do chores) and embedded with meaning (for instance, kids having a bath to calm down before bed). When peak energy use is also constrained by other norms and institutions (the timing of the working and school days, expectations of a 'good night's sleep'), we can see that shifting and reducing energy use becomes very much a household or family matter (ibid.).

The theme of time is important here: who has time, and at what time it is appropriate to engage in certain activities. We can also think of time on a grander scale, and a number of studies have investigated how someone's life stage affects how they consume. An illustrative example comes from Butler and colleagues, who tell the story of one of the interviewees in their 'energy biography' project (Butler et al., 2014). This older woman is widowed, and lives alone in a large house, but wants to remain there because of the memories it holds of her previous life, when husband and children lived there also. This is a useful example because it shows how people's relationships with others impact on consumption even after they leave the home. Butler and colleagues argue that by looking at how people live in relation to their biography, we understand the conditions which shape the decisions we make, as opposed to just the decisions themselves (ibid.). The importance of how people understand specific moments in the life course has also been used to think about both when it is appropriate to intervene

(Schäfer et al., 2012) and how life course changes (e.g. having a first child or retiring) impact on lifestyles (Burningham and Venn, 2017). Intriguingly, the latter study found that the perceived availability of time was very important, with previously environmentally oriented-first parents no longer finding time for environmental practices, and by contrast, newly retired interviewees seeing their new life situation as an opportunity to put principles into practice (ibid.).

Until now, we have been talking about multiple-occupant households, and indeed mostly about households with children. In the global North, the fastest growing household type is the single-person household, and the number of households is also increasing faster than the growth in population throughout the world (Bradbury et al., 2014). The assumption here is that single-person households use the same kinds of resources as multiple-person households, but because they live alone they use these resources less efficiently (Bradbury et al., 2014). Yates (2016) investigates this more extensively, using a large data set on single-person households in the UK. He finds that while there are inefficiencies in single-person households, this relationship is not such a simple one. For instance, single-person households are far less likely to own a tumble drier than are multiple-person households. On the other hand, single-person households are much more likely to eat alone, with the intensity of energy use that this entails. In a separate study, Büchs and Schnepf (2013) found that single-person households are also much more likely to have no transport costs. Further, smaller households in Belgium are more likely to report engaging in environmentally friendly practices (Bartiaux and Reategui Salmon, 2014). As Yates points out, consumption of a household (whether single or multiple person) also depends on the broader infrastructure that the household has access to. It is likely then that a small single-person dwelling in an urban area will have considerably less impact than a large multi-person dwelling in the countryside (as we saw in Chapter 2).

There are more radical responses to housing (and by extension to households) that have a strong connection with the sustainable consumption movement and deserve consideration here. The cohousing movement, which began in Denmark in the 1960s (McCamant and Durrett, 2011), and is active in many global North countries, is an attempt to redefine the meaning of home, and the household as a unit. These projects are characterised by the sharing of a range of facilities, which might include transport, laundry, kitchen and guest rooms, as well as having private space for more traditional household-based activities (Chatterton, 2013). The idea behind sharing facilities is to reduce consumption, as cohousing initiatives are often motivated by ecological concerns, and also frequently either inhabit or construct low-energy dwellings (Williams, 2005). However, the collective nature of this solution is not just environmentally motivated; projects often have strong social principles associated with building community by living more closely with others (Meltzer, 2000). A recent cohousing initiative in my university city of Leeds, LILAC (Low Impact Living Affordable Community), is a nice example of this, with its variety of goals including affordable housing, ecological living and participatory governance (Chatterton, 2013).

Critiques: What future collective action?

So it is clear that there are a range of initiatives which take the starting point 'the solution is collective', and that these attempt both to reduce consumption impacts, but also to increase social interaction on a number of scales (household, community, economy). As I have already hinted, there are some tensions inherent in these initiatives which need closer consideration. Indeed, a number of critical responses have emerged to the 'ideal' of participation that we have noted in the sustainable development literature. The initial enthusiasm that writers held for initiatives such as Transition Towns and the sharing economy, have given way to more measured assessments of the value of such initiatives. Note that a more detailed version of this discussion is also available (Taylor Aiken et al., under review), and that I am indebted to my co-authors for their collaboration in forming the key ideas below.

One of the key critiques of community-based sustainable consumption initiatives is that those engaged in these projects hold a variety of understandings as to what collective action is, and what it is for. This most often causes problems when government approaches the community instrumentally, as an arm's-length tool for policy implementation, and we sometimes see communities co-opted by government objectives in this context (Creamer, 2014; Kenis, 2016; Taylor Aiken, 2014a, 2016a). 'Community' in this context often refers to local action, as opposed to a broader interpretation of community to include communities of interest or practice (Taylor Aiken, 2014b; Kenis and Mathijs, 2014). Authors also note that 'community' often invokes the rural (locally produced food as a central strand) and the radical (as opposed to less radical action at national or international scales) (Kenis and Mathijs, 2014). None of these things are necessarily true of collective action; an initiative might be radical, rural and local, or it might be none of these things.

Indeed, communities (and their members) frequently have very different understandings of their own activities than other stakeholders (especially government) do. Communities might have transformative intentions that go much further than government policy on sustainability. On the other hand, communities might be tempted to aim for more conservative goals in order to attract a wider range of participants (Büchs et al., 2015). Anneleen Kenis (2016) notes how the Transition Towns movement is more likely to look for consensus and avoid politics, than the more radical Climate Justice Action, in her study of the Belgian movements. Martin (2016) notes a similar diversity of meaning and intent in public discourses on the sharing economy, which can be viewed as anything from a profitable business initiative, to an opportunity for reducing resource inputs and reinvigorating social life.

This point hints at our second critique: these projects cannot be understood outside of their context, which is based in a global North, and neo-liberalised world. This context has several important impacts on how these projects play out. For instance, in an individualised world, one in which people understand themselves as individuals first and foremost, and one which aims to please and placate such individuals, acting as a community is highly counter-cultural (Middlemiss, 2014). How do we then interpret attempts to make change collectively? Are these positive signs of a resurgence in collective action (Barnett et al., 2010; Seyfang, 2009) or merely a way of greenwashing the lack of action at a national level, and distracting from individualising policy (Scerri and Magee, 2012; Blühdorn, 2013)? A common description of 'governance by community' in this sense is to describe it as neo-liberal 'roll-back' of the state (where governments transfer responsibility to community), accompanied by a 'roll-out' of individualising ideas (where governments set expectations for communities to fulfil individualising targets) (Rosol, 2012; Taylor Aiken, 2014b).

A second example: the neo-liberal focus on quantifying change within these groups (on counting how they make change), has been shown to have a substantial impact on how they operate (Hobson et al., 2016; Taylor Aiken, 2016b). Again, this is reminiscent of Martin and colleagues' work on the sharing economy, where they find that commercial expectations of Freegle result in changed practices in the organisation (Martin et al., 2015). Clearly these initiatives exist within the world of 'business as usual', and there are pressures to conform, and aim for less radical objectives. Having said that, Hobson and colleagues find that when monitoring and evaluation of group activities are moulded from the bottom up there are signs that this has an empowering function: with the potential for groups to use data to show their successes, rather than their activities being constrained by such monitoring (Hobson et al., 2016).

The final set of critiques of collective action relates to diversity, inclusion and representation within these initiatives (there are links to Chapter 3 here). This is helpfully summarised by Bulkeley and Fuller (2012) as an issue of recognition justice, which encourages us to think about who these kinds of initiative recognise as stakeholders, and who they do not. This relates, first, to who is recognised as having a voice, or as they put it: 'The basis upon which exclusion and inclusion from decision-making is currently structured' (ibid., 3). Second, they note the need to recognise the disadvantage associated with the various starting points that people have: 'The structural conditions that create vulnerability and produce uneven landscapes of greenhouse gas emissions' (ibid.). Community-based sustainable consumption, sharing economy (Schor, 2016) and community currencies are all observed by critics to be dominated by, and often run to the advantage of, white, middle-class members. As Taylor-Aiken (2012) points out, this is partly due to these demographics being at the heart of formal volunteering; they are more likely to volunteer and as such are directing these activities to their own advantage (whether knowingly or not). In the case of the sharing economy, Schor points out that 'The platforms, especially Airbnb, have emerged as an easy new way to earn, using assets that people already possess' (2016, 19).

Issues of inclusion are also raised by the messages these groups give about their understanding of (and by extension their acceptance of) difference. In their analysis of the Transition Towns movement in Belgium, Kenis and Mathijs note that 'Inclusiveness, in Transition Town's discourse, primarily seems to mean being non-oppositional, strongly collaborative, and pursuing harmony through complementarity amongst individuals and their interests' (Kenis and Mathijs, 2014, 180).

In Transition Town groups, the ideal is to achieve consensus through dialogue, and Kenis (2016) elsewhere points out that this rather ignores that power is still exercised in reaching consensus. Inevitably, some will talk louder, more frequently and with more authority. Further, Kenis points out that this rather harks back to our 'People don't understand' chapter (Chapter 4), in the way that it assumes that if we talk long enough, we will do the 'right' (i.e. 'green') thing (ibid.). A more critical view on difference here, is that these projects will be excluding people (Grossmann and Creamer, 2016), and that as such, we need to understand them as representing the interests of their constituents, rather than the interests of bigger communities.

Conclusions

At the start of this chapter, I pointed out that the call for collective action is a common refrain in the context of sustainable development. We can see sustainable consumption itself as an attempt to translate an abstract set of ideas, into the lives of ordinary people, and in doing so to engage them in a process of change. One of the reasons that people turn to collective action is nicely encapsulated by Dennis Soron:

> the promise of 'alternative' models of sustainable consumption . . . resides not only in their capacity to transform the context and material intensity of everyday consumption practices, but in their ability to challenge the powerlessness that people feel as individuated 'consumers' by reconstituting a social, collective and non-commodified basis for personal identity.
>
> (Soron, 2010, 180)

It is important to recognise this need for a sense of collective endeavour, which addresses people's concerns about being individualised. Having said this, some of the approaches to this topic have been profoundly individualistic, and indeed individualising, thereby working against any sense of collective vision, purpose and practice.

The various attempts to engage a collective in sustainable consumption described above, are in part a reaction to such individualisation, that we can see in common understandings of the world, and as manifest in some of the attempts to encourage sustainable consumption (Middlemiss, 2014). These constitute a wide variety of experiences: from the radical to the conservative; from exclusive to inclusive, from holistic to highly particular. In this context, some of the critical questions I outlined in the introduction to this book are especially pertinent. For instance, in the final section of this chapter I have been asking 'what is this solution?', or more specifically 'what kind of a solution is collective action?', 'who does it include/exclude?', 'what kind of a problem is it reacting to?' I hope that you can see the value in being critical in this way. Certainly the risk otherwise is that we assume collective is good, without seeing that its boundaries are just as politically problematic as some of the individualistic approaches we have seen in earlier chapters.

Other resources

Great Transition debate on sharing economy: http://greattransition.org/publication/debating-the-sharing-economy
Luke Yates on small households: http://discoversociety.org/2016/01/05/the-environmental-threat-of-small-households-six-reasons-to-think-again/

References

AIKEN, G. 2012. Community transitions to low carbon futures in the Transition Towns Network (TTN). *Geography Compass*, 6, 89–99.
BARNETT, C., CLOKE, P., CLARKE, N. & MALPASS, A. 2010. *Globalizing Responsibility: The Political Rationalities of Ethical Consumption.* Indianapolis, IN: Wiley.
BARTIAUX, F. & REATEGUI SALMON, L. 2014. Family dynamics and social practice theories: An investigation of daily practices related to food, mobility, energy consumption and tourism. *Nature and Culture*, 9, 204–224.
BELK, R. 2014. You are what you can access: Sharing and collaborative consumption online. *Journal of Business Research*, 67, 1595–1600.
BLÜHDORN, I. 2013. The governance of unsustainability: Ecology and democracy after the post-democratic turn. *Environmental Politics*, 22, 16–36.
BÖCKER, L. & MEELEN, T. 2017. Sharing for people, planet or profit? Analysing motivations for intended sharing economy participation. *Environmental Innovation and Societal Transitions*, 23, 28–39.
BOTSMAN, R. & ROGERS, R. 2010. *What's Mine is Yours: How Collaborative Consumption is Changing the Way We Live.* London: Harper Collins.
BRADBURY, M., PETERSON, M. N. & LIU, J. 2014. Long-term dynamics of household size and their environmental implications. *Population and Environment*, 36, 73–84.
BÜCHS, M. & SCHNEPF, S. V. 2013. Who emits most? Associations between socio-economic factors and UK households' home energy, transport, indirect and total CO_2 emissions. *Ecological Economics*, 90, 114–123.
BÜCHS, M., SAUNDERS, C., WALLBRIDGE, R., SMITH, G. & BARDSLEY, N. 2015. Identifying and explaining framing strategies of low carbon lifestyle movement organisations. *Global Environmental Change*, 35, 307–315.
BULKELEY, H. & FULLER, S. 2012. *Low Carbon Communities and Social Justice* [Online]. Available: www.jrf.org.uk/sites/default/files/jrf/migrated/files/low-carbon-communities-summary.pdf [Accessed 21 December 2017].
BURNINGHAM, K. & VENN, S. 2017. Are lifecourse transitions opportunities for moving to more sustainable consumption? *Journal of Consumer Culture*. Available: http://journals.sagepub.com/doi/abs/10.1177/1469540517729010 [Accessed 29 March 2018].
BUTLER, C., PARKHILL, K. A., SHIRANI, F., HENWOOD, K. & PIDGEON, N. 2014. Examining the dynamics of energy demand through a biographical lens. *Nature and Culture*, 9, 164–182.
CHATTERTON, P. 2013. Towards an agenda for post-carbon cities: Lessons from Lilac, the UK's first ecological, affordable cohousing community. *International Journal of Urban and Regional Research*, 37, 1654–1674.

CHATTERTON, P. & CUTLER, A. 2008. *The Rocky Road to a Real Transition: The Transition Towns Movement and What It Means for Social Change*. Available: http://trapese.clearer channel.org/resources/rocky-road-a5-web.pdf [Accessed 29 March 2018].

CONNORS, P. & MCDONALD, P. 2011. Transitioning communities: Community, participation and the transition town movement. *Community Development Journal*, 46, 558–572.

CREAMER, E. 2014. The double-edged sword of grant funding: A study of community-led climate change initiatives in remote rural Scotland. *Local Environment*, 20, 981–999.

DE GEUS, M. 2004. The environment versus individual freedom and convenience. *In*: WISSENBURG, M. & LEVY, Y. (eds) *Liberal Democracy and Environmentalism*. London: Routledge.

DEFRA. 2005. *Securing the Future: Delivering UK Sustainable Development Strategy* [Online]. Available: http://www.sustainable-development.gov.uk/publications/pdf/strategy/ SecFut_complete.pdf [Accessed 29 March 2018].

GLOBAL ENVIRONMENTAL CHANGE. 2013. Special issue on Grassroots Innovations.

GROSSMANN, M. & CREAMER, E. 2016. Assessing diversity and inclusivity within the Transition movement: an urban case study. *Environmental Politics*, 26, 161–182.

GRUSZKA, K. 2016. Framing the collaborative economy – Voices of contestation. *Environmental Innovation and Societal Transitions*, 23, 92–104.

HAMARI, J., SJÖKLINT, M. & UKKONEN, A. 2015. The sharing economy: Why people participate in collaborative consumption. *Journal of the Association for Information Science and Technology*, 67, 2047–2059.

HARDIN, G. 1968. The tragedy of the commons. *Science*, 162, 1243–1248.

HARGREAVES, T. 2011. Practice-ing behaviour change: Applying social practice theory to pro-environmental behaviour change. *Journal of Consumer Culture*, 11, 79–99.

HEINRICHS, H. 2013. Sharing economy: A potential new pathway to sustainability. *GAIA – Ecological Perspectives for Science and Society*, 22, 228–231.

HOBSON, K., MAYNE, R. & HAMILTON, J. 2016. Monitoring and evaluating eco-localisation: Lessons from UK low carbon community groups. *Environment and Planning A*, 48, 1393–1410.

ISAKSSON, C. & ELLEGÅRD, K. 2015. Dividing or sharing? A time-geographical examination of eating, labour, and energy consumption in Sweden. *Energy Research & Social Science*, 10, 180–191.

JACKSON, T. 2009. *Prosperity Without Growth*. London: Earthscan.

JAEGER-ERBEN, M., RÜCKERT-JOHN, J. & SCHÄFER, M. 2015. Sustainable consumption through social innovation: a typology of innovations for sustainable consumption practices. *Journal of Cleaner Production*, 108, 784–798.

KENDALL, J. 2003. *The Voluntary Sector: Comparative Perspectives in the UK*. London: Routledge.

KENIS, A. 2016. Ecological citizenship and democracy: Communitarian versus agonistic perspectives. *Environmental Politics*, 25, 949–970.

KENIS, A. & MATHIJS, E. 2014. (De) politicising the local: The case of the Transition Towns movement in Flanders (Belgium). *Journal of Rural Studies*, 34, 172–183.

MACHIN, A. 2013. *Negotiating Climate Change: Radical Democracy and the Illusion of Consensus*. London: Zed Books.

MARTIN, C. J. 2016. The sharing economy: A pathway to sustainability or a nightmarish form of neoliberal capitalism? *Ecological Economics*, 121, 149–159.

MARTIN, E. W. & SHAHEEN, S. A. 2011. Greenhouse gas emission impacts of car-sharing in North America. *IEEE Transactions on Intelligent Transportation Systems*, 12, 1074–1086.

MARTIN, C. J., UPHAM, P. & BUDD, L. 2015. Commercial orientation in grassroots social innovation: Insights from the sharing economy. *Ecological Economics*, 118, 240–251.

MCCAMANT, K. & DURRETT, C. 2011. *Creating Cohousing: Building Sustainable Communities*, Gabriola Island, B.C.: New Society Publishers.

MELTZER, G. 2000. Cohousing: Verifying the importance of community in the application of environmentalism. *Journal of Architectural and Planning Research*, 17, 110–132.

MICHEL, A. & HUDON, M. 2015. Community currencies and sustainable development: A systematic review. *Ecological Economics*, 116, 160–171.

MIDDLEMISS, L. 2010. Reframing individual responsibility for sustainable consumption: Lessons from environmental justice and ecological citizenship. *Environmental Values*, 19, 147–167.

MIDDLEMISS, L. 2011a. The effects of community-based action for sustainability on participant lifestyles. *Local Environment*, 16, 265–280.

MIDDLEMISS, L. 2011b. The power of community: How community-based organisations stimulate sustainable lifestyles among participants. *Society and Natural Resources*, 24, 1157–1173.

MIDDLEMISS, L. 2014. Individualised or participatory? Exploring late-modern identity and sustainable development. *Environmental Politics*, 23, 929–946.

MIDDLEMISS, L. & GILLARD, R. 2015. Fuel poverty from the bottom-up: Characterising household energy vulnerability through the lived experience of the fuel poor. *Energy Research & Social Science*, 6, 146–154.

NICHOLLS, L. & STRENGERS, Y. 2015. Peak demand and the 'family peak' period in Australia: Understanding practice (in) flexibility in households with children. *Energy Research & Social Science*, 9, 116–124.

OSTROM, E. 1990. *Governing the Commons: The Evolution of Institutions for Collective Action*. Cambridge, UK: Cambridge University Press.

POWELLS, G., BULKELEY, H., BELL, S. & JUDSON, E. 2014. Peak electricity demand and the flexibility of everyday life. *Geoforum*, 55, 43–52.

ROSOL, M. 2012. Community volunteering as neoliberal strategy? Green space production in Berlin. *Antipode*, 44, 239–257.

SAHAKIAN, M. 2014. Complementary currencies: What opportunities for sustainable consumption in times of crisis and beyond? *Sustainability: Science, Practice, & Policy*, 10, 4–13.

SAHAKIAN, M. D. & DUNAND, C. 2014. The social and solidarity economy towards greater 'sustainability': Learning across contexts and cultures, from Geneva to Manila. *Community Development Journal*, 50, 403–417.

SCERRI, A. & MAGEE, L. 2012. Green householders, stakeholder citizenship and sustainability. *Environmental Politics*, 21, 387–411.

SCHÄFER, M., JAEGER-ERBEN, M. & BAMBERG, S. 2012. Life events as windows of opportunity for changing towards sustainable consumption patterns? *Journal of Consumer Policy*, 35, 65–84.

SCHOR, J. B. 2016. Does the sharing economy increase inequality within the eighty percent? Findings from a qualitative study of platform providers. *Cambridge Journal of Regions*, 10, 263–279.

SCHOR, J. B. & FITZMAURICE, C. J. 2015. Collaborating and connecting: the emergence of the sharing economy. *In*: REISCH, L. & THOGERSEN, J. (eds) *Handbook of Research on Sustainable Consumption*. Cheltenham, UK: Edward Elgar.

SEYFANG, G. 2009. *The New Economics of Sustainable Consumption: Seeds of Change*. Basingstoke, UK: Palgrave Macmillan.

SEYFANG, G. & LONGHURST, N. 2013. Growing green money? Mapping community currencies for sustainable development. *Ecological Economics*, 86, 65–77.

SEYFANG, G. & SMITH, A. 2007. Grassroots innovations for sustainable development: Towards a new research and policy agenda. *Environmental Politics*, 16, 584–603.

SEYFANG, G., PARK, J. J. & SMITH, A. 2013. A thousand flowers blooming? An examination of community energy in the UK. *Energy Policy*, 61, 977–989.

SORON, D. 2010. Sustainability, self-identity and the sociology of consumption. *Sustainable Development*, 18, 172–181.

TAYLOR AIKEN, G. 2014a. Common sense community? The Climate Challenge Fund's official and tacit community construction. *Scottish Geographical Journal*, 130, 207–221.

TAYLOR AIKEN, G. 2014b. (Local-) community for global challenges: Carbon conversations, transition towns and governmental elisions. *Local Environment*, 20, 764–781.

TAYLOR AIKEN, G. 2016a. Polysemic, polyvalent and phatic: A rough evolution of community with reference to low carbon transitions. *People, Place and Policy*, 10, 126–145.

TAYLOR AIKEN, G. 2016b. Prosaic state governance of community low carbon transitions. *Political Geography*, 55, 20–29.

TAYLOR AIKEN, G., MIDDLEMISS, L., SALLU, S. & HAUXWELL-BALDWIN, R. under review. Researching climate change and community in neoliberal contexts: An emerging critical approach. *Wiley Interdisciplinary Reviews: Climate Change*.

TRANSITION NETWORK. 2016. *Transition Network* [Online]. Available: www.transition network.org/ [Accessed 31 March 2012].

WILLIAMS, J. 2005. Designing neighbourhoods for social interaction: The case of cohousing. *Journal of Urban Design*, 10, 195–227.

WORLD COMMISSION ON ENVIRONMENT AND DEVELOPMENT 1987. *Our Common Future*. Oxford, UK: Oxford University Press.

YATES, L. 2016. Sharing, households and sustainable consumption. *Journal of Consumer Culture*, 39, 881–898.

12 Sustainable consumption makes you happy!

This chapter is co-authored with David Wingate

In this chapter, we address a widespread framing of sustainable consumption as a route to happiness. This is a framing that is seen in academic work, and in a broader public discourse, where we often see the idea of happiness invoked as a goal or outcome of environmental action. Further, the relationship between sustainable consumption and happiness is part of a wider public conversation about what makes us happy, and how we might achieve 'well-being'. Witness extensive conversation around how 'money doesn't make you happy', the self-help industry's promise of a 'better', happier you, the idea of the 'quantified self' (when people monitor their own behaviour by counting in order to 'improve' themselves), the enthusiasm for 'mindfulness' and so on.

For some time, environmentalists have been preoccupied with thinking about what makes us happy. As this is a question that is being asked more generally in the public domain, it is not surprising that it arises in the context of sustainable consumption. However, the public image of environmentalists as serious, grumpy, self-sacrificing, advocating a 'return' to less resource-intensive and traditional ways of living, potentially even judgmental of others' behaviour, has also played a role. In the face of this stereotype, the environmental world has felt the need to fight back – by finding a more positive story to tell. Intriguingly, this more positive story reverses the common perception of consumption: instead of 'consuming makes you happy', the argument put forward in the sustainable consumption world is that if we reduce consumption levels, this will both reduce environmental damage, and also potentially make us happier. In other words, the conversation around sustainable consumption here suggests that the route to happiness is through consuming less, or 'downshifting'.

Some of these ideas are probably instinctively familiar to you – the 'promotion' of happiness through reduced consumption is widespread in western environmentalism. In this chapter, we will look at the logic of the idea that 'sustainable consumption makes you happy', its roots in evidence on happiness, and ideas of human nature and needs, and how academics and practitioners have used this idea (in a discussion of voluntary simplicity, or downshifting). In the review of this work at the end of the chapter, we argue that it is important to remain critical both of the idea that sustainable consumption brings happiness, and the idea that it is appropriate to aim for happiness in the first place.

There are some disagreements over the meanings of the terms 'happiness' and 'well-being'. Sometimes they are used interchangeably (Veenhoven, 2012), but in general, well-being is thought of as an umbrella concept, which includes a number of forms of happiness (life satisfaction, 'episodic' happiness), which aggregate to an overall understanding of people's happiness status (Diener et al., 1999; Veenhoven, 2012). Broader interpretations of well-being also include social, political, geographic and infrastructural impacts on well-being, especially for instance the 'eudaimonic' interpretations we will introduce below (Brand-Correa and Steinberger, 2017). Here we will err towards the word 'well-being', unless 'happiness' is used specifically by the authors we cite.

So how could sustainable consumption make you happy?

As a starting point, we will introduce a well-known piece of work by Tim Jackson, a highly influential author in this field, who coined the term 'double dividend' (2005). This 'hedonic' (explained below) interpretation of well-being dominates in research about sustainable consumption and well-being, and as such merits a detailed description. You will also see that Jackson's work reappears throughout the chapter – given its influence, it is the main argument we will discuss throughout. We will also refer to work on 'eudaimonic' (explained below) well-being in this field, which is based on a more social understanding of how well-being comes about, and therefore opens up different kinds of questions about what can be done (Brand-Correa and Steinberger, 2017).

In his paper, Jackson argues that we could 'devise a society in which it is possible to live better (or at least as well as we have done) by consuming less, and become more human in the process' (2005, 33). This argument hangs on the evidence that while per capita consumption in industrialised countries has been increasing for several decades, self-reported well-being has not been increasing at the same rate and therefore we can safely reduce environmentally damaging consumption without causing any loss of well-being (known as the 'Easterlin Paradox'). The double dividend takes this one step further, claiming not only that consumption *does not make us happy*, but in fact too much consumption *actually makes us unhappy*. As a result, a reduction in consumption would not only benefit the environment, but would also *make us happier* (hence, a double dividend, as two types of benefit are accrued).

The double dividend takes on, and contradicts, the mainstream point of view: that people consume to be happy. This mainstream conception is rooted in economic theory, which, as we saw in Chapter 5, would argue that a higher income provides an individual with greater opportunities to consume, which in turn allows that person access to greater well-being. Following this way of thinking, people are expected to act to 'maximise their utility', which could be interpreted as maximising their well-being. The double dividend challenges this logic – indeed it reverses it, such that the central claim moves from 'consumption makes you happy' to 'sustainable (reduced) consumption makes you happy'.

As we have said, this idea has been highly influential in the sustainable consumption literature, and beyond (Madjar and Ozawa, 2006; Berg, 2009; Knight and Rosa, 2011; Alexander and Ussher, 2012; MacKerron, 2012). The double-dividend concept is not a new one, and it impacts on environmental policy and practice, at many scales and in many contexts. For instance, the Rio Declaration on Environment and Development advocated for 'new concepts of wealth and prosperity which allow higher standards of living through changed lifestyles and are less dependent on the Earth's finite resources and more in harmony with the Earth's carrying capacity' (UNCED, 1992, section 4.11).

Here the aspiration is both to raise standards of living and to reduce impact on the environment by redefining wealth and prosperity. In a much more local context, Frances Bonner notes how in green lifestyle television, presenters 'are consistent in emphasizing the fun they are having and the pleasures of the practices they promote' (2011, 233). We can also see these ideas playing out in recommendations in the more general sustainable consumption literature: 'pro-environmental actions can be made (to be perceived as) more convenient, fun, cheaper or less effortful as to make such actions more attractive' (Steg et al., 2014, 105). While authors and commentators reference this idea with varying levels of enthusiasm, in some circles, the idea that 'consuming less makes you happy' is accepted as truth.

The double dividend represents an attempt to shift the story about people's involvement in environmental solutions from one of self-sacrifice, to one of increasing well-being. In relation to the wider literature on well-being, this amounts to a 'hedonic' approach, one that focuses on maximising the pleasure of the individual, and minimising their pain (in this case, hedonism through sustainability!). Lina Brand-Correa and Julia Steinberger summarise the central argument in this field: 'it should be possible to decouple well-being from increased consumption simply by shifting utility functions: by convincing people what other elements (beyond consumption after a minimum level has been reached) are constituents of well-being' (2017, 44).

In other words, this hedonic perspective on sustainable consumption argues for a reframing of what counts as 'making me happy' (after basic needs have been met). There is a strong focus both on individual well-being, and on changing the story of what counts as a 'good life'.

Similar ideas to the double dividend are elaborated in theoretical work by the philosopher Kate Soper (also covered in Chapter 9). Soper (2008) argues that a transition to sustainability requires an alternative vision of the good life; she calls this a 'new erotics of consumption':

> the chances of developing or reverting to a more ecologically sustainable use of resources, and hence of removing some of the key sources of social and environmental exploitation, are dependent on the emergence and embrace of new modes of thinking about human pleasure and self-realization, especially, in the first instance, on the part of the affluent global elites.
>
> (Ibid., 571)

Soper (2004) believes that we are already seeing the emergence of an 'alternative hedonism', a counter-consumerist trend. She argues that people act because they find pleasure in acting, and therefore if we can make sustainable consumption pleasurable, people will engage with it. Soper also claims that appeals to altruism and compassion are not enough, and that an appeal to self-interest is required in order to engage those who already consume the most.

An alternative way in which ideas of sustainable consumption and well-being are brought together is through a 'eudaimonic' interpretation of well-being (Brand-Correa and Steinberger, 2017). Eudaimonia focuses on 'the enabling of humans to reach their highest potential within the context of their society' (ibid., 44). These authors claim that to experience well-being, someone must be able to flourish in a given social context, regardless of their personal circumstances (ibid.). As a result, this work places more attention on how social context enables well-being. This work suggests that instead of changing people's ideas about what well-being constitutes, we must first see how well-being, or flourishing, can be achieved in the current social context, and also think about how the social context could be transformed in order for well-being to be more easily achieved. Note that thinking 'eudaimonically' about well-being maintains a challenge to the idea that consumption is the route to happiness.

Much of the rest of this chapter will address the hedonic interpretation of well-being, as used by the double dividend and in Jackson's work (2005, 2008), given that this has been the most influential in sustainable consumption research and practice to date. Our next step is to engage with the evidence on well-being mobilized by the double dividend.

Evidence on well-being

In thinking hedonically about well-being, Jackson draws on the happiness studies literature (see especially Diener et al., 1999; Inglehart et al., 2008; Layard, 2006). One of the key pieces of evidence used in the sustainability debate is shown in Figure 12.1, which cites data on a large number of countries around the world, and plots their average reported life satisfaction (based on international surveys asking people 'how happy are you on a scale of 1 to 10?') against their average GDP per person (a proxy for their levels of consumption, and taken from national statistics). The point that scholars (including Jackson) make from this graph is that when people's income (and related potential to consume) increases, initially their happiness also increases (for instance, the difference between Macedonia and the Czech Republic). However, after a certain level of wealth is attained – for instance, the place of Argentina or Uruguay on the chart – happiness does not increase anymore as a result of added income. Thus New Zealand and the United States have similar reported happiness levels despite having very different GDP per capita.

So income and happiness do not have a simple correlation, and beyond a certain point (after basic needs are met), additional income does not much add to people's reported happiness. At this point, we could talk of a 'single dividend'; from this evidence: we could claim that if consumption is reduced, this

Figure 12.1 Life satisfaction (mean score), per capita gross domestic product (GDP), differentiated by different types of societies (from Inglehart, 2018; reproduced with permission from Cambridge University Press)

will not necessarily affect well-being. Perhaps the idea of 'consuming less', that we see in strong sustainable consumption, could be achievable without a dip in well-being. Note that the evidence above is based on averages which mask the variations within countries – it could be that equivalent countries (Argentina and Uruguay) have very different distributions of happiness (with a bigger standard deviation). Further, there may be cultural differences in interpretations of the question 'how happy are you?', as well as culturally appropriate responses to this. Cultural differences could explain the group of relatively 'happy' but income-poor Latin American countries, versus the 'sad' but income-poor ex-communist European countries.

So where is the evidence for a 'double dividend', in which we would expect to see less consumption *and* greater well-being? For this, Jackson draws on the happiness studies literature, foregrounding, for instance, a rise in reported depression and anxiety in income-rich countries, high levels of reported happiness in some income-poor countries, and studies correlating 'materialistic values' with low levels of psychological well-being (Jackson, 2005, 2008). He also draws on the work of Juliet Schor and Tim Kasser, who make similar arguments as to the possible detrimental effects of consumption. Schor's (1999) sociological study of the 'life/work balance' explores a growing discontent with the culture of working longer hours to consume more, which has prompted some people to 'downshift' – to work fewer hours and consume less – for the sake of their happiness. Schor argues that the unhappiness caused by working longer hours outweighs any benefits brought about by increased income, suggesting that society would prosper, given more leisure time. Kasser's (2003) empirical work consists largely of quantitative psychological experimentation, which suggests a strong correlation between what he terms 'materialistic values' and unhappiness. Kasser believes that this link is causal, and claims that a less materialistic lifestyle would satisfy what he refers to as 'intrinsic' human needs, resulting in greater psychological well-being.

At this point, we need to ask some questions about understandings of human needs and human nature in this hedonic interpretation of well-being. In Jackson's work on the double dividend, and Kasser's work on 'materialistic values', the implication is that materialism and 'over'-consumption is counterproductive to both fulfilling human needs, and to being happy. This also suggests that there is a universal set of human needs (if 'over'-consumption is 'bad' for people, no one needs it) and in turn a universal human nature. These are arguments rather than facts, and, as we will see, both concepts (universal human needs and human nature) are contested.

Human needs and human nature

When we think about happiness, how it is created, and what people might understand to be a state of well-being, we very quickly get into discussions of human needs and human nature. In environmentalist circles, there is a tendency to mark out products or practices as either 'needs' or 'wants', justifying some forms of consumption and dismissing others. You may have made these judgements yourself, or have had such judgements made about your own consumption. When we make universal statements about some forms of consumption being fundamental (needs), and others less important (wants) to achieving well-being, the implication is that there is a common set of needs that all human beings should fulfil, which in itself implies a common human nature. In other words, people need some things, and merely want others, because, based on an understanding of what people are like (their human nature), it is possible to categorise consumption according to what is objectively 'necessary' or not for their well-being.

The hedonic well-being perspective on sustainable consumption says that we are currently consuming both to meet our needs, and to meet our 'wants' or desires, and that the latter type of consumption is not helping us to create well-being (Jackson, 2005). This suggests that some consumption is 'good for us' (good for all of us) and some is not. Further, according to this way of thinking, our needs can be met with lower levels of consumption (ibid.). The implication is that much of our consumption is unnecessary, and is failing to meet our needs, failing to create well-being and damaging the environment in the process.

Let's stop for a minute to think about this. Talking about needs and wants as universal raises some important political questions. For instance, is it really the case that much of our consumption is unnecessary? Who gets to decide what is necessary and what is not? Do we all really have the same needs as each other? If we are to take on this kind of politics – one which argues that we are over-consuming according to our 'real' nature and 'human' needs – are we not likely to be oppressing people with different needs?

Even if we agree that you can make a clear distinction between wants and needs, exactly where the line is drawn between these is a matter for debate. There will be material things that we would expect to be categorised as merely 'wants' in environmental circles – for instance, luxury goods, inefficient cars, or perhaps travelling by air. Writers are often at pains to point out that this is not just about material needs being fulfilled. For example, in Jackson's book *Prosperity Without Growth*, he writes:

> more than material security is needed for human beings to flourish. Prosperity has vital social and psychological dimensions. To do well is in part about the ability to contribute useful work and to have a sense of belonging and trust in the community.
>
> (Jackson, 2009, 36)

There is a sense of an exchange happening here – that is, swapping consumption of unnecessary things for well-being (belonging, trust, and useful work). Note that even a 'sense of belonging' and 'contributing to useful work' are universalist statements of need.

There is a complex and substantial debate about human needs and human nature in the social science literature. Early understandings of needs tend to place material needs (shelter, food, water) further up the hierarchy than symbolic needs (love, self-expression, self-actualisation), albeit with a recognition that the latter are still essential (see, famously, Maslow, 1943). More recently, scholars have attempted to enumerate the fundamental human needs that must be satisfied in order to produce well-being (Nussbaum, 2011: Doyal and Gough, 1984: Max-Neef, 1991). Those espousing a universal understanding of human needs (and nature) have also introduced some complexity into this thinking. For instance, the concept of a needs 'satisfier' allows us to understand needs in a more culturally specific way (Max-Neef, 1991), putting a distance between the need and the thing that satisfies that need. A human need might be the opportunity to participate in society, while in one particular cultural context, the satisfiers of this need might be a basic education, significant primary relationships and economic security (Gough, 2015). These satisfiers might differ from person to person and from culture to culture, but the fundamental need (participation) remains the same. The concept of satisfiers allows scholars to avoid prescribing specific ways with which to fulfil your (universal) needs, thereby allowing for the subjectivity of individuals' lived experience.

One of the key points to make here is that not everyone agrees that human needs are universal (notably Sen, 1999). The introduction of needs satisfiers relates to our discussion of social difference and sustainable consumption, where we can see clear challenges to the idea of universality (see Chapter 3). Fenney Salkeld's discussion of the bike as an 'ableist' symbol, and cycling as an environmentalist practice which excludes disabled people, is a good example of this. Cycling is not a satisfier that is appropriate for some physically disabled people to fulfil the need for mobility. A number of forms of social difference (bodily, cultural, status-related) can impact on how we understand needs and satisfiers. There is a strong risk in environmentalist discourses of a list of universal needs (or indeed satisfiers) becoming a moral distinction – with the universal 'needs' being 'good' and the universal 'wants' being 'bad'. Sara Ahmed, to whom we will return in the critique below, sees a well-being lens as a means of turning judgements of taste into value judgements: if our 'needs' have been deemed mere 'desires', then they are less 'worthy', because they are 'inauthentic' (2010). These dangers are by no means inevitable, but it is important to maintain an understanding of social difference, so as not to fall into the trap of marginalising, oppressing, or simply ignoring others.

Voluntary simplicity

So how are these ideas used in practice? You can probably guess that governments would hesitate to tell their citizens to 'consume less in order to be happy'. This idea is problematic in a number of ways. For instance, governments do not want to look like 'nanny states', as if they are interfering in their citizens' daily lives by telling them how to 'be happy'. In addition, given their objectives for economic growth, and the way in which this is ensured through consumer spending, they are hesitant to ask for people to 'consume less'. However, there are grass-roots responses which draw on these ideas. Here we profile voluntary simplicity as a living example of the idea that 'less consumption makes you happy'.

Voluntary simplicity is a small anti-consumerist movement which has taken on this idea with enthusiasm. This varies from people making small adjustments to their lives (going part-time at work, choosing to live in a smaller house) to more radical steps (buying nothing for a year, practicing zero waste). People who practice such 'voluntary simplicity' are often enthusiastic advocates of the idea that 'consuming less makes you happy'. Voluntary simplists often say that reducing consumption reduces the stresses associated with living in a consumer society (Zavestoski, 2002). This also seems to be a widespread movement. Juliet Schor (1999) found that in 1998, 20 per cent of Americans had chosen to downshift (in one way or another); Emily Huddart-Kennedy and colleagues found that

26 per cent of Canadians in Alberta had downshifted in the previous five years (Huddart-Kennedy et al., 2013). Michael Maniates (2002) notes that voluntary simplists in the US are financially average, but substantially more educated than the norm, giving them more 'power over work' than most people. The motivations to downshift or simplify are not necessarily environmental, indeed in Huddart-Kennedy's work no one mentioned environment, and Maniates finds that many people are trying to find 'ways that ordinary people caught in the midst of it all might reasonably react to preserve their sanity, their families, and their sense of self-esteem' (2002, 216).

Box 12.1 Some examples of initiatives to reduce consumption

There are many initiatives that promote the idea that reducing consumption brings happiness. For instance:

- **Buy Nothing Day** is celebrated on Black Friday, the day after Thanksgiving in the US, and a day on which retailers offer big discounts to customers at the start of the Christmas shopping season. This sale is also popping up in places where Thanksgiving is not celebrated. The UK version of the campaign (Buy Nothing Day Website, 2017) has as its motto 'shop less, live more'. The picture painted is of a world in which people are coerced into fighting for bargains, in response to which the website asks 'Can you resist the urge to splurge? Or will Black Friday bully you into buying things you probably don't need?'
- **Campaigns to reduce working hours** say that if people worked less, they would be happier, and that environmental impacts would be reduced as people had less disposable income. The New Economics Foundation (2010) in the UK argued that reducing working hours would tackle unemployment and overwork, increase well-being, and reduce impacts on the environment. These arguments have had limited traction in the UK, but the national government in France implemented a 35-hour working week in 2000, and Swedish companies have independently implemented a 6-hour working day. The evidence for these claims for reducing working hours is mixed, but it could be argued that such a strategy is worth a try given the variety of potentially positive outcomes (Kallis et al., 2013).

The impacts of voluntary simplicity have been measured in empirical work. The results show that when based on self-reported measures of well-being (effectively answers to 'how happy are you?'), people report a range of impacts.

This includes either non-significant differences (Huddart Kennedy et al., 2013), or substantial effects (Alexander and Ussher, 2012). Huddart-Kennedy and colleagues find non-significant differences when they control for class variables such as education, income, owning a home (ibid.). However they do find that downshifting is significantly associated with sustainable household practices (ibid.). They argue that social context is important when thinking about downshifting, and that this is unlikely to have as much traction as we might hope in a world which social structures do not enable more sustainable practices (see chapter 8). Perhaps a more substantial shift is needed (see also Chapter 13). Halina Brown and Philip Vergragt (2015) argue that, given their unique generational position, millennials may be best placed to make a shift in values: from valuing stuff to valuing well-being. Others argue for the need for 'utopias of sufficiency' rather than 'utopias of abundance', recalling Kate Soper's arguments (de Geus, 2003).

Much of the work on voluntary simplicity is written by advocates (Alexander and Ussher, 2012; Schor, 1999; Elgin, 1993) which results in an evangelical tone reminiscent of religious or self-help texts. Elgin, a campaigner and influential author within the movement, describes voluntary simplicity as 'a manner of living that is outwardly more simple and inwardly more rich, a way of being in which our most authentic and alive self is brought into direct and conscious contact with living' (1993, 25).

Elgin's language – 'inwardly rich', 'authentic', 'alive self' – implies that 'we' are currently not living authentic lives, and that voluntary simplicity provides a solution to this. There are similar statements in Jackson's work around the double dividend: 'we could collectively devise a society in which it is possible to live better (or at least as well as we have done) by consuming less, and become more human in the process' (Jackson, 2005, 33). The implication of both perspectives is that this is a 'better' way of living, and that those who consume less are more authentic, more 'human' even.

Another problem with the voluntary simplicity movement links back to our discussion on individualisation in Chapter 5. The logic of 'consume less and you will be happier' (and have less impact on the environment) is individualising – positioning the problem and solution as belonging to the individual, as well as happiness being the property of the individual. Intriguingly, voluntary simplicity imagines very specific motivations for the individual, based around psychological needs for an uncluttered and calm life (Etzioni, 2006), rather than environmentalist commitments. This in turn results in solutions to unhappiness being pitched at individuals, rather than at society as in the eudaimonic perspective (Brand-Correa and Steinberger, 2017). As we have seen, individualising the solution to environmental issues is problematic because it ignores social barriers to change, and places the responsibility too clearly on the individual – 'encouraging powerless people to believe they can significantly control their lives, and blaming themselves when they fail' (Gough, 2015).

The tendency of voluntary simplicity to individualise is particularly problematic in the context of sustainable development where the problem is seen as collective (Middlemiss, 2014). Indeed, there is a strange tension in the voluntary simplicity movement, given that it does rely on collective action (Alexander and Ussher, 2012), and yet works with an individualised logic. Clearly, as Lawrence Buell puts it, 'We need feasible alternatives models for collective sustainable living above and beyond individually chosen redirections of lifestyle' (Buell, 2014, 13). How personal happiness translates into social transformation is not clear (Humphery, 2011). Indeed the double dividend imagines a self-interested hedonist, rationally seeking a better life for themselves, and in the process somehow creating social change. The parallels with more conventional visions of the consumer are unnerving.

Critiques

You may have been able to detect throughout this chapter that we are not entirely convinced by the argument that people are happier if they consume less. We hope to have given it a good enough exposition, so that you can make your own mind up. However, we also have some major reservations about this argument, and the way that it is so liberally used in environmentalist circles. These fall into three main points:

1 A *problem with universal ideas of the good life*.
2 A *problem with the incentivising discourse* used especially in the hedonic understanding of happiness and well-being.
3 A *problem with the politics of well-being* as a social goal.

We will deal with each of these in turn in the sections below.

Universal ideas of the good life

Whilst there may be some basic, or very abstract characteristics, which all humans share, those characteristics do not translate into specific cultural practices like those associated with consumption. And even if everyone can feel something called 'happiness', there is great variety in the specific things that cause or evoke happiness in different people. Because of this, when we try to make generalisations about 'what humans need' or 'what makes people happy', they either have to be so abstract as to be, in practical terms, meaningless, or else they end up being so culturally specific that they ignore the real needs of huge numbers of people for the sake of (over)simplicity. That is why, for example, we end up with some rather bland statements about how people want to 'participate in society', when in reality people have very different interpretations of what 'participation' is. It is difficult, even impossible, to talk meaningfully about 'what makes people happy' in a universal way. Any specified 'need' can have radically different satisfiers, so there is very little analytic value in placing them all in a single category, at least not for the study of sustainable consumption.

In talking about human needs in a universalist way, there is a tendency to make distinctions between 'real needs' and 'mere wants', as we discussed earlier. Sara Ahmed (2010) argues that when deciding on what counts as a 'real need', we engage in a moralistic and political assessment of how people choose to live their lives. There is a risk that when a group of (predominantly) middle-class, educated researchers try to rationalise this messy topic, we end up with a list of needs derived from our own tastes.

In the discussion of voluntary simplicity above, it is clear that this option is only open to particular types of people. You can only reduce consumption if you already consume 'too much' in the first place. As a result, while reducing consumption to create well-being might be a positive step for those who have plenty, it is clearly not an option open to everyone (Littler, 2009). One of the simplest objections when talking about reducing consumption (and increasing well-being) is humanity's persistent failure to provide everyone with the most basic needs such as food, warmth and shelter. How might someone who can't afford to consume as much as they would like, feel about a drive to 'reduce consumption'? Are they to accept being told that they are happier as they are, and that being lifted out of poverty would only make them unhappy? Hopefully, it is becoming clear why universalist ideas of human nature and needs can be highly problematic.

Finally, there is a problem in conflating all aspects of consumption with the damage caused by some forms of consumption, then deeming all 'symbolic' consumption as unnecessary and frivolous. While it would be fair to say that the overall levels of consumption that we see in the global North are excessive, and that many forms of consumption are unlikely to contribute to well-being, it is important to acknowledge the great social value that consumption can provide (see Chapter 9): 'consumer culture is "popular" precisely because it does . . . resonate with powerful collective desires and identity needs' (Soron, 2010, 179). In other words, one person's list of universal needs may deem one form of consumption 'meaningless', which may in fact have great meaning to someone else. In these ways, universal ideas of human nature and needs are fraught with politics, value judgements, and power relations, which make them highly problematic.

Incentivising discourse

Part of the power of the idea that 'consuming less makes you happier' is that it frames sustainable consumption as a positive intervention. This is a deliberate attempt to escape some of the negative associations of environmentalism, which can make people feel ashamed for causing environmental problems, feel powerless in the face of globalisation and industrialisation, or feel as though they must sacrifice the things they like in order to solve the problem. These moralistic, sacrificial, dystopian narratives are widely believed to have failed to persuade people of the need for change. The association of environmentalism with 'tree huggers', or other such negative stereotypes, can act as a barrier to involvement for people who do not identify with such radical politics (Hobson, 2011).

In putting a positive spin on environmentalism, 'hedonic' approaches move away from making a moral case for sustainable consumption, to making a case based on incentivisation. Its basic argument ('consume less and you will be happy') is used as a sales technique for sustainable consumption. The consumer is assumed to be a self-interested, rational actor, faced with a simple market choice: consume more and lose, or consume less and gain. Counterintuitively, this precisely mirrors the economic view of the consumer (see Chapter 5) so that, in a 'hedonic' approach to sustainable consumption, people are expected to behave like consumers, even when being anti-consumerist.

Encouraging self-interested behaviour could easily prove counterproductive. If the hedonic approach to incentivisation merely reproduces a culture of self-interest, then collaborative endeavours such as sustainable development could easily be derailed (Middlemiss, 2014). Further, if people are encouraged to consume less in order to find happiness, what happens if they do not find it? Will they move on to the next thing that promises happiness? By positioning happiness as the purpose of sustainable consumption, sustainable consumption itself risks becoming expendable. So if, for instance, a government chooses to enforce limits on consumption, this could be resisted on the basis that it limits human well-being.

Politics of well-being

In the body of writing that links sustainability to well-being, authors frequently call for the measurement of well-being to replace the measurement of GDP, as the chief indicator of social progress (see also Chapter 13 on degrowth). This is not so simple as it might seem. As Sara Ahmed (2010) points out, happiness has in the past been used to promote a range of unsavoury practices, including the subjugation of women who were deemed to be happier in 'caring roles' as wives and mothers, and the oppression of colonised populations who were thought happier as a result of being 'civilised' by their oppressors. Ahmed argues that if happiness is the purpose of society, then it is not just an aim, but a duty, and so to be unhappy, and to afflict others with your unhappiness, is to be a troublemaker. The feminist is then labelled a 'killjoy', rather than an 'activist'.

There are strong arguments in favour of moving away from GDP as our main indicator of progress, since economic growth still correlates with growth in consumption and environmental problems. But if we are going to move away from GDP, why choose an ambiguous indicator like well-being, which can be just as open to detrimental effects? Instead of placing happiness at the centre of environmental policy (in the hope that it might reduce consumption as a side effect), we should keep sight of the indicators that truly reflect the state of the environment. And if we really believe that certain social indicators causally relate to well-being (health, education, equality, and so on) then let us find indicators for those too, rather than sticking to a single, imperfect measure. Whatever the solution, we should not ignore the risk that if one, simplistic measure of well-being becomes the end in itself, then other goals might be neglected.

Conclusions

So hopefully by the end of this chapter it is clear to you that there is no simple relationship between sustainable consumption and happiness! The evidence for a 'double dividend' of both happiness and environmental protection is somewhat mixed, and relies too heavily on assumptions about human nature and needs that not everyone will agree with. That is not to say that this 'hedonic' approach is entirely without advantage. As Kate Soper points out, it enables us to talk about the 'potentialities of human pleasure and the rich and subtle forms of their possible realisation in a post-capitalist society' (2015, 50), rather than only focusing on the mundane or technical aspects of production and consumption – or indeed the 'sacrifice' of consuming less. The risks, however, are that we forget people are different in their abilities, expectations and aspirations, that these differences are real, and that we cannot expect everyone to find happiness in the same place.

There are two future avenues of research, which hold promise for this topic. First, the 'eudaimonic' approach to well-being opens up new and interesting ways to think about well-being, in a more complex and socially situated way, rather than the narrow psychological view of well-being that makes up most of the happiness studies literature to date (see Brand-Correa and Steinberger, 2017). Second, we could try and determine which needs are being satisfied by the most environmentally destructive forms of consumption, and to think about ways in which this kind of consumption could be catered for differently. In other words, how might you substitute one needs-satisfier for another, in order to achieve a similar social outcome, but with less environmental damage?

Useful resources

Great Transition Initiative debate on well-being: www.greattransition.org/publication/sustainability-and-well-being

References

AHMED, S. 2010. *The Promise of Happiness*. Durham, NC: Duke University Press.

ALEXANDER, S. & USSHER, S. 2012. The voluntary simplicity movement: A multinational survey analysis in theoretical context. *Journal of Consumer Culture*, 12, 66–86.

BERG, A. 2009. Down-to-earth economy: The discursive contribution of sustainable consumption and production debate. *Finland Futures Research Centre, Turku School of Economics Proceedings*, 82–90.

BONNER, F. 2011. Lifestyle television: Gardening and the good life. *In*: LEWIS, T. & POTTER, E. (eds) *Ethical Consumption: A Critical Introduction*. London: Routledge.

BRAND-CORREA, L. I. & STEINBERGER, J. K. 2017. A framework for decoupling human need satisfaction from energy use. *Ecological Economics*, 141, 43–52.

BROWN, H. S. & VERGRAGT, P. J. 2015. From consumerism to wellbeing: Toward a cultural transition? *Journal of Cleaner Production*, 132, 308–317.

BUELL, L. 2014. Enough is enough? *In*: SYSE, K. L. & MUELLER, M. L. (eds) *Sustainable Consumption and the Good Life: Interdisciplinary Perspectives*. Abingdon, UK: Routledge.

BUY NOTHING DAY WEBSITE. 2017. *Buy Nothing Day* [Online]. Available: www.buynothingday.co.uk/ [Accessed 17 October 2017].

DE GEUS, M. 2003. *The End of Over-Consumption: Towards a Lifestyle of Moderation and Self-Restraint.* Utrecht: International Books.

DIENER, E., SUH, E. M., LUCAS, R. E. & SMITH, H. L. 1999. Subjective well-being: Three decades of progress. *Psychological Bulletin*, 125, 276.

DOYAL, L. & GOUGH, I. 1984. A theory of human needs. *Critical Social Policy*, 4, 6–38.

ELGIN, D. 1993. *Voluntary Simplicity: Toward a Way of Life that is Outwardly Simple, Inwardly Rich.* New York: Quill.

ETZIONI, A. 2006. Voluntary simplicity: Characterisation, select psychological implications and societal consequences. *In*: JACKSON, T. (ed.) *The Earthscan Reader in Sustainable Consumption.* London: Earthscan.

FENNEY SALKELD, D. 2017. Ableism and disablism in the UK environmental movement. *Environmental Values*, 26, 503–522.

GOUGH, I. 2015. Climate change and sustainable welfare: The centrality of human needs. *Cambridge Journal of Economics*, 39, 1191–1214.

HOBSON, K. 2011. Environmental politics, green governmentality and the possibility of a 'creative grammar' for domestic sustainable consumption. *In*: LANE, R. & MURRAY, A. G. (eds) *Material Geographies of Household Sustainability.* London: Routledge.

HUDDART KENNEDY, E., KRAHN, H. & KROGMAN, N. T. 2013. Downshifting: An exploration of motivations, quality of life, and environmental practices. *Sociological Forum, Wiley Online Library*, 764–783.

HUMPHERY, K. 2011. The simple and the good: Ethical consumption as anti-consumerism. *In*: LEWIS, T. & POTTER, E. (eds) *Ethical Consumption: A Critical Introduction.* Abingdon, UK: Routledge.

INGLEHART, R. 2018. *Cultural Evolution: People's Motivations are Changing, and Reshaping the World.* New York: Cambridge University Press.

INGLEHART, R., FOA, R., PETERSON, C. & WELZEL, C. 2008. Development, freedom, and rising happiness: A global perspective (1981–2007). *Perspectives on Psychological Science*, 3, 264–285.

JACKSON, T. 2005. Live better by consuming less?: Is there a 'double dividend' in sustainable consumption? *Journal of Industrial Ecology*, 9, 19–36.

JACKSON, T. 2008. Where is the 'wellbeing dividend'? Nature, structure and consumption inequalities. *Local Environment*, 13, 703–723.

JACKSON, T. 2009. *Prosperity Without Growth.* London: Earthscan.

KALLIS, G., KALUSH, M., O'FLYNN, H., ROSSITER, J. & ASHFORD, N. 2013. 'Friday off': Reducing working hours in Europe. *Sustainability*, 5, 1545–1567.

KASSER, T. 2003. *The High Price of Materialism.* Cambridge, MA: MIT Press.

KNIGHT, K. W. & ROSA, E. A. 2011. The environmental efficiency of well-being: A cross-national analysis. *Social Science Research*, 40, 931–949.

LAYARD, R. 2006. *Happiness: Lessons from a New Science.* London: Penguin.

LITTLER, J. 2009. *Radical Consumption.* Maidenhead, UK: Open University Press.

MACKERRON, G. 2012. Happiness economics from 35,000 feet. *Journal of Economic Surveys*, 26, 705–735.

MADJAR, M. & OZAWA, T. 2006. Happiness and sustainable consumption: Psychological and physical rebound effects at work in a tool for sustainable design. *International Journal of Life Cycle Assessment*, 11, 105–115.

MANIATES, M. 2002. In search of consumptive resistance: The voluntary simplicity movement. *In*: PRINCEN, T., MANIATES, M. & CONCA, K. (eds) *Confronting Consumption.* London: MIT Press.

MASLOW, A. H. 1943. A theory of human motivation. *Psychological Review*, 50, 370.

MAX-NEEF, M. A. 1991. *Human Scale Development: Conception, Application and Further Reflections*. New York: Apex Press.

MIDDLEMISS, L. 2014. Individualised or participatory? Exploring late-modern identity and sustainable development. *Environmental Politics*, 23, 929–946.

NEW ECONOMICS FOUNDATION. 2010. *21 Hours: the case for a shorter working week* [Online]. New Economics Foundation Website. Available: http://neweconomics. org/2010/02/21-hours/ [Accessed 29 March 2018].

NUSSBAUM, M. C. 2011. *Creating Capabilities*. Cambridge, MA: Harvard University Press.

SCHOR, J. B. 1999. *The Overspent American: Why We Want What We Don't Need*. New York: Harper Perennial.

SEN, A. 1999. *Development as Freedom*. Oxford, UK: Oxford University Press.

SOPER, K. 2004. Rethinking the 'good life': The consumer as citizen. *Capitalism, Nature and Socialism*, 15, 111–116.

SOPER, K. 2008. Alternative hedonism, cultural theory and the role of aesthetic revisioning. *Cultural Studies*, 22, 567–587.

SOPER, K. 2015. Towards a sustainable flourishing. *In*: SYSE, K. L. & MUELLER, M. L. (eds) *Sustainable Consumption and the Good Life*. Abingdon, UK: Routledge.

SORON, D. 2010. Sustainability, self-identity and the sociology of consumption. *Sustainable Development*, 18, 172–181.

STEG, L., BOLDERDIJK, J. W., KEIZER, K. & PERLAVICIUTE, G. 2014. An integrated framework for encouraging pro-environmental behaviour: The role of values, situational factors and goals. *Journal of Environmental Psychology*, 38, 104–115.

UNCED (UNITED NATIONS CONFERENCE ON ENVIRONMENT AND DEVELOPMENT) 1992. *Rio Declaration on Environment and Development*. Rio de Janeiro, Brazil.

VEENHOVEN, R. 2012. Happiness, also known as 'life satisfaction' and 'subjective well-being'. *In*: LAND, K. C., MICHALOS, A. C. & SIRGY, M. J. (eds) *Handbook of Social Indicators and Quality of Life Research*. London: Springer.

ZAVESTOSKI, S. 2002. The social-psychological bases of anticonsumption attitudes. *Psychology and Marketing*, 19, 149–165.

13 Revolution or evolution?

In the final chapter of this 'visions of the future' section, I outline some emerging systemic solutions to sustainable consumption. These are interdisciplinary attempts to think about change at an appropriate scale to the size of the problem, often (but not always) as perceived from a strong sustainability, or indeed a 'strong sustainable consumption' perspective (Lorek and Fuchs, 2013), as opposed to a 'green consumerism' perspective (Akenji, 2014). Scholars in this field are increasingly convinced that substantive, structural and/or systemic change is needed to address the problem of unsustainable consumption, and that such change requires both social and economic transformation over time. As Lewis Akenji writes, 'The political economy of consumption sees patterns such as intensifying environmental stress, growing economic volatility and widening social inequality as being interlinked and needing to be addressed under the same framework' (2014, 16). In engaging with these ideas, writers are attempting to imagine a better way of governing for sustainable consumption, a new type of system that is 'centered around resilient societies operating within ecological limits' (O'Rourke and Lollo, 2015, 251).

Given what we have seen in the rest of the book, writing about systemic change feels like an appropriate way to bring this book to a close. The middle section (Chapters 4–10) gave us a sense of how the different disciplines see this problem. None of these visions feel particularly satisfactory in terms of tackling such a diffuse and substantial issue. Perhaps one of the problems with the single-discipline perspectives is the focus on the act of consumption; this makes us more likely to exclude important political and systemic questions about how resources are distributed and provisioned. A systemic view forces us to think in an inter-disciplinary way, integrating insights from different disciplines into an overall understanding of change. It also tends to be associated with a politics of strong sustainable consumption, in response to the problem of unsustainable consumption profiled in Chapter 2.

Before I delve into the details of a number of systemic approaches to thinking about consumption, it is useful to put this in historical context. Maurie Cohen's book *The Future of Consumer Society* (2016) does just this, showing how the consumer society came about, and how changes in society might result in it coming to an end. He argues that consumer society is precarious because of a generational shift, from baby boomers, with their aspirations to home and car ownership, to millennials (likely including many of you) who have different lifestyle priorities. This, combined with what he sees as the dissolution of political consensus on economic growth, stagnant wages and reduced resource availability, means that the consumer society is unlikely to survive in its current form (ibid.). Cohen paints a picture of a world in which systemic change away from the more environmentally destructive practices of consumer society is already in train, an interesting (although debatable) starting point for us in thinking about how change might come about.

We began dealing with systemic issues in Chapter 10, which profiled concepts such as the circular economy, and product service systems. In this chapter, I take a broader view, outlining what a systemic approach might entail from a macro social and economic perspective. I then continue to profile three key bodies of work in this field: work on degrowth, new economics, and transitions. These ideas are all concerned with systemic change, but understood from different political perspectives, both with regard to the desired ends of change (to more or less green or communitarian utopian visions) and with regard to the means by which we achieve these (by revolution or by evolution). I then give some insights and examples from research and practice, followed by a critique of this field.

A systemic approach

The systemic approach to sustainable consumption entails a shift from understanding this problem and solution as a function of the individual, to thinking about this as a structural issue (O'Rourke and Lollo, 2015). We have seen hallmarks of this in the practice approach (Chapter 8), which moved away from thinking about the problem as a function of attitudes or choices, and instead understood people's daily lives to be embedded in a context in which infrastructure, materials and meanings are critical in shaping the way that people act. We also saw signs of this in thinking around the circular economy and product service systems (in Chapter 10). A systemic approach attempts to bring together both sustainable consumption and production, and looks to understand how this system might be transformed:

> Most research to date has either addressed the supply side and technological solutions or has focused on behavioural change of individual consumers. To date, research has hardly begun to investigate a possible and necessary societal transition to new and sustainable production and consumption systems, which includes new economics, and a new post-consumerist culture.
>
> (Lorek and Vergragt, 2015, 29)

Lorek and Vergragt can see that practice approaches have a more systemic understanding of change, but that there is scope for more extensive development of visions and strategies for the future (ibid.). In a systemic approach, authors want to look to the future, and think about how a different economy and society might be achieved. Lorek and Vergragt identify socio-technical transitions, grass-roots innovations, new social movements and degrowth as promising avenues for thinking about how a new kind of future might be reached (ibid.).

In this writing about the future, and about ways of achieving social, economic and ecological change, there are a range of politics on offer. Degrowth, which advocates abandoning the social objective of economic growth, is perceived as radical by politicians. An important moment for the degrowth perspective came after the financial crash in 2008, and the release of Tim Jackson's *Prosperity Without Growth* in the UK in 2009 was (briefly) seen as a window of opportunity for real change, as financial institutions were being called into question. Frank Geels and colleagues (Geels et al., 2015) call this a 'revolutionary' approach, which is rooted in Marxist ideas, and an ethos of 'small is beautiful' (Schumacher, 1973). Writers emphasise the failure of a growth-based economy to deliver environmental and social goods, and seek to understand the possibilities for a zero growth or degrowth economy.

The emphasis on efficiency and decoupling common in 'business as usual' approaches is a key target here. In their excellent introduction to this emerging body of work, Dara O'Rourke and Niklas Lollo characterise it, in opposition to the work on decoupling, as follows:

> Focusing entirely on decoupling avoids examining how current lifestyles and systems generate significant environmental and social problems. The decoupling framework fails to understand complex systems of production and consumption, thereby allowing for an inappropriate amount of substitutability amongst economic, ecological, and social resources and benefits. Efficiency strategies alone often ignore issues of equitable distribution and development . . . while distracting from a needed focus on absolute reductions in environmental impacts. To be clear, efficiency measures are an absolutely necessary part of an effective strategy. Yet, efficiency alone fails to effectively address the scale and scope of our consumption and sustainability challenges.
> (O'Rourke and Lollo, 2015, 241)

Critically, in this vision of the problem, authors see unsustainability as both a social and an ecological crisis; they engage in discussions of happiness and well-being (see Chapter 12), mobilise the idea of community as a solution (see Chapter 11), and talk about the inequalities inherent in the way that resources are currently distributed (see Chapters 2 and 3). This body of work therefore provides a normative vision for a different kind of world, as well as some detail on how it might be achieved.

Not all thinkers in this area are looking for radical change, however. Indeed, there is a strong strand of writing which suggests a middle ground; as Schroeder and Anantharaman (2017) suggest, the objective is 'finding balance between reformist efforts that focus solely on green purchasing and eco-innovations and radical approaches that call for the end of consumer capitalism' (2017, 7). Geels and colleagues position their socio-technical transitions research (profiled below) and practice approaches, as a 'reconfiguration' approach which:

> argues for transitions in socio-technical systems and social practices in societal domains such as mobility, housing, agro-food, heating, and lighting. Such transitions entail co-evolutionary changes in technologies, markets, institutional frameworks, cultural meanings and everyday life practices, but do not necessitate the overthrowing of some hypostasized totality (such as capitalism, consumerism or materialism).
>
> (Geels et al., 2015, 2)

Writers advocate reconfiguration for a number of reasons, which help to throw light on what a systemic approach might mean in practice. This is a less radical approach, in the sense that it does not set out to revolutionise the way we understand our world; instead it suggests incremental, evolutionary change, albeit to potentially the same ends. Authors in this field argue that:

- Changes in systems offer more potential than changes in technology or behaviour, because they attempt to understand the whole rather than the parts.
- Changes in systems must embrace pluralist understandings of causality; they must understand causality as a web of interlocking factors rather than a simple linear model.
- Changes in systems focus on interactions between production and consumption, thereby avoiding the pitfalls of individualisation or technological determinism.

Researchers across the political spectrum that take a systemic approach tend to look at processes of change – the logics and decisions made by a range of actors, the existing lock-in to unsustainable consumption (O'Rourke and Lollo, 2015). The focus of this research is on how the system works, and, whatever your political starting point:

> This requires a more complete understanding of system dynamics – actor roles, relations between actors, and relationships with dominant structures – and methods to address those dynamics – behavioral, structural, and institutional interventions, at key leverage points – to break from unsustainable processes and to generate positive sustainability feedback loops.
>
> (Ibid., 247–248)

In the following three sections we will look in more detail at the various approaches to systemic thinking that have engaged with sustainable consumption topics.

Politics of growth

There is a substantial body of macro-economic research on 'degrowth' which challenges the central role of economic growth as a social objective, including some useful popular economics introductions to this topic (Jackson, 2009; Dietz and O'Neill, 2013). The contention here is that economic growth is not a useful or sensible goal for societies, either ecologically or socially. These authors point out that efficiency and 'decoupling' of environmental harm from economic growth (where additional economic growth does not result in additional environmental harm) are unlikely to be enough to address environmental or social problems. Given that richer nations have environmental impacts that break ecological limits (as we saw in Chapter 2), and that people in richer nations are not substantially happier than those in middle-income countries (see Chapter 12), this body of work proposes that societies (and governments) need to focus on other forms of progress.

Degrowth would also involve scaling back consumption and production, in order to reduce the material-dependency of our economies. Table 13.1, reproduced from Kersty Hobson's work, is a useful characterisation of 'strong' sustainable consumption in contrast to 'weak' sustainable consumption, the former focusing on a degrowth agenda. Note the interests in social as well as environmental change here, which is a hallmark of this movement.

Much academic work on degrowth does not use the term 'sustainable consumption', and is not particularly consumption oriented, although the actions that are recommended in the context of degrowth do chime with some of the initiatives you will have read about in this book. This includes Transition Town-type activities (see Chapter 11), co-housing, zero waste and no consumption initiatives, as well as voluntary simplicity and reducing working hours. Writers on degrowth tend to point towards relocalised economies, redistribution of opportunities for consumption through reformed democratic institutions, and an

Table 13.1 'Weak' and 'strong' approaches to sustainable consumption (from Hobson, 2013, 1083; reproduced with permission from Sage)

Key facets	Weak approaches	Strong approaches
Central tenet	Improve material, social and institutional efficiency of the prevailing production–consumption nexus	Displace current foci of 'growth' and 'the economy' with nonconsumption concepts and practices
Methods	Technological innovation, voluntary, multiscale interventions; limited use of nonvoluntary measures	Diverse grass-roots movements and communities; ontological displacement of growth and the economy in modernity
End goal	Continued economic growth alongside improved socio-ecological well-being	Multilevel sociopolitical transformation that brings nonconsumption-based well-being to the fore

emphasis on sufficiency (consuming enough, rather than 'too much') (Hobson, 2013). There is also enthusiasm in this field for developing alternative indicators to GDP to track national development in a way that does not engage with economic growth (Jackson, 2009). This has included the possibilities of monitoring well-being or happiness, as discussed in Chapter 12.

There are clearly links between the strong sustainable consumption and the degrowth agendas. Sylvia Lorek and Doris Fuchs (2013) characterise these as follows:

1 They are based on similar values, with sufficiency (Princen, 2005) as an organising principle.
2 They face similar political obstacles, with organisations locked into a 'more is better' paradigm, making it difficult for consumers, businesses and governments to find spaces to act.
3 As a result, they recommend similar political strategies.

In addition, both agendas require changes to levels and patterns of consumption in order to achieve their goals, including reduction in material consumption. Writers on consumption inspired by degrowth ideas have engaged with concepts of needs and wants (also discussed in Chapter 12, on happiness), for instance, by calculating an appropriate amount of resource consumption to meet basic needs (Druckman and Jackson, 2010). Angela Druckman and Tim Jackson estimate that we could meet key quality-of-life goals, and reduce greenhouse gas emissions by 37 per cent at 2004 levels in the UK (ibid.). Some interventions and research in this field experiment with not consuming, as, for instance, in a 'fashion detox' study (Armstrong et al., 2016), which shows the challenges and opportunities of engaging fashion students with degrowth ideas. Sylvia Lorek and Joachim Spangenberg (2014) argue that all mechanisms of sustainable consumption (as listed at the beginning of Chapter 10, and including, for instance, green supply chains, and producing with less) could be consistent with strong or weak sustainability, and that as such there is much potential for implementing the strong vision understood by degrowth advocates. Lorek and Spangenberg see a need for clearer narratives of degrowth, linked to those of strong sustainable consumption, which can offer visions of the future to people aspiring to create change (ibid.).

New economics

The term 'new economics' tends to be associated with visions of the future stemming from bottom-up, often environmentalist, thinkers, influenced by degrowth and 'small is beautiful' ideas. The New Economics Foundation think tank in the UK, and the New Economy Coalition non-profit in the US, have had an important impact on public debates around these topics. These initiatives tend to support a particular vision of the future, emphasising local solutions, collective action, and alternative forms of measurement (happiness and degrowth).

While 'old' economics focuses on the monetary economy, it fails to measure things like caring work, and environmental impacts and contributions (Seyfang, 2009). A new economics attempts to build a broader understanding of wealth, work and money. So, for instance, the New Economics Foundation has been at the forefront of a campaign to reduce working hours in the UK, and regularly refers to the ideas of transition and degrowth in its work. The foundation's mission is one which resonates well with the theme of this chapter: 'we will offer an agenda for people to take more control over the decisions and resources that affect their lives today and a plan for how we can all begin to change the whole system tomorrow' (New Economics Foundation, 2017).

Gill Seyfang, in her book, *The New Economics of Sustainable Consumption*, sees five key characteristics of this approach to thinking about sustainable consumption, which in turn double as indicators of whether this form of sustainable consumption is in operation. New economics approaches aim towards localisation, reducing ecological footprints, community-building, collective action and building new infrastructures of provision (Seyfang, 2009). We can see numerous links to other chapters of this book here, but a particular emphasis on ideas of community, collective action and localisation harks back to Chapter 11 on 'the solution is collective'. In addition, the idea of the ecological citizen, and the 'personal is political', which I profiled in Chapter 7, is also called upon here, including the feminist perspective on the value of caring work. The new economics indeed amounts to a politics of sustainable consumption, which emphasises a group of political ideas that are characteristic of the contemporary environmental movement.

Gill Seyfang and Adrian Smith (2007) also initiated a strand of work on 'grass-roots innovations' which profiles bottom-up action for social and environmental change. A grass-roots innovation occurs when some form of usually social innovation results in change; some examples might include community currencies, maker spaces (allowing people to repair or repurpose goods), or new forms of community ownership. In their view, grass-roots innovations offer an alternative vision of success, and in doing so alter the cultural and social rules around what can and cannot be done. They also offer an alternative space in which the way that people operate can be transformed: '[Grassroots innovations] help overcome the principal problem with an individualised approach to greening the market, namely, that acting individually, consumers are powerless to change the rules of the game, they are stuck within current socio-technological regimes' (ibid., 595).

Grassroots innovation work draws closely on our next area of interest: socio-technical transitions research, and shares some terminology, including the idea of a niche innovation which, if successful, can develop into a change in the socio-technical 'regime' (see below). Socio-technical transitions research has historically focused on technological innovation, as opposed to the social innovations profiled here, so the addition of the grass-roots innovation approach has also expanded that field.

Socio-technical transitions

Research on transitions to sustainability emerged in the Netherlands, as a way of thinking about how long-term goals on sustainability (e.g. decarbonisation, reducing human impact on ecological systems) could be met (Geels, 2002). This work is an attempt to think about systemic change, which tends to see such change as an evolutionary process (Foxon, 2011). As Tim Foxon puts it, in his work on 'co-evolution':

> a transition to a low carbon energy system will involve the innovation and deployment of low carbon technologies, business strategies relating to investment in these technologies and market and regulatory frameworks that encourage such investment. It will also involve changes to practices relating to energy use, for example changing the time of use of appliances to suit variations in supply or allowing the external control of these appliances through some form of 'smart grid'. It is clear that there will be many causal influences relating the evolutionary dynamics in each sub-system.
>
> (Ibid., 2265)

The concept of 'co-evolution' positions change as produced by a number of inter-related drivers (including user practices – as seen in Chapter 8), which influence each other as they innovate and produce change (ibid.). This vision is very much one which envisages coordinated and incremental change, towards a more sustainable future. A transitions approach encourages us to think about how we might understand change historically, and what we can learn about that to try and influence change incrementally in the future: 'Such transitions entail co-evolutionary changes in technologies, markets, institutional frameworks, cultural meanings and everyday life practices, but do not necessitate the overthrowing of some hypostasized totality (such as capitalism, consumerism or materialism)' (Geels et al., 2015, 2).

Geels's theory is that when radical innovations emerge from niche activities, these can lead to transformations in the socio-technical regime (the dominant mid-level institutions in society, such as the market, or specific forms of governance, and practices), which in turn aggregate to impact on the socio-technical landscape (the more stable social structures that transform only slowly over time). A transition is a change from one dominant regime to another dominant regime, which serves the same social function – for instance, the transition from public transport to private transport in cities.

To bring this to life, I draw on an example from research by Maurie Cohen (2010) who uses socio-technical transitions research to explain how innovations in personal aeromobility are transforming the current air-travel regime. Personal aeromobility is the use of private and corporate flights, to increase opportunities for corporate leaders or wealthy individuals to get around in small aeroplanes. In tracking the emergence of new innovations in aeromobility, Cohen finds that personal aeromobility is growing beyond a 'niche' activity, and becoming 'an increasingly stable socio-technical regime with an interlinked network of companies, personnel, customers, manufacturers, airports, agents, brokers, publications, trade associations, financial institutions, and legal conventions' (ibid., 464).

Cohen argues that this is happening because of social innovation. For instance, the possibility for part-ownership of an aircraft, has meant more people are able to afford to have a stake in a small plane, and therefore to increase their use of it. Such an innovation gives cause for concern in environmental terms, given the substantial amount of carbon emitted from air travel, in contrast to any other form of travel.

A number of authors have made the link between transitions thinking and the practice approach, which, if you have read Chapter 8, will make sense (Shove and Walker, 2010; McMeekin and Southerton, 2012; Hargreaves et al., 2013; Geels et al., 2015). Given that the practice approach sees what people do as embedded in infrastructures and social norms, we can see that change to socio-technical systems over time is a common interest. Geels and colleagues (2015) list the key similarities as:

- Both approaches see change happening in a co-evolutionary way.
- Both believe that what people do is structured by routines, rules and habits.
- Both are interested in the tensions between stability and change.
- Both are interested in processes.

Hargreaves and colleagues would also add:

- Both recognise contemporary environmental and sustainability challenges as 'demanding fundamental systems change that cannot be achieved through incremental tinkering with existing systems' (Hargreaves et al., 2013, 407).

The policy implications of both transitions and practice ways of thinking are that policy-makers cannot steer change at will, given the systemic nature of the socio-technical world. As Elisabeth Shove puts it:

> relevant societal innovation is that in which contemporary rules of the game are eroded; in which the status quo is called into question; and in which more sustainable regimes of technologies, routines, forms of know-how, conventions, markets, and expectations take hold across all domains of daily life.
> (Shove, 2010, 1278)

Of course the point of bringing two sets of ideas together in this way is to create more than the sum of the parts. Hargreaves and colleagues maintain that the value of using transitions and practice approaches simultaneously is to add a wider analytical frame which incorporates systemic depth (transitions) to an already deep understanding of how people act (practices) (Hargreaves et al., 2013). Practice approaches frequently focus on how practices exist in the here-and-now, while socio-technical transitions research pushes us to think also about how they might be transformed in the future in the context of greater system change.

There are tensions between the two approaches also. Shove and Walker (2010) criticise the tendency of socio-technical transitions research to focus on how technology shapes the social, despite comprehensive evidence to show that the social also has a substantial influence on technology. The same authors show how transitions research is good at explaining innovations, but less good at explaining normality (ibid.). Note that the practice approach is frequently criticised for the opposite (being good at explaining normality, but less good at explaining innovation).

Socio-technical transitions research has some limitations, which impact on how we can use it to think about the future. For instance, transition research tends to be rather quiet on power inequalities, and in thinking about how power shapes change (Cohen, 2010). As we saw in Chapter 8, practice approaches have attracted similar criticism (Sayer, 2013). Given the complexity of system change, it is also hard to predict if it will produce results, or to make generalisations about what 'should' be done and how (Geels et al., 2015). In general, this is a highly challenging endeavour – very often transitions research attempts to map future trends, and anticipate unintended effects on a huge scale, and researchers active in this field are not naïve as to the difficulties of doing this effectively (Cohen, 2010; Geels et al., 2015). Having said that, it is also an important thing to do; when we look at the state of the environment profiled in Chapter 2, it is clear that we need a nuanced and thoughtful plan to ensure that humanity can sustain itself.

Some insights from research and practice

In this section, I profile some recent work which takes a systemic approach to thinking about how sustainable consumption might be achieved. These are examples of research which do not quite fit into the categories above (degrowth, new economics, transitions), but that have interesting things to say about a systemic approach to understanding and proposing solutions to sustainable consumption.

Lifestyle leapfrogging

Patrick Schroeder and Manisha Anantharaman offer the concept of 'lifestyle leapfrogging', which aims to explain 'how sustainable lifestyles of consumers in emerging economies could be realized from the outset, circumventing the unsustainable lifestyles of Western consumers' (2017, 4). Leapfrogging is a concept that has mainly been used to describe technological development in the global South: where a country acquires the newest and most efficient technology first, rather than going through many increasingly efficient iterations. The authors note that leapfrogging to weak sustainable consumption is happening, for instance, in China where there has been considerable increase in the use of highly efficient lighting technology, and in solar water heaters. However, to achieve strong sustainable consumption, a systems approach (engaging a range of stakeholders in concerted action) is needed, as is behavioural change (to complement efficient technology):

> Lifestyle leapfrogging to strong sustainable consumption would entail a qualitative shift in consumption practices through the use of the most efficient technologies available and behavioural changes which would still result in an increase of 'quality of life,' but would not result in an increase of overall material consumption comparable to the level of consumption levels in western consumer societies.
>
> (Schroeder and Anantharaman, 2017, 9)

In exploring how this might happen through case studies, they produce the diagram reproduced in Figure 13.1. Here, the x axis represents the passage of time, and the y axis the level of environmental impact. The idea is that policy, market and society interventions might preserve the business as usual pathway, or alternatively they might produce a less impactful 'leapfrogging' pathway to development. The critical point here, is that policy, market and society would need to work together, systemically, to cumulatively increase the number of energy-efficient buildings on offer in China. For clarity, the least environmentally impactful route (the lower curve in the diagram) would require the adjustments to policy, markets and society which follow that curve.

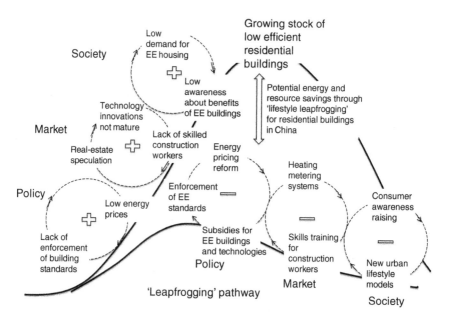

Figure 13.1 'Leapfrogging' causal loop diagram, contrasting lifestyle leapfrogging towards low-energy housing in China and business-as-usual development (from Schroeder and Anantharaman, 2017; reprinted by permission from Springer)

Box 13.1 Some practical examples of transformational and systemic thinking

Transform together

With the aim of helping to achieve the 2030 Agenda for Sustainable Development, this is a network of businesses, NGOs and governments which is attempting to work together to implement systemic change: 'We aim to be a powerful multistakeholder partnership of civil society, business and governments, which will catalyse and demonstrate the political, business and societal changes needed to transform unsustainable patterns of consumption and production' (Transform Together, 2017).

Shorter working days

Governments and businesses have experimented with shorter working days. This includes a small Internet company in Sweden, Brath, which embraced a short working day (six hours) for its employees and has achieved considerable success (Brath, 2017). The French government also mandated a 35-hour working week in 2000. These initiatives fit most closely with the idea of degrowth, which would support initiatives that result in people having more time, but less disposable income. Note that this is a very challenging idea for low-income earners, as in many global North nations people on low-incomes struggle to make ends meet.

The idea of lifestyle leapfrogging raises further issues about the potential for global South countries to adopt sustainable consumption, and the different kinds of challenges that these nations will face in the process. I have commented throughout that middle-class lifestyles in emerging economies are not dissimilar to those in the global North. Addressing sustainable consumption issues in these nations is challenging, because there is such wide inequality, thus arriving at a combination of under-consumption and unsustainable consumption. How to address this topic in both global South and emerging economies is an important area for future research.

Culturally appropriate change

The various development trajectories that we see in different nations have an impact on how these ideas are received. You can imagine that degrowth might be a hard sell to a nation that has not yet had all the advantages of a high consumption economy, as accrued by the global North nations. In the Asia-Pacific region, for instance, growth is very high, consumption is increasing, there is a growing consumer or middle class, and new forms of exclusion are emerging (Hobson, 2013).

Wei Zhao and Patrick Schroeder (2010) point out that in this region, sustainable consumption is not on the agenda; the focus of environmental policy is more clearly on production processes and pollution. Even for urban consumers, who are able to access some of the benefits of consumption, a global North call for degrowth is not likely to play to a sympathetic audience!

Further, some of the recommendations of degrowth are culturally inappropriate. For instance, as Kersty Hobson (2013) points out, suggesting relocalisation in a context such as China, for instance, is unlikely to work in a culture where you are not supposed to show dissent. In Romualdas Juknys and colleagues' work on new EU member states (lest we forget, those that used to be part of the communist Eastern bloc), the authors are also reluctant to embrace a degrowth perspective (Juknys et al., 2014). Given the history of this part of the world – that is, a massive economic decline post-communism, followed by rapid growth, which in itself has been characterised by substantial efficiency gains – again you might be able to sense why a 'revolutionary' change might be unacceptable.

Critiques

The degrowth and new economics literatures tend to attract similar criticisms, as might be expected, given that they are based on a similar body of ideas, and that these ideas sit outside of mainstream thinking in consumer societies. Attempting to develop a radical new vision of how the world might work without one of its central beliefs (that economic growth is good) is clearly a challenging endeavour, and some of the criticism is around the lack of specificity in what degrowth actually means. Jeroen van den Bergh (2011) points out that degrowth could mean a reduction in GDP, consumption, or working time, a radical transformation to the economy, or a reduction of the resource throughput in the economy. Such criticism is slightly disingenuous; there is no reason why this movement should be unified on what precisely it is 'for', given these are ideas under development. Van den Bergh favours 'a-growth': a disregard for economic growth as an indicator, rather than an active attempt to reduce growth. This is similar to Kate Raworth's take, in a recent (and potentially influential) popular economics book (2017).

More fundamental questions strike at the rather naïve expectations of the social and political world which tends to be promoted in this field of work. For instance, Kersty Hobson (2013) questions the assertion that a degrowth strategy will result in a more equal distribution of wealth (Lorek and Fuchs, 2013). As Hobson puts it, 'there exists the possibility that degrowing or downsizing signify the capture of forms of social, cultural, and possibly economic capital by those already with some relative advantage' (2013, 1090–1091).

In other words, given that, historically, more richly resourced people (more educated, more wealthy, better connected) tend to hold on to their resources, we should be open to the idea that degrowth will result in no real change to the status quo with regards to distribution of wealth. If economies reduce in size, inequalities could even increase, as the very rich hold on to everything they can, and others are left in penury. It is not clear, in any case, what the strategy would be to ensure better distribution of wealth under a degrowth system.

These more radical ways of thinking have a tendency to tell much more positive stories about the future, in order to give a counter-balance to the stories told by more mainstream voices. We have seen this in the work on happiness (consume less to be happy, Chapter 12) and in the idea that community is a good thing (Chapter 11). This is not inevitable, however – just because the vision of the future is counter to the status quo does not mean it should be a happy one. Stephen Quilley (2013) counters this utopianism, in his work on relocalisation, which he sees as counter to the socially liberal values of degrowth movement. We could easily tell a very different story about scenarios of forced relocalisation (through the collapse of a more globalised system):

> In any collapse scenario, it is difficult to see how the denizens of Totnes might protect their newly planted nut trees. But at the same time it is impossible to imagine that resource shortages on the scale anticipated by the peak oil and Transition movements would not result in geo-political violence and regional and even global wars.
>
> (Ibid., 266)

As Quilley sees it, just because we live in a liberal, democratic and cosmopolitan space at the moment, does not mean that this will be automatically translated into a localised world, or that we are immune from the violence and tensions likely to ensue from a reduction of resources. History, in this regard, shows limited evidence of peaceful downsizing.

Conclusions

The degrowth and transition approaches to thinking about sustainable consumption systemically are very different in character, in Geels and colleagues' terminology the first proposes 'revolution', a radical change of the system, whereas the second proposes 'reconfiguration', a gradual transition from one system to another more sustainable one (Geels et al., 2015). Which of these is likely to achieve the best results is a political question, of course, and something you might like to develop a position on. Certainly, there are both risks and rewards inherent in both forms of change. A revolution might produce quick change, but also destabilise parts of the current system which work very well for people and planet, as radical change often has unintended consequences. On the other hand, a careful transition to a more sustainable system might also make it difficult to quickly achieve an impact on key environmental targets (such as carbon emissions reduction). These approaches do have ideas in common, however – in particular, their commitment to a need for systemic change in order to achieve goals associated with ensuring that environmental and social problems are overcome. This is a substantial contrast to, for instance, a 'nudge' approach (Chapter 5).

It is useful at this point to return to Maurie Cohen's (2016) work on the future of the consumer society. In discussing social change with students in my teaching on this topic, I frequently encounter presentism in their interpretations of what might happen next (presentism being a bias towards interpreting the past and future through present-day experiences). My students tend to instinctively assume that neither revolutionary nor incremental change can occur, despite historical evidence to the contrary! Some aspects of the status quo seem so firmly embedded that they cannot imagine them changing in their lifetimes. Cohen's suggestion – that a transition to a different (potentially more environmentally benign) system is already in play – is a helpful counter-narrative to the presentist narrative I frequently encounter. Even if we do not have Cohen's optimism about the ends of change (a sustainable future), we surely can see that radical social changes have occurred within living memory; a systemic shift (of one sort or another) is under way.

As a consequence, spending time and energy in attempting to understand if and how we can control both the process and outcome of a systemic shift is a valuable endeavour. In my view, this is an important future direction in sustainable consumption research and practice.

References

AKENJI, L. 2014. Consumer scapegoatism and limits to green consumerism. *Journal of Cleaner Production*, 63, 13–23.

ARMSTRONG, C. M. J., CONNELL, K. Y. H., LANG, C., RUPPERT-STROESCU, M. & LEHEW, M. L. 2016. Educating for sustainable fashion: Using clothing acquisition abstinence to explore sustainable consumption and life beyond growth. *Journal of Consumer Policy*, 39, 417–439.

BRATH. 2017. *6 Hour Working Days* [Online]. Available: http://brath.com/why-we-started-with-6-hour-work-days/ [Accessed 10 November 2017].

COHEN, M. J. 2010. Destination unknown: Pursuing sustainable mobility in the face of rival societal aspirations. *Research Policy*, 39, 459–470.

COHEN, M. J. 2016. *The Future of Consumer Society*. Oxford, UK: Oxford University Press.

DIETZ, R. & O'NEILL, D. W. 2013. *Enough is Enough: Building a Sustainable Economy in a World of Finite Resources*. Oxford, UK: Earthscan, Routledge.

DRUCKMAN, A. & JACKSON, T. 2010. The bare necessities: How much household carbon do we really need? *Ecological Economics*, 69, 1794–1804.

FOXON, T. J. 2011. A coevolutionary framework for analysing a transition to a sustainable low carbon economy. *Ecological Economics*, 70, 2258–2267.

GEELS, F. W. 2002. Technological transitions as evolutionary reconfiguration processes: A multi-level perspective and a case-study. *Research Policy*, 31, 1257–1274.

GEELS, F. W., MCMEEKIN, A., MYLAN, J. & SOUTHERTON, D. 2015. A critical appraisal of Sustainable Consumption and Production research: The reformist, revolutionary and reconfiguration positions. *Global Environmental Change*, 34, 1–12.

HARGREAVES, T., LONGHURST, N. & SEYFANG, G. 2013. Up, down, round and round: Connecting regimes and practices in innovation for sustainability. *Environment and Planning A*, 45, 402–420.

HOBSON, K. 2013. 'Weak' or 'strong' sustainable consumption? Efficiency, degrowth, and the 10-Year Framework of Programmes. *Environment and Planning C: Government and Policy*, 31, 1082–1098.

JACKSON, T. 2009. *Prosperity without Growth*. London, Earthscan.

JUKNYS, R., LIOBIKIENĖ, G. & DAGILIŪTĖ, R. 2014. Sustainability of catch-up growth in the extended European Union. *Journal of Cleaner Production*, 63, 54–63.

LOREK, S. & FUCHS, D. 2013. Strong sustainable consumption governance – Precondition for a degrowth path? *Journal of Cleaner Production*, 38, 36–43.

LOREK, S. & SPANGENBERG, J. H. 2014. Sustainable consumption within a sustainable economy – Beyond green growth and green economies. *Journal of Cleaner Production*, 63, 33–44.

LOREK, S. & VERGRAGT, P. J. 2015. Sustainable consumption as a systemic challenge: Inter-and transdisciplinary research and research questions. *In*: REISCH, L. & THØGERSEN, J. (eds) *Handbook of Research on Sustainable Consumption*. Cheltenham, UK: Edward Elgar.

MCMEEKIN, A. & SOUTHERTON, D. 2012. Sustainability transitions and final consumption: Practices and socio-technical systems. *Technology Analysis & Strategic Management*, 24, 345–361.

NEW ECONOMICS FOUNDATION. 2017. *New Economics Foundation Website, About page* [Online]. Available: http://neweconomics.org/about-us/ [Accessed 1 December 2017].

O'ROURKE, D. & LOLLO, N. 2015. Transforming consumption: From decoupling, to behavior change, to system changes for sustainable consumption. *Annual Review of Environment and Resources*, 40, 233–259.

PRINCEN, T. 2005. *The Logic of Sufficiency*. Cambridge, MA: MIT Press.

QUILLEY, S. 2013. De-growth is not a liberal agenda: Relocalisation and the limits to low energy cosmopolitanism. *Environmental Values*, 22, 261–285.

RAWORTH, K. 2017. *Doughnut Economics: Seven Ways to Think Like a Twenty-First Century Economist*. London: Random House.

SAYER, A. 2013. Power, sustainability and wellbeing. *In*: SHOVE, E. & SPURLING, N. (eds) *Sustainable Practices: Social Theory and Climate Change*. Abingdon, UK: Routledge.

SCHROEDER, P. & ANANTHARAMAN, M. 2017. 'Lifestyle leapfrogging' in emerging economies: Enabling systemic shifts to sustainable consumption. *Journal of Consumer Policy*, 40, 3–23.

SCHUMACHER, E. F. 1973. *Small is Beautiful*. New York: Harper & Row.

SEYFANG, G. 2009. *The New Economics of Sustainable Consumption: Seeds of Change*. Basingstoke, UK: Palgrave Macmillan.

SEYFANG, G. & SMITH, A. 2007. Grassroots innovations for sustainable development: Towards a new research and policy agenda. *Environmental Politics*, 16, 584–603.

SHOVE, E. 2010. Beyond the ABC: Climate change policy and theories of social change. *Environment and Planning A*, 42, 1273–1285.

SHOVE, E. & WALKER, G. 2010. Governing transitions in the sustainability of everyday life. *Research Policy*, 39, 471–476.

TRANSFORM TOGETHER. 2017. *Transform Together Website* [Online]. Available: http://transform-together.weebly.com/ [Accessed 10 November 2017].

VAN DEN BERGH, J. C. 2011. Environment versus growth – A criticism of 'degrowth' and a plea for 'a-growth'. *Ecological Economics*, 70, 881–890.

ZHAO, W. & SCHROEDER, P. 2010. Sustainable consumption and production: Trends, challenges and options for the Asia-Pacific region. *Natural Resources Forum. Wiley Online Library*, 4–15.

14 Conclusion

Building images of the future

> ... an image of the future which springs indeed from a deep understanding of the present, determines men's thoughts and actions even in periods when the course of events seems to be leading far away from such a future.
>
> (Horkheimer, 1972, 220)

The study of sustainable consumption is the study of how lifestyles might be transformed in order to reduce environmental impacts to an ecologically viable level, and to temper the damage caused by inequalities of all kinds. The word 'transform' is critical here; studying sustainable consumption means thinking about how we will live in the future, whether in response to an intervention today, or in response to evolutionary change in the next twenty years. I begin this Conclusion with the above insight from Max Horkheimer, a critical theorist who points out how problematic it is to base our ideas of the future in the politics of the present, given how fast social change can (and does) happen. When natural scientists look forward, they predict radical and unprecedented change, expressing deep concerns about the availability of key resources and waste sinks (Steffen et al., 2015). If we think back over the last fifty years, there have been radical transformations in geo-politics, which have had enormous implications for people's lives – from the Cold War, to the 'end' of communism, to the emergence of China as a world power. As some former developing countries gain in wealth and power (the BRICS nations, for instance), and others look to the global North for leadership, who knows what the future will hold. The 'consumer society' that we inhabit is relatively new in human history, and some argue that it is already showing signs of change (Cohen, 2016). It would surely be foolish to imagine a future that looks a lot like the present, given this pace of change in both the natural and social worlds. On the other hand, what can we build stories of the future on, other than present-day understanding and experiences?

A key purpose of our work in studying sustainable consumption is building images of the future. In this book, I profiled the existing stories of a sustainable consumption future, both in the public domain and in the world of research. This included stories told by the key disciplines that engage with this topic about the nature of the problem and the potential solutions to it (Chapters 4–9).

It also covered less discipline-based thinking about what the future should hold (Chapters 10–13). Many of the stories I have told, whether consciously or not, project a clear image of the future. For instance, those disciplines and approaches that espouse universal truths about human behaviour (economics, Chapter 5; psychology, Chapter 6; hedonic well-being, Chapter 12), and see society as built on these truths, do not foresee a change in the ways that human beings act and react. This leaves rather limited room for social transformation; if people are motivated by self-interest, for instance, a story of the future is more likely to consider change as reliant on making sustainable consumption 'work' for people. Some areas of study in sustainable consumption have transformative visions: hoping for people to 'come together' (Chapter 11), for alternative forms of happiness to develop (Chapter 12), or for new ways of measuring progress (Chapter 13). Here, the expectation is often that 'good' will somehow prevail, that sustainable consumption will come about as people realise it is the 'right' thing to do. All of these stories about the future are only stories however, and stories that in some cases tell us more about the nature of those writing them (as Horkheimer would say, that give us a 'deep understanding of the present'), than they do about how the future will unfold.

One of the challenges of studying sustainable consumption is the sheer profusion of different approaches to the topic (or indeed, images of the future) which I hope to have captured in this book. The social science of sustainable consumption is prolific, diverse and contradictory. Many of the social science disciplines present their knowledge as if it represents the 'truth' about the world, despite the evident contradictions between disciplines. In the light of urgent messages about the state of the planet ('runaway climate change', 'toxic waste spills'), arguing about who really knows the 'truth' can seem rather pedantic. However, stories, as Horkheimer puts it, have real consequences, spelled out in the daily lives of people around the world. The fact that economic explanations of change have currently 'won' the ear of powerful people (and even, possibly, more public discourses) is hugely important; it has direct impacts on the numbers of people affected by environmental problems, on the nature of the impacts they feel, on the 'feasibility' of solutions, on the possibility of engaging in certain forms of political debate.

Back in another form of 'reality', we also must remember how much of a counter-trend sustainable consumption represents. As I write, the Trump administration in the US, for instance, has little to no interest in environmental issues, let alone social justice goals. Meanwhile, more environmentally and socially benign administrations do relatively little to counter unsustainable consumption. This is apparent in the comparison between national ecological footprints we saw in Chapter 2 – even 'environmental' nations in the global North consume more than their share. Instead of focusing on people or planet, in consumer societies, our attention is frequently given to the markets (who service the consumers) or the consumers themselves (albeit only with regards to their 'confidence' and their 'spending'). If you search for 'consumer' on Google News, headlines are more likely to be about consumer confidence (high=good=more consumption), consumer prices (high=bad=less consumption), or consumption growth forecasts (high=good=more consumption). There is no sense in this mainstream world that reducing consumption, or even transforming consumption, is an appropriate response.

So back to the idea that the way we think in the present places restrictions on our ability to think about the future. Horkheimer suggests that critical thinking can overcome this. At this point, the logical question for our field is: where are our blind spots? How, in our framing of this topic, are we trapped in the present? I am only one person, and, as I am sure you can tell from my writing, I have a bias towards some of the stories I have told over others. Having said that, I do not have a firm allegiance to any of them. I am also inclined to a critical approach, as I outlined in Chapter 1. Perhaps this puts me in a helpful position with regard to commenting on the blind spots of the field. In my view, the real challenges that this wide-ranging field faces are as follows:

- **Social complexity and politics**: one of the hallmarks of a critical approach is to pay attention to power relations, and, as we saw in Chapter 3, for sustainable consumption this also means understanding the impacts of the field for different types of people. In my view, studies of sustainability have tended to have a blind spot when it comes to social difference, which creates an unhealthy politics. Many scholars and practitioners come to this topic with a knowledge of the environmental crisis and a passion for finding solutions to this. The social side of sustainability tends to be the first to be forgotten (e.g. in Chapter 10 on the circular economy). I make a plea to take these issues more seriously in my first section below.
- **Disciplinary wars**: the tendencies of disciplines to barricade themselves behind their theories, language and understandings of the world are unhelpful. By this, I do not mean to call for a naïve 'community' of academics working on this topic. Most of the disciplines I have profiled are built on truths that contradict those of at least some of the other disciplines (Shove, 2010; Whitmarsh et al., 2011; Wilson and Chatterton, 2011; Shove, 2011). Below, in the section 'Navigating complexity', I will suggest some ways that you personally can respond to this difficult set of ideas. The blind spot here, however, is the presence of fortifications around the disciplinary knowledges on this problem. Yes, I know that these knowledges are incompatible, but given the complexity and urgency of this problem, can we at least forego trading insults, and attempt a civilised conversation? Perhaps the critical approach that I have encouraged here is a useful starting point in this; in my view, none of the disciplinary approaches (Chapters 4–9) are 'right', indeed they are all a little bit 'wrong'. Some humility about the boundaries of each discipline and the necessarily limited role each can play in building *the* image of the future (if such a thing exists) would not go amiss.
- **Beyond the global North**: much of the literature in this field originates from, and describes, the global North. There is lots of excellent work emerging from or about the global South, including many authors cited

here (notably, for me, Manisha Anantharaman on India, Livia Barbosa and colleagues in Brazil, Marlyne Sahakian on the Philippines, Kuishuang Feng on China). There is also political interest in the global South, with UNEP's programme on sustainable consumption, for instance, having a global South, youth and cities focus. In reading for this book, I have deliberately sought out examples and authors from the global South, I hope both to have a wider selection available in future, and my apologies if I have missed anything exciting this time!

In the rest of this Conclusion, I will first elaborate on my argument that social complexity and politics need more attention. After this I will propose some means for you the reader to navigate this complex multi-disciplinary field. This amounts to a series of potential strategies, or dispositions you can choose to take in response to this prolific, diverse and contradictory set of ideas. I finish by telling you the story of someone who was important in my life, and whose story I hope will inspire you to take an open and inclusive approach to thinking about sustainable consumption.

Towards a socially complex and political understanding

So we now understand multiple 'images of the future', and we understand how these are based in a wide range of disciplinary traditions, knowledge paradigms and politics. Is this the only insight we have after all this academic endeavour? Of course not! Within each of the disciplines themselves, there are clearly evolving 'truths', which of course I could only write about in the preceding chapters because of all the hard work done by my colleagues within these disciplines. We can speak of, for instance, the failings of a neo-classical economic model, the importance of identity in structuring values, or the potential for change based on practice theory, only because people have invested the intellectual energy in addressing these research topics. Some of this intellectual work also impacts how things work in practice, as ideas built in theory flow into the world.

For me, there are two further key insights that come from the multi-disciplinary nature of this topic of study. These insights are representative of my own position in this research. As I have said, I do not have a firm allegiance to any of these perspectives; rather, I have an affinity with other scholars who take a critical perspective on this literature. The hallmarks of this critical approach for me include first, an appreciation of social complexity, and by extension of social difference, and their role in structuring consumption, and second, an acknowledgement of the politics of this body of work.

So, first, the social world is complex, and consumption is structured by this social complexity. The very fact that an array of social science disciplines can engage with the idea of sustainable consumption, and come up with a number of contradictory, and in many cases convincing, 'truths' about it, is evidence in itself of a complex social world. This makes any kind of definite assertion about 'how things are' rather difficult to maintain. We have seen multiple ways, for instance, in which the assertion 'people care about what things cost' can be disproved by the way that specific types of people react. In my own research on energy poverty in the UK, for instance, we often see income-poor people choosing to pay more for their energy (using pre-payment meters) in order to have more control over their spending (Middlemiss and Gillard, 2015). On the other hand, in other instances, it is clear that cost (and bringing down costs) plays a huge part in making environmental innovations accessible. One of the challenges here is that, in trying to find universal truths, we are trying to provide a single answer to a complex question.

In my view – and inspired by an ex-colleague of mine, Ray Pawson (a social policy scholar) – the complexity of the social world should encourage us to step away from the simple question 'what works?' in sustainable consumption, and to move towards a more open question: 'what works, for whom in which circumstances?' (Pawson and Tilley, 1997). Pawson and Tilley argue for a more nuanced approach to the social world which starts with the assumption that people are different, they are inspired and motivated differently, they inhabit different geographical and social worlds, and have access to different types of resources, and that as such it makes no sense to even conceive of a single solution to a social (or environmental) problem. The next challenge for sustainable consumption studies, I think, is to embrace the idea of social difference spelled out in Chapter 3, and to begin to think in a more sophisticated way about this problem (as perceived by different constituencies) and solutions to it (which address multiple standpoints). This is likely to require thinking beyond disciplinary boundaries. Taking difference into account has both pragmatic and ethical benefits; nuanced and targeted interventions are more likely to result in change, and understanding difference forces us to take into account the contrasts between (in the extreme) those living extravagantly and those suffering hardship.

The second insight that arises from this multi-disciplinary field, is that all aspects of sustainable consumption are imbued with politics, and that each of the disciplinary, or thematic approaches outlined in the chapters of this book has its own political baggage. Politics is apparent in the way that problems are defined ('people don't understand environmental issues'), solutions are proposed ('people just want to be happy'), and in the motivational framing of initiatives ('you could save money by switching supplier'). If you accept my first point about social difference above, you can also see that taking difference into account makes sustainable consumption highly political. As well as 'what works, for whom, in what circumstances', we must ask 'who is marginalised by a particular type of politics?', 'who is let off the hook?', 'what doesn't work, for whom, in what circumstances? This is frequently related to one of my critical questions in Chapter 1: 'how is the subject of change understood?' For example, the well-being agenda (Chapter 12) places an emphasis on individual action, whereas the practice approach (Chapter 8) risks forgetting that the individual has a role. As Horkheimer recognises, these kinds of politics constrain the boundaries of possibility in both visible and invisible ways.

To give an example of how this works: my research on fuel poverty in the UK has sensitised me to see inequality or difference along wealth/class lines in lots of different circumstances. By immersing myself (as far as is possible) in the viewpoint of another, I have learned to at least try to understand daily life and politics from that viewpoint. One of the things one begins to understand when one studies people at a disadvantage is just how far this disadvantage is embedded in the way things work, and how strongly we reproduce disadvantage in both everyday life and in everyday politics. In the study of sustainable consumption, the more optimistic messages ('we could be happier', 'we should work together') frequently assume that these kind of inequalities can merely be 'overcome'. The attitude of thinkers in this area risks being 'in the new world, everyone will be equal' without a sense of how this will be achieved.

Navigating complexity

To return to the substance of my opening quote, then, one thing I am confident to say about you, the reader, and what the future holds for you, is that you are statistically likely to hold power, to have the opportunity to change the world. Whether you come from a developed or developing country, whether you are male or female, whether your family was part of your nation's elite or not, a university education sets you up with the resources to take on a powerful role in society. This might be working in government, in industry, in a non-governmental organisation, in academia, or in a less formal capacity as a community leader. You may not have power straight away, but eventually, you will likely be in a position to be making decisions about other people's daily lives, or to be taking leadership in one way or another. One of my hopes, in writing this book, is that you will take a critical awareness of sustainable consumption into your (working) lives, and apply your critical understanding in any interventions you lead. In short, since you are going to have the chance to create change in some way, I hope you will draw on the insights in this book to do that thoughtfully, and with an awareness of the varied impacts of your actions.

Taking knowledge and understanding into the world is easier said than done, however, particularly in this multi-disciplinary context where learning in one discipline contradicts another. The complexity of the field, and of the social world, can make it difficult to know even how to define sustainable consumption problems, never mind attempting to solve them. In my teaching on this topic at Leeds in the UK, I like to offer students some ideas about how they might do this in practice. Over the years, I have come up with three possible strategies as to how you might use your learning on sustainable consumption in a real world context. I present these below. These are not necessarily exclusive strategies – you may want to combine elements of the three in your own response.

Pick sides

The first strategy in this multi-disciplinary field, is to pick sides: choose a particular disciplinary perspective as your 'home', and apply the knowledge and understanding of that perspective to all real-world problems. There are plenty of people in

226 Visions of the future in sustainable consumption

the world who pick sides; indeed, in an academic context, they are probably more common than those who do not. In my life I have come across some very inspiring people who 'picked sides'. The economist Jeroen van den Berg, who works on environmental issues and taught me economics in Amsterdam, seemed to my classmates and I to live and interpret his whole life through the discipline. Elizabeth Shove is also deeply embedded in practice thinking, a field that we saw in Chapter 8 has substantially altered the terms of debate in sustainable consumption, in the wake of her seminal book *Comfort, Cleanliness and Convenience* (2003). You may feel comfortable in picking sides, especially if you define yourself by a discipline already, or if one of the disciplinary perspectives really appeals to your way of thinking.

In the light of our discussion above, and of the multiple perspectives apparent in the field, picking sides is not really enough on its own, however. Critically, if you take this strategy, you must be alert to the strengths and weaknesses of the discipline that you pick. The way to pick sides, in my view, is to take on board the critiques and counter-arguments I have presented in each of the chapters of this book, to accept the disciplinary positions as a 'good-enough' starting point to understand the problem and possible solutions. Here the strategy is to take the stance 'well nothing is perfect, but this particular perspective seems to me to be the one most likely to achieve results.'

HEALTH WARNING: when people do pick sides, they often forget about the failings of their own particular perspective! Picking sides requires you to retain an open mind, while also committing to particular ways of understanding the world.

Be pragmatic

The second strategy, again in the light of the multi-disciplinary evidence base, is to be pragmatic, drawing on the various disciplinary theories and bodies of evidence according to the real world problem in question. While pragmatists recognise the tensions between the disciplines, they look for solutions according to the problem presented. They do not get hung up on belonging to a discipline; instead they look for ways in which a problem can be solved, drawing on appropriate theories in order to justify the response. Many interdisciplinarians are pragmatists, and there is evidence of pragmatism all over the sustainable consumption literature (see especially Wilson and Chatterton, 2011; Whitmarsh et al., 2011). Wilson and Chatterton, for instance, argue for 'appropriateness' of theory, instead of asking for the 'integration' of disciplines. This certainly seems more realistic in the context of sustainable consumption. When ecological economists draw on anthropological thinking to better explore the questions they have (Brekke and Howarth, 2006), this is also a kind of pragmatism: an acceptance that one set of theories on their own do not really answer the question, and therefore that there is value in trying to integrate insights from elsewhere.

Note that interdisciplinary work can be undertaken in more or less deep and considered ways, and there are pitfalls associated with taking a pragmatic approach. For instance, pragmatism can cover up political assumptions that you are not aware of making; if you claim to be acting on 'common sense', this can mean that you are not thinking critically about the implications of your choices. Anna Wesselink (2009) argues that interdisciplinary knowledge brings together different disciplines through values (or politics), by representatives from different disciplines agreeing on normative goals. In my view, this is not a problem, unless it is unrecognised, and unacknowledged by those that make these judgements. Pragmatism can also mean that you look only at the problems you are attempting to solve in a superficial way, given that in this approach, there is a tendency to throw away theory that doesn't 'work'. What does 'working' constitute? Does this just mean throwing away uncomfortable findings? Further, some disciplines, theories, or insights are deeply incompatible and it is difficult to see how they can be used together. We have seen these kinds of arguments in the ABC debates (featured in Chapter 8).

HEALTH WARNING: when people act pragmatically, they sometimes choose theory lazily, to back up what they already believe, rather than making a critical assessment of its value. Make sure you retain a critical approach to your own work.

Be critical

The third strategy is to take a critical approach. This involves attempting to understand the theoretical and political implications behind each real-world problem, in order to uncover some of the deeper implications of policy and practice. This is a strategy I have encouraged throughout this book; indeed, the critical questions outlined in the Introduction have been asked of all the disciplines and literature topics I have covered here. Perhaps this is the strategy I am most comfortable with; after all, as academics we are trained to think critically about each other's work, and about social change.

There are different forms of critical approach to sustainable consumption research. The scholars that engage with degrowth debates, and with the well-being agenda, are one kind of critical; they are looking at society and offering alternatives to the way it currently works, usually in opposition to capitalism (see Chapters 12 and 13). Others are more likely to be critical of the way that sustainable consumption initiatives themselves are positioned, looking for evidence of exclusion in these initiatives, whether by mistake or by design (see Chapters 3 and 7). If you wish to take a critical stance, you must attempt to understand what is happening politically beneath the narrative of how things are. These are often couched as 'common sense' or 'human nature' – and we can be alert to the assumptions being made when we hear such phrases.

HEALTH WARNING: critical approaches are themselves criticised for not suggesting a way forward – merely picking apart other people's solutions and showing how they fail. You may be comfortable with this (we do not all have to focus on solutions), but it is worth developing a rebuttal to such an argument. There is also potential for critical scholars to engage in conversation about solutions: 'if not this, then what?'

Learning from Florence Scott

In 2016, shortly after I began writing this book, my Nana (my mum's mum) died at the age of 93. To conclude this chapter, I will tell her story, linking it into the history of consumption, and bringing out some important points about our studies. Please do Florence the honour of reading about her life, I am sure she would have found being featured in an academic textbook quite surprising!

Florence was one of eight children born into a working-class household in Sunderland, a city in the industrial north-east of England. Her dad was violent, a gambler and a drunk, and her mum eventually kicked him out. With just her mum to support them, Florence's was a poor household. Nana's mum often went without food to feed her children, and Florence had to leave school at 14 to contribute to the family income. Her first job was in a rope factory, and after the Second World War she moved to East Yorkshire to marry my Yorkshire grandad, a farm labourer.

Nana made her own family of two children, in the late 1940s. Florence lived in social housing all of her life, provided by the UK government for low-earning families. She and her family were able to access free healthcare in the newly created National Health Service. As new labour-saving devices emerged, Nana was able to afford some of these: a washing machine, fridge and a vacuum cleaner. This gave her time to go out to work as a cleaner in the local school, and in one of the local pubs. Money was tight, but her family did not go without what they saw as the basics in life.

When I knew Florence, she lived with my grandad in a well-insulated bungalow close to the village centre. They did not have a car, and Nana travelled rarely, usually to visit us when Grandad's health allowed. She went abroad only twice in her life. Florence's approach to life was frugal: if we gave her a gift of a new jumper, it would go into her drawer to be used when her current jumper was beyond repair. She was a generous-spirited woman, and was content with her lot, although she played the lottery with enthusiasm and often talked about what she would do when she won big. Towards the end of her life, Florence had a mobile phone, which she just about worked out how to use. The Internet was a step too far.

Florence witnessed the Industrial Revolution, the Second World War, the creation of the welfare state in the UK, the birth of the 'consumer society' and the Internet age. Her life story is interesting because it confounds some of the stereotypes we have about what happened to people in wealthy countries like the UK in this era. In environmental terms, my Nana had a very low ecological footprint (see Chapter 2). Florence always worked in low-paid jobs, and she 'made ends meet', but she never had luxuries or consumed to excess, as might have been expected in this consumerist era. She was not really one of the beneficiaries of the 'consumer society'; indeed, in some ways she did not really live in one. The 'labour-saving devices' she was able to access allowed her to labour more outside of the home, for low pay, to supplement her husband's low income. People like my Nana sustained the era of strong economic growth in the UK, but she saw limited benefits for herself and for her family. Although, given her starting point in a single-parent family, living in private rented accommodation, and occasionally going without food, she saw things differently: for her, having a stable home provided by the government was a great asset.

There are still households like Florence's in the UK, and in many other global North countries. Many of the stories we tell about the 'march of progress' in the twentieth century are generalisations, and they can tend to exclude people like my Nana, or to assume that everyone took the same path. We can also forget that there are people in global North countries that have limited power to change their lives; just as Nana 'made do' all of her life, plenty of others do the same. In leaving this book, and indeed as you leave the study of sustainable consumption, I would like you to keep Florence in mind, or to look for your own examples of people who do not fit the stories you have read about. The real work of sustainable consumption, for me, is to find ways forward for everyone, including my Nana.

References

BREKKE, K. A. & HOWARTH, R. B. 2006. Two alternative economic models of why enough will never be enough. *In:* JACKSON, T. (ed.) *The Earthscan Reader in Sustainable Consumption.* London: Earthscan.

COHEN, M. J. 2016. *The Future of Consumer Society.* Oxford, UK: Oxford University Press.

HORKHEIMER, M. 1972. Traditional and critical theory. *In:* IDEM. *Critical Theory: Selected Essays.* New York: The Continuum Publishing Company.

MIDDLEMISS, L. & GILLARD, R. 2015. Fuel poverty from the bottom-up: Characterising household energy vulnerability through the lived experience of the fuel poor. *Energy Research & Social Science*, 6, 146–154.

PAWSON, R. & TILLEY, N. 1997. *Realistic Evaluation.* London: Sage.

SHOVE, E. 2003. *Comfort, Cleanliness and Convenience: The Social Organization of Normality.* Oxford, UK: Berg Publishers.

SHOVE, E. 2010. Beyond the ABC: Climate change policy and theories of social change. *Environment and Planning A*, 42, 1273–1285.

SHOVE, E. 2011. On the difference between chalk and cheese? A response to Whitmarsh et al.'s comments on 'Beyond the ABC: climate change policy and theories of social change'. *Environment and Planning A*, 43, 262–264.

STEFFEN, W., RICHARDSON, K., ROCKSTRÖM, J., CORNELL, S. E., FETZER, I., BENNETT, E. M., BIGGS, R., CARPENTER, S. R., DE VRIES, W. & DE WIT, C. A. 2015. Planetary boundaries: Guiding human development on a changing planet. *Science*, 347, 1259855.

WESSELINK, A. 2009. The emergence of interdisciplinary knowledge in problem-focused research. *Area*, 41, 404–413.

WHITMARSH, L., O'NEILL, S. & LORENZONI, I. 2011. Climate change or social change? Debate within, amongst, and beyond disciplines. *Environment and Planning A*, 43, 258–261.

WILSON, C. & CHATTERTON, T. 2011. Multiple models to inform climate change policy: A pragmatic response to the 'beyond the ABC' debate. *Environment and Planning A*, 43, 2781–2787.

Index